The Literatures of India

Edward C. Dimock, Jr.

Edwin Gerow

C. M. Naim

A. K. Ramanujan

Gordon Roadarmel

J. A. B. van Buitenen

The Literatures of India

An Introduction

The University of Chicago Press

Chicago and London

This volume was initiated
by the Asian Literature Program
of the Asia Society

The University of Chicago Press, Chicago 60637
The University of Chicago Press, Ltd., London
 Published 1974
Phoenix Edition 1978
Printed in the United States of America
82 81 80 79 78 98765432

ISBN: 0-226-15233-2
LCN: 73-87300

For permission to reprint excerpts from previously published and copyrighted books, grateful acknowledgment is made to the following:

Columbia University Press for excerpts from *Two Plays of Ancient India*, translated by J. A. B. van Buitenen, © 1968.

Peter Owen, Ltd., and Indiana University Press for excerpts reprinted from *The Interior Landscape: Love Poems From a Classical Tamil Anthology*, translated by A. K. Ramanujan, Copyright © 1967 by A. K. Ramanujan. Reprinted by permission of Indiana University Press, Bloomington, and Peter Owen, Ltd., London.

The University of Michigan Press for excerpts from Kalidasa's *The Cloud Messenger*, translated from the Sanskrit *Meghaduta* by Franklin and Eleanor Edgerton, © 1964.

Penguin Books, Ltd., London, for excerpts from *Speaking of Siva*, by A. K. Ramanujan, © 1973.

In Memoriam
GORDON ROADARMEL

A fine scholar
a rare colleague
a good man

Contents

Preface

This book was begun over cocktails in 1963. Several of us were discussing the need for an introductory book on Indian literature, one that would approach the problems of Indian literature from an essentially critical point of view, a point of view that would help students in understanding the texts of this vast and complex area. Mrs. Bonnie R. Crown, publications director of The Asia Society in New York, suggested that we stop talking and start writing. It is largely due to Mrs. Crown's encouragement, despite her occasional and understandable despair at ever seeing press copy, that the work is finally finished.

It was at a conference in Chicago in the spring of 1964, called with the generous support of the Rockefeller Foundation, that ideas about the book began to solidify. Working papers, which form the basis of the current chapters, were prepared, and principles such as that of concentrating on a few selected topics in some depth, rather than attempting to cover the whole span of Indian literature, were established. Attending that conference, in addition to the authors represented here and Mrs. Crown, were Professors Charlotte Vaudeville of the University of Paris, and S. M. Pandey of Allahabad University (now at University of London), both of whom were at the time visiting at the University of Chicago, and Norman H. Zide, also of the University of Chicago. Although their contributions are not here represented in writing, it goes without saying that their insights contributed substantially to the thinking of those who are so represented, and they also should be considered among the writers of this book.

There are two main reasons why the book has been so long in the making. The first is that editorial attempts to unify the book stylistically were time consuming, and were ultimately given up; no single individual wanted to take the responsibility of changing his colleague's style, for fear of damaging the content. And, second, no single individual wanted to take the responsibility for a final chapter on modern writing:

the situation, everyone said, is too complex, with too many variables, too many diverse influences. It was fortuitous that at the Association for Asian Studies Meetings in 1970, at a panel organized by Professor Rachel van M. Baumer, two papers were read that, combined, satisfied the need. The paper by Edwin Gerow, which showed the influence of the classical esthetic tradition on three modern Bengali novels, is in expanded form included as the next to last chapter of this book. And that by Gordon Roadarmel, which is the last chapter of this book, suggested that although the classical traditions might continue to show themselves in modern prose, it would be simplistic to argue that this is the only formative influence, and that in fact the new literary forms and values have their roots in the new India. The new India does not deny the old, but is not identical with it. It is to be hoped that the reader will be left with the impression, which we have tried to convey, that it is impossible to generalize about Indian literature, and that he will read each text from the many viewpoints suggested.

None of the writers feels that this is the definitive work on the subject. All in fact feel that it is a bare beginning, the first in what will be a long series of critical studies. The panel mentioned above, and a subsequent meeting at the University of Hawaii, also arranged by Rachel van M. Baumer, suggest that this is not an unrealistic hope. The thinking of many of the writers here represented has already gone well beyond what is recorded in this book. But all continue to feel that the critical approach is a valid one. It does not supersede, but complements, the historical and sociological approaches familiar through the writings of many Indian and Western Orientalists. This book depends in fact upon such studies. Not only has the vast literature of the philosophies, theologies, and ritual been left entirely aside, but literary giants such as Rabindranath Tagore are often mentioned merely in passing. This is obviously not meant as a slight to those traditions and individuals, but is permissible simply because they are so well known through the work of others; the reader can fit them, or not fit them, into the categories we propose.

It was mentioned above that the attempt to further unify the book stylistically was given up. Thus, the passages for which each of the writers is responsible will be initialed. Sometimes the editors have supplied transitional paragraphs; these will not be identified, except where they are of a length to warrant it. The editors have been several; in fact, almost every writer included has read the whole text and has made suggestions and revisions, not only of his own but of others' work. This is as it should be in a cooperative venture. If those who did the bulk of the editorial work, however, were to be singled out, they would be J. A. B. van Buitenen, Edwin Gerow, and Edward Dimock. The last of these is grateful to the Center for Advanced Study in the Behavioral Sciences at Stanford, California. Some of his time at the Center in 1969–70 was devoted to this editorial task.

We wish to thank not only Mrs. Bonnie R. Crown for her support, but also the organization that she represents, The Asia Society, for financial assistance. Thanks for financial assistance to the original conference also goes to the Rockefeller Foundation, specifically to Mr. Chadbourne Gilpatric of that organization, and to Miss Judith H. Aronson of the University of Chicago for typing the final copy.

Edward C. Dimock, Jr,
Edwin Gerow
J. A. B. van Buitenen
University of Chicago

Introduction

An overview: the sūtra

Until relatively modern times in India—meaning by India the Indo-Pakistan subcontinent—it is sometimes difficult to distinguish literature from religious documentation. This is not because there has been an imposition of a system of religious values on the society; it is rather because religion in India is so interwoven with every other facet of life, including many forms of literature, that it becomes indistinguishable.

At the time when the earliest Vedas were composed, a period usually assumed to be a century or two this way or that from 1500 B.C., they were folk expressions of religious wonderings. They gave voice to the perceptions and the fears of a nomadic people in a hostile universe, dependent upon the rain, the sun, all the forces of nature, and the gods, angry or benevolent, who control these. The Vedas—especially *The Ṛg-veda*, the oldest and greatest of the four books—are collections of poems occasionally of great literary power. They embody the simple awe that a wandering people feels of the storm, the temporal and eternal night, of the welcome dawn, of the winds and of the miracle of human speech. And as time passed, and the Aryan tribes, as they are called, moved slowly down through Central Asia, through the passes in the northwest and into the Gangetic Plain, the racial memory of the mountains and the storms remained, fortified and encapsulated by the Vedic hymns. And memory being what it is, these hymns, formulated in eternity, became not the terror-stricken or exultant cries of ancestors, but the speech of the gods themselves.

This is the most ideal kind of history through literature. For also in the course of time, as the people settled down to a surer existence, they began to see that man, also possessing the miracle of speech, the word, *vāk*, might do more than merely propitiate the hostile gods by sacrifice. The ancestors existed successfully because they possessed the Vedas. Therefore one can control the universe by means of these same words. The Vedas, no longer folk poetry, became ritual formulas.

Truth is there from the the beginning. Some men, as the ideal yogin sitting on his mountain top, know it completely, blissfully, and absolutely. Others, less fortunate or disciplined, can uncover only a corner of it here and there. Thus, with the exception of the successful yogin, who cannot or does not communicate his absolute knowledge, one man's insight can only supplement, and not replace, that of another. All thought and all literature can only be commentary on the Truth there from the beginning. The formulas for controlling the universe, for keeping man and the gods in equilibrium—the so-called *Brāhmaṇas*—were elaborated and conceived as expansions of the kernels of this Truth.

The Vedas are not only originally poetry on nature and, later, ritual formulas. As the Vedic poets gazed into the vast night, they speculated on man's relation to it all, to the creation, to birth and death, to animals and natural forces and other men. And especially the tenth book, the latest, of *The Ṛg Veda*, provided grounds for later philosophical speculation. This speculation is embodied in *The Āraṇyakas*, the "forest books" evolved from meditation, and in *The Upaniṣads*. And these books, in four sets following the four Vedas, in their turn provided the basis for later commentaries, the six systems of philosophy called Nyāya, Vaiśeṣika, Sāṁkhya, Yoga, Pūrva-mimāṁsa, and, best known of all, the Vedānta. Even more recently evolved systems justify their positions by putting forward the "real meaning" of the Vedas; the process of uncovering bits and parts of Truth goes on.

The classical Sanskritic tradition

This process of commentaries written on commentaries is at the root of a large part of classical Indian literature. In the texts called *śāstras*, lawbooks on every conceivable facet of life from caste regulation to sexual pleasure, the basic statement is usually given in a pithy, aphoristic form called *sūtra*. The commentaries dilate this. So too with later literature. It is impossible to date accurately the great classical epic *The Mahābhārata*, a massive compendium of folktales, myths, beliefs, and doctrines (embedded in the epic is *The Bhagavad-gītā*), hung on the framework of a titanic war, after the fashion of other Indo-European epics; the most that scholars can say is that it was compiled between 400 B.C. and A.D. 400. *The Mahābhārata* is an encyclopedia of things Indian as they existed, before being precipitated into the epic, and to a certain extent defining things as they exist today. Like all epics, *The Mahābhārata* and the more unified *Rāmāyaṇa* (200 B.C.–A.D. 200) state what the culture thinks of itself. Thus the great classical poet and playwright Kālidāsa can choose an episode from the epic, commenting on it from his own point of view, and given his genius there emerges the drama *Śakuntalā*.

And thus a modern Bengali playwright, sure that his theme will bring a response from both the conscious and the unconscious mind of his audience, can choose an episode from the epic, as Archibald Macleish can comment on the Book of Job in his play *J.B.*

The statement that Indian literature is intimately bound up with things religious should perhaps now be modified, to say that if some Indian literature does not start out being religious, it often ends up being so. The classical drama is an exception, but the epic *Rāmāyaṇa* is a case in point. The epic was written by a man named Vālmīki sometime just before or just after the beginning of the Christian era, and like *The Mahābhārata* it is the story of a war, here between the forces of good, personified by the hero Rāma and his allies the monkeys, and those of evil, represented by Rāvaṇa and his cohorts, who have abducted Sītā, Rāma's wife. It is a morality tale, and in the beautiful version of Vālmīki it is little more than that. But in the course of time and as the theme spreads over the subcontinent, *The Rāmāyaṇa* takes on different characteristics. Many later writers, especially those of the fourteenth through the eighteenth centuries, choose to comment on, and to give their own versions of, the theme. By their time a great religious force, that of *bhakti* (devotional worship of a personal deity) had swept across northern India, as it had done earlier in the south. And Rāma, to these later devotional poets, became an incarnation of the great god Viṣṇu; he is no longer a hero "with arms as hard as iron bars" to draw the bow of war. He has become a gentle god, come to save mankind; Rāvaṇa's hosts attain salvation by being killed by him, and the war has become a mere formality. The temper of the whole epic is radically changed.

The Rāmāyaṇa was not the only thing altered by the bhakti movement. The whole course of Indian literature and, indeed, of Indian civilization was transformed by it. For the representatives of bhakti were singers and poets; their object was to inspire the people, who were by this time removed from the great Sanskrit religious tradition by the rigid and austere system of Brāhmaṇism, Vedic, sacrificial worship to which Brāhmaṇs alone had access. These poets sang in the languages that the people spoke—Tamil, Bengali, Hindi, and the rest, and not often in Sanskrit. And in doing so they raised those languages to the status that they enjoy today as vehicles for serious and creative literature. This type of lyric expression of devotion was unfamiliar to Sanskrit. The Sanskrit poets Bhartṛihari, Mayūra, and Bāṇa wrote such poetry, and perhaps the highest expression of it was in *The Gīta-govinda* of Jayadeva (late twelfth century). But the genius of Sanskrit poetry was different; its highest aim was to create a perfect, highly polished gem to present as an offering to the deity. The poetry of the regional languages was more fervid, more direct, less sophisticated; and the course of Indian literature was changed.

Non-Sanskritic languages and literatures and their influence

From the tenth century on, too, another element was entering the stream of Indian literature; when the Muslims invaded the subcontinent they brought with them not only their Islamic religion, but the Perso-Arabic literary tradition. The Persian elements especially flourished in their new environment. The Sufi tradition was in many ways like that of bhakti, and the imagery of the two poetries is strikingly similar: God as the Beloved (or, in the case of bhakti, the Lover), eternally and deliberately separated from man, in order that man's longing would grow stronger. On many levels, in literature and in society, there was interaction between Hindu and Muslim elements. On others, such interaction did not take place. For when Islam came to India it was already well-established as a religion, and although its literary forms often flourished in Indian soil, they were often preserved pure.

It is in fact a characteristic of Indian literature—or at this point it might be well to say, literatures—that there is both syncretism and discreteness, depending on the level of examination. A case in point is that of the Dravidian literatures, of which the four primary are Tamil, Telugu, Kannada, and Malayalam, the most noteworthy and oldest recorded one being Tamil. The Dravidian languages, spoken for the most part in the southern part of the subcontinent, are of an entirely different language family from Sanskrit and its derivatives, and the literature written in them is almost equally old. As is clear from its early literature, the so-called Cankam poetry, collected in anthologies and dating perhaps from the first century B.C., Tamil had been developing literary forms peculiarly its own; they draw upon a set of conventions unfamiliar to Sanskrit literature, and its epic tradition and its traditions of war, lyric, and religious poetry are unique. But at the same time, literature written by Indians is Indian, no matter what the language or what the audience, and the Dravidian writings are not foreign to northern India. By retention of its peculiarities and its own genres and literary concepts, Tamil contributes importantly to Indian literature as a whole. Furthermore, the Dravidians adopted literary and religious facets of the Sanskritic culture also, putting their own stamp upon them. The Kamban *Rāmāyaṇa*, written in Tamil, is as familiar and as dear to the people of the south as Vālmīki and the later versions are to people in the north, and the values that all express are essentially the same. The Sanskrit language was brilliantly cultivated in the south, but it never superseded the culture of Tamil. Like the Islamic Urdu, Tamil has to be treated both on its own and as a part of the general literary continuity of India.

The fact is that it is often unclear as to which tradition borrowed what from whom, for another fact of Indian history is that there is a constant dynamic interchange between Indo-Aryan (the generic name given to the Sanskritic languages) and Dravidian and between what the anthropologists have called the "great" and "little" traditions. The Vedic literature was oral literature, remarkably preserved through many centuries by precise learning and repetition. Oral too were the stories embodied in *The Mahābhārata* and in *The Purāṇas* (A.D. 500–1000), those other compendia of religious lore, until written down. But the history of all this is obscure. It seems that the dynamic exchange works in both directions: the myths and legends of a local deity in, let us say, Bengal, become famous throughout the region and are then taken up into the great tradition, become associated with a deity already existing in that tradition, and are disseminated throughout the subcontinent. And in their turn, the rites and characteristics of the already existing deity become attributed to the local god. So too with literature: a local legend is taken up and disseminated through the subcontinent, through Tamil or Sanskrit. There remains, of course, much that is not so taken up, and there is a vast body of literature, still largely unknown in the West, in the regional and tribal languages—folk songs and folktales, legends, aphoristic poetry, even epics. Such is the case with the literature of the Austric languages. Some of these languages do not even now have a written literature, and in many cases it has been the modern anthropologist who has first recorded some of their rich oral literature. It is probable that many of the local deities, myths, rites, and perhaps literary themes now considered the property of the "great" Indian cultural tradition were originally those of the Austric-speaking peoples. On this, scholars are only now beginning to work.

As Islam and the Dravidian culture were both absorbed and not absorbed, in the north, into the dominant Sanskrit tradition, so it was with Western civilization. The French, British, Dutch, and Portuguese were all at one time or another significant forces in India. But the vestiges of all but the British are a few borrowed words in regional languages, and the vanishing remains of a factory or two. The British, who began as traders, soon established not only great commercial and political centers, but the educational system that has had such a profound effect on modern India.

Both for trade and for education, English became the linguistic medium, and that language and the literary values it embodies are today vital forces as well as matters of controversy. Scholars are still busy tracing the influence of Scott, Dickens, and Milton on nineteenth-century writers in the regional languages, and the likes of Poe and Eliot in more modern times. And argument about the use of English as a medium of instruction waxes hot. But it is a proposition at least worth considering that a culture accepts only those influences toward which it is predisposed; and the question of what there is in Indian culture, with such a seemingly different aesthetic stance from that of the West, that allows it to accept certain literary values or certain authors, has yet to be examined.

This of course does not mean that all modern Indian writers write in English, or that in all modern Indian writing the West is discernible. Many writers feel that they can write creatively only in Bengali or Marathi or Tamil or whatever their native language, though they might be bilingual in that language and English. Others feel that English is as native to them as any language. And in the second place, aesthetic systems and literary values of India and of the West have become interwoven with one another, so that writing in India produces little that can be called purely Western, or purely within the Indian tradition as the classicist might define it.

The dynamic process that has characterized India for so many centuries, goes on, becoming more and more complex every day. What the ultimate synthesis will be, or whether there will be an ultimate synthesis, is unknown. One thing is clear: the most enjoyable means to the understanding of another culture is through the literature that represents that culture. The case for understanding need not be made. (ECD)

A brief history of the languages of India

A great many problems have already been raised, and many concepts advanced, not the least of which is the complexity of the linguistic situation in which all this interaction took place. Let us turn back to the beginning, when the wandering Aryan tribes, with their cattle and their great possession, the Veda, were drifting through the high passes into the fertile plain below. For they must have collided almost at once with representatives of two other major language families, with which their tongue, the southeasternmost branch of the Indo-European family, had not a word in common. Those two families were Dravidian and Austric.

In the valley of the Indus River, in the northwestern corner of the Indian subcontinent, lie the ruins of a vast and ancient civilization, which had planned cities, a script, and, most important, plumbing. Archeologists have long speculated on the coincidence of the estimated dates of that civilization (2500–1500 B.C.?) and the estimated dates of the arrival of the Aryan tribes in the plain. It is tempting to believe that the cities were destroyed by the invader-nomads, and their people driven southward. It is also tempting to believe that the writing on the seals recovered from the ruins is Dravidian. Recent linguistic studies support that possibility, but the writing code has not yet been deciphered (though recent studies in Copenhagen and elsewhere suggest that a breakthrough may be near). If Dravidian it is, this would have been the first encounter of the Indo-European speakers with that mysterious language family, to which no related languages have so far been discovered outside India.

The tribes would have met, early in their invasions, speakers of the Austric languages, members of a global family that, according to one theory, stretches from India to Hawaii. Unlike the dwellers in the Indus Valley, these tribal people probably had no script; many of the tribes have none today. But it is difficult not to believe that the Indo-Aryans did not exchange lore and legend, perhaps even elements of language, with them. Other language families, Tibeto-Burman in the mountain regions of the northeast, and Dardic in the extreme northwest, were perhaps too far removed from the settlements of the Indo-Aryans in the plains for much interaction to take place.

Despite the antiquity of the Vedas, none of the Indo-European languages brought by the Aryan tribes were recorded until relatively recent times. The unique emperor Aśoka, who assumed the throne about 269 B.C., repented of his bloody war-faring ways and in a series of rock and pillar edicts testified to his new Buddhist-inspired humanism. But the language of the inscriptions is a far cry from Vedic; for that ancient language, older than any writing in those other Indo-European tongues, Latin and Greek, not recorded in writing but orally transmitted with incredible fidelity by a long line of priests, underwent great internal development during the thousand years of its cultivation. By the time of the first inscriptions, therefore, several forms of language were already in use. The ancient Vedic language, as ritual language, existed unchanged. But the language of the commentaries shows transformation: the disquisitions of the *Brāhmaṇas*, *Āraṇyakas*, and *Sūtras* (1000–500 B.C.) are in an arid prose, while there are homely idioms and highly colloquial passages in *The Upaniṣads* (600–500 B.C.).

But with the possible exception of the Upaniṣadic passages, this language of the texts was not the speech of home, or even of court, but was a deliberately adopted and cultivated literary language. Speech was a means of communication. But it was at the same time far more than that, and the Vedic language, packed with power and preserved almost miraculously through the long wanderings of the Aryans, was the Voice of the Nation, the *rāṣṭrī vāk*. Not a God-given grace, not even to be derived from the articulations of some Indic Adam, speech was the Goddess herself, first utterance of Prajāpati, Lord of Creation, and herself coterminous with creation. Speech is the Goddess, larger and higher than the sum total of her expression, for "three quarters of Her are in heaven,

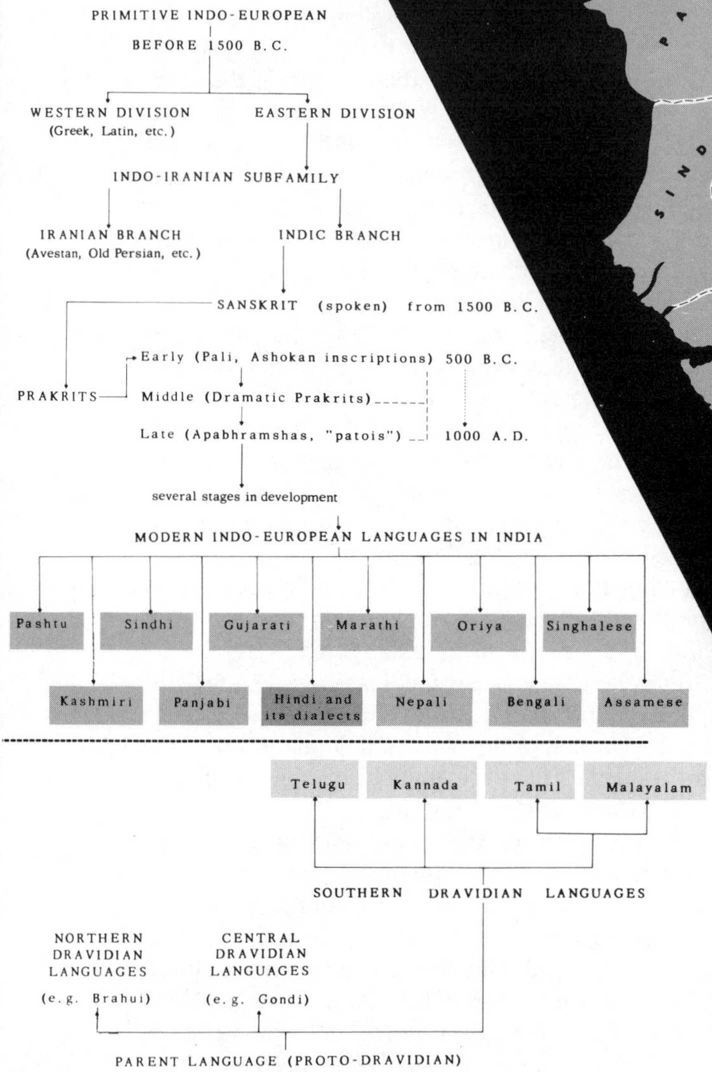

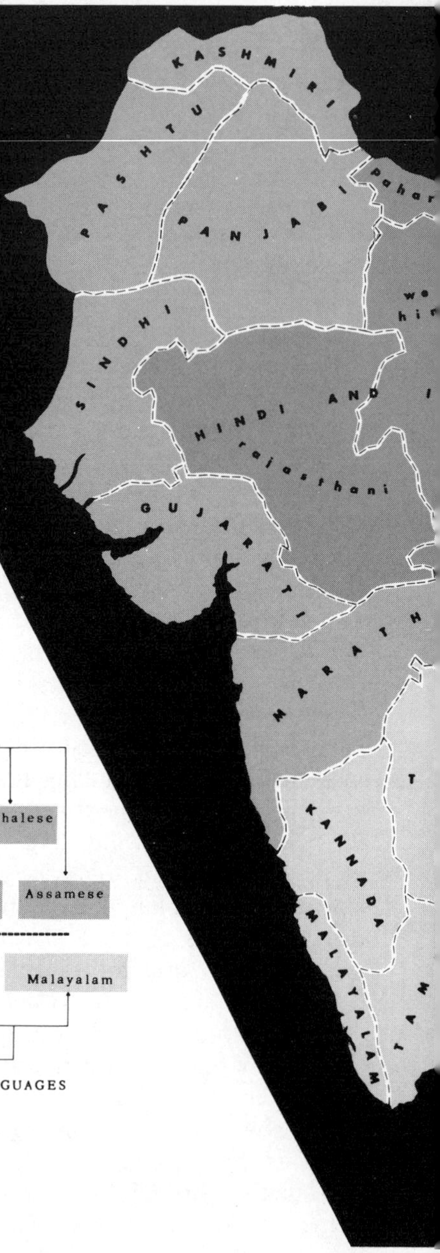

GUIDE TO THE DIAGRAMS

- areas in which the Dravidian languages are used in government, education and literature.
- areas in which Indo-European languages other than Hindi are used in government, education and literature.
- areas in which Hindi (including Urdu) is the principal language of government, education and literature.

Major Languages of South Asia

Map boundaries are approximate

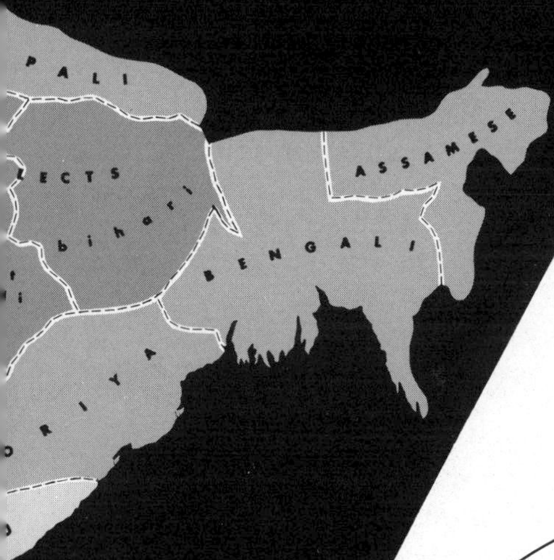

In addition to the major regional languages shown on the map there are thousands of local-village dialects and dozens of regional dialects spoken throughout South Asia. These are used by a large percentage of the population both as daily speech and as the spoken local or inter-village trade language.

This chart shows the approximate proportion of the total population of India* that speaks each of the major languages and the proportionate relationship of these major languages to the linguistic families. It is based on the 1951 census.
* Excluding Ceylon, Nepal, and Pakistan.

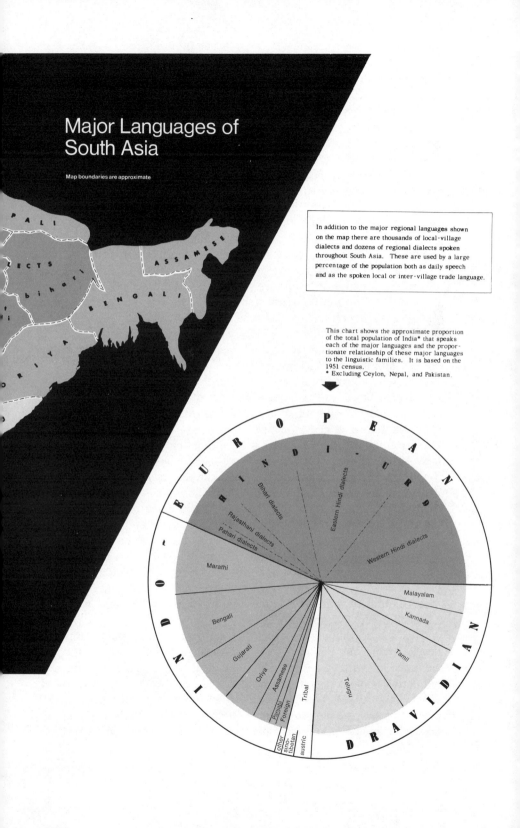

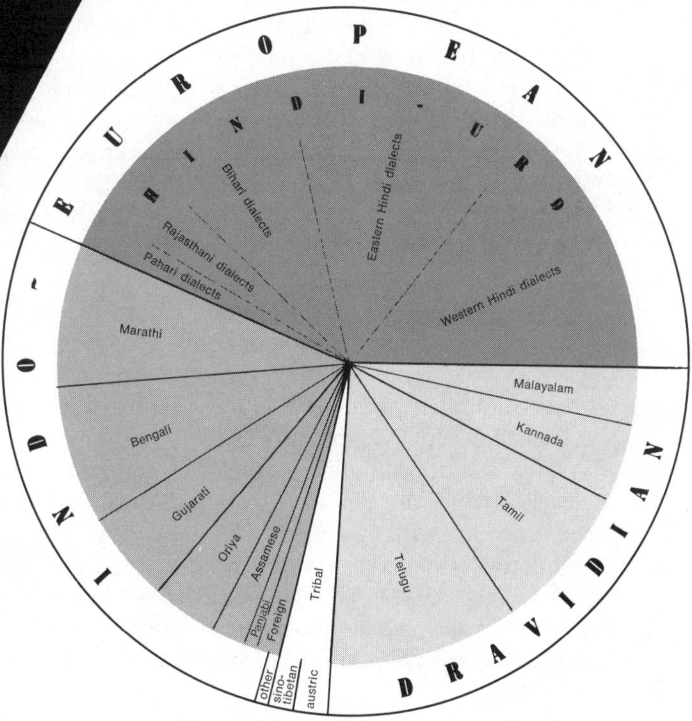

and the fourth quarter is spoken on the earth." She must, in the serious and sacred setting, be treated as such. And thus, from the beginning, there was a deep awe for the solemnly spoken word and an almost obsessive respect for the correctness of language. The poets of the Veda, possessors of this Vedic language, were later in history regarded not merely as poets but as seers who literally saw the eternally present hymns. When they bequeathed their verse, when the compilations of the Ṛg Veda and the Atharva Veda had been completed, transmission of the sacred lines with absolute perfection came to be the central concern: not a vowel or accent could be lost, lest the word with its awful power become a thunder-bolt to strike him who treats it lightly. The grammarian Patañjali in listing the uses of grammar points to the example of a demon whose epithet was Indraśatru, "Conqueror of Indra," who performed penance. Prompted by the demon's austerities, the Creator appeared and asked what he wanted; the demon replied that he wished himself, Indraśatru, to prosper. What he meant was *indraśátru*, "The Conqueror of Indra"; what he said was *índraśatru*, "whose conqueror is Indra." And so according to his own wish, expressed faultily only in one accent, he was destroyed. The word was all, the intention nothing, and it carries its own deadly power. This is why Hindu wives will not utter the names of their husbands, for with every utterance of his name a piece of his life falls away. Children are given the names of gods, for on his deathbed a father would surely call out his children's names; even if he forgot the god, the father would utter his name and thus secure his seat in heaven. And in reverse, in the Judeo-Christian tradition, one should not take the name of the Almighty in vain, for in the name is the Almighty.

From such a concern there developed a science of the analysis of language, of breaking up words into their smallest components, of finding the roots from which they are derived, of creating as it were an inventory of building blocks that make up the edifice that is Language. The tendency culminated in a textbook that is until this day the very basis of traditional learning (and a model for at least one branch of modern analytic linguistics), the grammar of Pāṇini (400 B.C.), the "Science in Eight Chapters."

The spoken language continued its normal process of internal development; but Pāṇini's grammar froze for all time the cultivated language known as Sanskrit. The name of the language, one of the few not derived from a region or a people, states its own program: *saṃskṛtā bhāṣā* is the ritually perfected and intellectually cultivated language. If one is to speak the language, he must speak it correctly. It is the proud possession of one whose birth predisposes him to education and whose education proceeds from, and in, Sanskrit. It was always his second language, though it was also always the language of his preference. In it he could speak to other educated Indians across the growing barriers between regionally developing dialects, and across the eternal barriers between the language families themselves, both in India and outside, in Java as well as Tibet. He would take extraordinary delight in reproducing complex clusters of consonants that his regional vernacular might have lost, or might never have possessed, in tasting the rolling phrases with the fastidious tongue of the paṇḍit, the Sanskrit specialist; and the wonder of the language, at once so rich and so neatly ordered, would perhaps inspire him to feats of complexity. He would communicate with a fellow Sanskritist, perhaps a friend standing next to him as they admired a lotus pond, perhaps that forgotten author who was the first ever to liken the face of a beautiful girl to a lotus flower. And in this communication he would find himself drawing on a metavocabulary that his regional tongue could not supply. He becomes an Erasmus conversing, through Latin and on things Latin, with a Thomas More, reserving his peasant Flemish for his maid and fellow villagers. But it is also true that the character of Sanskrit and of discourse in it result in a sometimes frustrating unconcern with specificity, with details of time, place, and person. This is one of the limitations that will be discovered in Sanskrit literature—limitations at least from one point of view. To the speaker of Sanskrit they were not felt as limitations, for he also had his regional vernacular in which he could meaningfully discuss matters of everyday and be sure that his fellow speaker, from the same region, would understand his references.

Some regional languages in their turn became literary languages. Pāli, a language akin to Sanskrit, became the instrument of the older forms of Buddhism. The Buddha had demanded that "each be taught in his own tongue." The emperor Aśoka took this demand seriously, and in his inscriptions he adapted identical words to different dialects. Pāli itself was conceived as a new universal language of religion, a kind of Buddhist Sanskrit. But, unlike Sanskrit, it was close enough to the dialects to be intelligible to speakers of them, yet far enough away from any particular one to sound much like local idiom. This is a phenomenon that has occurred repeatedly in India, the emergence of a new literary language derived from a group of diverse colloquials, yet differing from all of them.

Pāli, though usually because of its vast literature considered separately, is sometimes included in the group of regional languages called the Prākrits, which represent the next stage of the development of Indic. These languages are named after the regions in which they were spoken, e.g., Śaurasenī, Māgadhī, and Māhārāstrī. It is in fact unclear whether they were separate languages or dialects, mutually intelligible. In any case, in the classical Sanskrit drama it is clear that they were literary dialects, and mutually intelligible, at least by the connoisseur, for, as will be seen, in that drama each person speaks a language appropriate to his character and various Prākrits are used. The Prākrits were literary languages, and in fact much is left of their literature. But inestimably more has been lost. Apart from Pāli and Ardhamāgadhī, which was used by the religious group called the Jains, the Prākrits were neither languages of high culture nor of religion. Thus, unlike the texts of Vedic and Sanskrit, Prākrit texts have not been carefully preserved orally; the subject of the preservation of literature in manuscripts in India is a painful one.

It must be remembered that every ancient Indian book now extant emerged into print after a long line of users with the interest, the means, or the leisure to transcribe an earlier copy. At times this line became very thin. At times it vanished altogether, and a book was irretrievably lost. Also, the materials used for writing, birchbark and palm leaf, were very perishable. The rigors of climate, the heat and the humidity, and vermin threatened them. It has been remarked that 90 percent of Indian literature has been eaten by white ants. What is left has had to overcome the even greater obstacles of inertia or indifference. A handful of Indian manuscripts are as old as A.D. 1000, but the great bulk of those extant date from no earlier than the seventeenth century. This was a period when Sanskrit learning itself had dwindled, when the number of the erudite who might be interested in copying old books had decreased and their interests perhaps narrowed. Disinterest in certain works and in certain types of works, especially if written in Prākrit, knowledge of which was largely lost, would effect an unconscious but definitive censorship. Uncopied manuscripts would disintegrate and finally disappear. A very real consequence is that certain of the ideas formed of India, particularly classical India, may be distorted or at the least incomplete. The texts transmitted down to modern times—and this is as true of the regional "vernacular" languages as it is of Sanskrit and Prākrit—are texts illustrative of the high culture or of the main religious stream. Others, less acceptable to the main learned and religious traditions, would have died a natural death, leaving modern scholars with sure knowledge only of that which the guardians of these traditions permit.

Moving through time, after the Prākrits there is traditionally distinguished another phase in the development of the Indic languages called "Apabhraṃśa" or "Decadence," a catch-all term, like Prākrit, not meant to denote a specific time span, but a general stage of development between the Prākrits and the modern vernaculars. The name Apabhraṃśa was given by Sanskrit authors who considered language to be so rigidly defined that any change in it could only be thought of as deterioration. But the Apabhraṃśa languages were the matrices from which the modern Indian languages of the north were to rise into literature, and in their late form, around A.D. 1000, they carried themes and forms back and forth between late classical Sanskrit and the early modern languages. And with such interchange, together with natural growth and development, writings began in the regional languages that the regional cultures would later consider their own most ancient classics. From this point the histories of literature in Marathi, Bengali, and the rest of the modern Indic languages took off.

There was in fact to come a time when the sacredness of Sanskrit as a language and as the carrier of the ancient religion and learning would be scorned and the pedantry of the paṇḍits who were its keepers mocked. From the fourteenth century down through the seventeenth, the enthusiastic religious revival of bhakti, which had begun some centuries earlier in the south, swept all across northern India; its expression was in the regional languages. "Sanskrit is like the water of a deep well," wrote the poet Kabīr in the sixteenth century, "but the vernacular is like a running brook." Fired by a missionary zeal, the poets of this movement spoke to the people in their own languages, as indeed the Buddha had suggested that his disciples do, many centuries before. And a spate of writing, not only religious poetry but philosophical texts and works of literature and biography, broke out. The bhakti movement more than any other single factor gave the regional languages self-confidence enough to begin to develop literarily on their own, to grow away from the massive trunk of the Sanskritic tradition.

But they remained attached to that trunk, and remain so still, and in more than a historical way. There are a thousand natural legacies received by the modern Indic languages from Sanskrit: metrical preconceptions if not actual metrical systems, notions of the efficacy of certain sounds, mythological and symbolic repertories, and ideas of the purposes, norms, and values of literature.

One final note on linguistic matters. It should not be forgotten that the variety of languages in India is matched almost equally by a diversity of scripts. As far as is known, all Indian scripts derive from an ancient script called "Brāhmī," used by the emperor Aśoka in his inscriptions. Brāhmī seems to have been the basis not only of the scripts of India itself, but of those of Java and Bali, Ceylon, Tibet, Burma, Cambodia, and Thailand. But as with other forms of language, scripts have a way of developing over time, so that with the passage of centuries the script used by modern Gujaratis is no longer readable to Bengalis, though similarities are clear. The scripts of most of the northern languages differ from the southern in about the same degree as roman and Cyrillic differ from Hebrew. This, among other things, created obstacles to the preservation of manuscripts in languages other than the ones in which they were found.

As if this were not sufficiently complicated, when the Muslim invasions began in earnest in the ninth and tenth centuries, an entirely different script was introduced. For the invaders naturally brought their languages with them, and these languages were written largely in the Persianized Arabic script. The invaders settled down to become an integral part of the population of the subcontinent; their script took its place. Urdu, Sindhi, and the other languages of the northwest are Indo-Aryan, not Semitic, in their structure. But the script in which they are embodied is the Perso-Arabic one.

If there has ever been anything in India close to universal script, it is the one called Devanāgarī, the principal script used for the transmission of Sanskrit and now used for Hindi and Marathi. The problems all this raises are in no sense purely academic, and one of the main controversies on the linguistic side of modern India's search for unity has been in terms of a single script. Some feel that only the adoption of a script entirely outside the heritage of Brahmi will solve the problem.

A brief survey of the literatures of South Asia

At the risk of repeating some things that have already been said and anticipating others that will later be elaborated in greater detail, it might be found useful to have a quick survey of the main course of the literatures of South Asia and give some chronological framework to the variety of works written in an increasingly large number of languages.

South Asian literature began in the region of the Panjāb in northwestern India with the arrival of a people who spoke a tongue akin to the language groups of Europe and Iran. This tongue was an early representative of the so-called Indo-Aryan family of languages, which now covers most of South Asia with the exception of peninsular India. From this early date onward—usually placed at ca. 1400 B.C.—the subcontinent has had a continuous literature.

In its entirety the literature of South Asia can be divided in three broad periods: the ancient and classical, which runs from ca. 1200 B.C. until A.D. 1000; the medieval, from ca. A.D. 1000 until the coming of the British; and the modern period, which begins with the influence of Western letters on the literatures.

The ancient and classical literatures

These literatures comprise the Vedic, Sanskrit, Pāli, and Prākrit literatures as well as the beginnings of the literature of the second important language family of India, Dravidian.

Vedic literature. The literature of the Veda consists almost entirely of sacred texts that were in use at, or centered around, the specific Vedic religion of sacrifice and ritual. It is commonly divided into four layers, which are largely successive though there is an overlap in time between the last phase of one and the early phase of the other. The most ancient works are the so-called *Saṃhitās*, "Compendia." They, as well as the Vedic literature in general, are classified according to the division of the Veda as a whole into the Ṛgveda ("Wisdom of the Hymns"), the Yajurveda ("the Sacrificial Formulas"), the Sāmaveda ("the Chants"), and the Atharvaveda ("The Wisdom of the Atharva priesthood").

The first three of the Saṃhitās belong intimately together, their common reference being the Vedic ritual. The Ṛgveda comprises principally hymns of invocation and prayer to the high gods of the Pantheon—Indra, the Fire God, and others—and to the principal substance of sacrifice at the great ceremonies, the *soma*. The Yajurveda is a compilation of the formulas pronounced by that group of priests belonging to the Yajurveda, whose function it was to perform the ritual manipulations. The Sāmaveda is an anthology of Ṛgvedic verses that were set to music and chanted during the high rituals.

The Atharvaveda is a quite different collection. On the one hand it contains spells for rites within the province of the Atharvaveda, which spoke to day-to-day needs of the people and contained a good bit of magic, and on the other hand hymns in which the source of being, creation, man's relation to the supernatural world, and cosmology are speculated upon.

The earliest literature—and this can be said of most of the ancient and classical and even the medieval literatures—does not allow of precise dating. The Ṛgveda is the oldest, from about the fourteenth century B.C. The Yajurveda and Sāmaveda must have developed in the centuries after that, though before 1000 B.C., while for the Atharvaveda usually the date of 1200 B.C. is set. Apart from general uncertainty it must further be kept in mind that works described as one book have undergone an internal evolution, so that the same book contains older and more recent portions.

The *Saṃhitā* literature is followed by that of *The Brāhmaṇas* ("Discussions about the holy rites and spells"), voluminous tomes that deal with the principal rituals and the speculation to which they give rise, mainly their relationship to the potent forces at work in the cosmos that they were thought to originate and regulate. These texts, once more divided according to the four-Veda scheme, are mostly dated from ca. 1000–700 B.C.

The next group of texts, *The Āraṇyakas*, continues the concern of *The Brāhmaṇas* while dealing with other, more recent, or more mysterious rites, but also gives increasing attention to the relationships between rite and cosmic process on the one hand and man's relationship to both on the other. They generally are posterior to *The Brāhmaṇas* and hence usually placed between 700 and 600 B.C.

The speculative content of the Āraṇyakas begins to dominate the last layer of strictly Vedic texts, *The Upaniṣads* ("Mystical Equations"), in which the interest in sacerdotal detail has receded and the attention is almost wholly focused on man, his relationship to the cosmos and its source, and his relationship to the ultimate and irreducible principle in himself, the *ātman*. There are a good many of these mostly brief texts. The oldest ones, among which *The Bṛhadāraṇyaka Upaniṣad* and *The Chāndogya Upaniṣad* may be singled out, go back to the sixth century, but others are more recent and may even belong to the Christian era.

Around the Vedic literature and its principal concern, the sacrifice, there arose a body of subsidiary literature. It centers around the six so-called *Vedāngas* ("limbs of the Veda") such as phonetics, metrics, grammar, and ritual procedure, which in turn spawned a further subsidiary literature of *sūtras* ("Brief Manuals"), in which the result of these investigations is summarized. Oldest are the *kalpa-sūtras* (on the ritual procedure), the most important among which are the *śrauta-sūtras* (on the great priestly ceremonies) and the *gṛhya-sūtras* (on the domestic ritual, rites of passage, and the like).

One of the *sūtras* to emerge from the Vedāngas was *The Aṣṭādhyāyī* ("sūtra in eight chapters") of Pāṇini (ca. fifth century B.C.), in which the late-Vedic language was analyzed and forever fixed normatively. It was the language thus codified that will henceforth be Sanskrit, the unchangeable "tongue perfected."

Sanskrit literature. The literature in Sanskrit as defined according to Pāṇini's grammar begins in the fifth century B.C. and experienced its highest efflorescence from the second century B.C. until the seventh century A.D., although it continued as the language of scholarship, religion, and philosophy until much later and until today has remained alive among the traditionally educated.

The first among the older Sanskrit works (though not always written according to strict Pāṇinean lines) are the Indian epics, *The Mahābhārata* and *The Rāmāyaṇa*. Both are large works, but *The Mahābhārata* is gigantic, comprising a length of about seven times that of *The Iliad* and *The Odyssey* combined. *The Mahābhārata* in the main narrates the story of two rival groups of cousins both laying claim to the succession in a region somewhere near present-day Delhi, and of the war that ensues. But for the later literature its main inspiration has become the large number of extraneous tales that have become agglutinated to the epical core. The characters of the main story go back to ca. 1000 B.C., but the text we have at present is of later date, probably not older than ca. 400 B.C. The great number of stories that made the work swell to its present size, and not least the long didactic insertions bearing upon the Dharma and religion, bring the date of the text as a whole, i.e., when its composition was finally closed, down to ca. A.D. 400.

The Rāmāyaṇa, which will be treated more circumstantially below, took on form during the period that *The Mahābhārata* underwent its evolution, ca. 200 B.C.–A.D. 200. Unlike *The Mahābhārata*, to which many authors must have contributed, it has a unitary style that may well derive from a single author, to whom Indian tradition has given the name Vālmīki.

Vālmīki has been given the honorary title of Ādi-kavi, the "first poet." While occasional great poetical force cannot be denied to *The Mahābhārata*, Vālmīki's title is inspired by the fact that in the judgment of the later Sanskrit authors he first adhered to the literary standards and themes that became normative for the genre that is called *Kāvya*.

Kāvya arose in the first centuries A.D. as a literary style that would decide literary tastes for a millenium, and even longer through the profound influence it exerted on the literatures of medieval India. *Kāvya* has been called court poetry, which is apt not only because much of it was composed at urban centers and not infrequently patronized by local princes, but also because it exhibits a hyper-refined style of language, poetics of metaphor and simile, virtuosity of meter, and precious erudition.

The classical expression of this *Kāvya* style is the so-called *mahākāvya* ("great poem"); the short lyric; and the Sanskrit theater. It was also extended to the narrative literature, in which the authors at times indulge in typically *kāvya*-type literary fancies, and in particular to the "novel," itself mostly based upon the narrative literature.

The earliest example of a *mahākāvya* is given by the Buddhist Aśvaghoṣa (ca. 1st century A.D.) in his two extant works, *The Buddhacarita*, "Life of the Buddha," and *The Saundarānanda*, "The Story of Sundarī and

Nanda." Compared with later literature his poems are relatively simple but show the basic characteristics of the Kāvya style: a predilection for nature scenes, amorous episodes, grand spectacles, and gnomic aphorisms. In its classical form a *mahākāvya* comprises a variable number of "cantos" of usually short length, each often written in a different meter such as is in harmony with the subject matter, and takes its subject matter from the two epics, which are followed with a great deal of freedom. There are set pieces: the description of urban and nature scenes, the seasons, sun and moon in rising and setting, games and festivals, war and triumph.

The tradition lists six exemplary *mahākāvyas*, three by Kālidāsa and one each by Bhāravi, Māgha, and Śrīharṣa. Kālidāsa (ca. fifth–sixth centuries A.D.) draws on epic themes in two of his *Mahākāvyas*, *The Kumārasaṃbhava*, "The Birth of the War God Kumāra," and *The Raghuvaṃśa*, "The Dynasty of Raghu." The first describes the courting of Śiva by Pārvati, the daughter of Himālaya, their wedding and love play; the second the vicissitudes of one great mythical dynasty, to which also Rāma belonged. Kālidāsa is the master of the simple-appearing crystalline strophe, a genius that he displays particularly in his *Meghadūta*, "the Cloud as Messenger," in which a lovesick exile sends a cloud on its detailedly described way with a message for his beloved. Bhāravi hails from the sixth century; he based his *Kirātārjunīya*, "Of Arjuna and the Mountain Man," on an episode of *The Mahābhārata* in which the two are embattled. Also based on the great epic is Māgha's *Śiśupālavadha*, "The Slaying of Śiśupāla," which retells in ornate style an episode of *The Mahābhārata* in which Kṛṣṇa kills his rival Śiśupāla. Śrīharṣa wrote *The Naiṣadhacarita*, "Life of Nala," on the first part of King Nala's life when he marries Damayantī, but stops when the story is to turn to the tragedy of his gambling. Partly in the genre of the *mahākāvya* is also *Gītagovinda*, "Song of the Cowherd Kṛṣṇa," of Jayadeva (twelfth century), which marries to this genre a highly musical style of interspersed songs.

The short lyric, usually styled *subhāṣita*, "well-turned couplet," shows the power of the poet in miniature. Its subject matter might be anything that strikes the author's fancy, but the most favored is that of love, and mostly that of love in separation, which in later ages will become a model for the separation of the soul from God. Side by side with the worldly lyric there are large collections of *stotras* or devotional lyrics, of which Mayūra's *Sūryāṣṭaka*, "Eight Stanzas of the Sun," Śankara's *Saundaryalāharī*, and Bilvamangala's *Kṛṣṇakarṇāmṛta* are well-known examples. The erotic and devotional lyric may shade into each other when the yearning of the soul for God is described as that of a woman for her lover.

The Sanskrit theater was the epitome of Sanskrit literature, combining great verse with an operatic spectacle, dance, music, and mime. Fragments have been preserved from Aśvaghoṣa, who stands at the beginning of a grand tradition that is more fully treated elsewhere in this book.

Of special distinction in Indian literature is the narrative one, many examples of which have survived in Sanskrit, though they hardly originated in that language. A fuller account of the narrative literature is found in chapter 4.

Pāli and Prākrit literature. Although the literature in Sanskrit dominates the classical period, this language was by no means the only medium. Like Vedic, however, Pāli, and some of the Prākrit works, has a religious rather than literary intention. Pāli is resorted to by the Theravāda school of Buddhism for the sacred canon, *The Tipiṭaka* and other canonical works, whereas *Ardhamāgadhī* and *Māhārāṣṭrī* have been used by Jains for their texts.

In spite of their religious thrust, some of the Buddhist texts contain episodes of great literary value. The discourses of the Buddha can be direct, homely, lively, and with a wry humor. *The Dhammapada,* "Words on the Doctrine," is an example of the strain of gnomic aphorisms that is evident also in the Sanskrit short lyric. Of the utmost interest are the personal verses of the Buddhist elders and nuns in *The Theragāthā,* "Songs of the Elders," and *Therīgāthā,* "Songs of the Nuns," which often reveal the quality of the appeal that Buddhism had for its early converts. Of a very different character are the episodes collected in *The Jātakas,* "Birth Stories," in which a popular story or fable is pulled within the ambience of Buddhism by describing it as an incident in the Buddha's previous lives. There are approximately five hundred such episodes, many of which also live on in Sanskrit narrative literature.

In a historical context is set *The Milindapañha,* purporting to describe the questions of the Greco-Bactrian king Menander (ca. 140–110 B.C.), who was skeptical of Buddhism but is converted by the Elder Nāgasena, mainly with the aid of metaphor and parable.

Considerably less interest attaches to the canonical texts of the Jains from a literary point of view. However, the Jains were great transmitters of tales, and *The Vāsudevahiṇḍī,* "The Wanderings of Vāsudeva," is an important part of the narrative heritage.

Of much interest, however, is the remaining Prākrit literature. The most popular work is *The Hālasattasaī* (fourth century A.D.), the "Seven Hundred Couplets of King Hāla," a collection of at times quite outspokenly erotic literature. An important part was played by Prākrit in the Sanskrit plays where, as will be noted, characters other than kings and brahmins speak one of the variously graded Prākrits. As some of the greatest Sanskrit writers in this way had to employ Prākrit, the statements, particularly in verse (for which Māhārāṣṭrī is used), can be very forceful. Much of the Prākrit literature undoubtedly has been lost due to the waning knowledge of the language on the part of later men of letters and lack of interest. The Prākrit literature is succeeded by Apabhraṃśa literature, which is in an even sorrier state, and Apabhraṃśa in turn was succeeded by the modern Indo-Aryan languages, with which a wholly new chapter starts. (JABvB)

The Indo-Aryan literatures: the medieval period

At the turn of the millenium there began to appear, at slightly differing times, the literatures of the languages now known as the regional languages of the subcontinent. As far as is now known, the earliest literature to develop was Bengali. Although some would contest the argument that they are in Bengali, rather than Oriya, Assamese, or Hindi, the poems called *caryā-padas*, short Buddhist esoteric poems preserved in manuscripts in the cold climate of Nepal, date from perhaps the eleventh century A.D. Slightly later, on the other side of the subcontinent, Old Gujarati was taking literary shape. Other literatures do not begin to appear until later. So the most that can be said is that the literatures of the regional languages began to develop in the two or three centuries following A.D. 1000.

These literatures show three characteristics: a debt to their progenitor Sanskrit, a less obvious one to their Apabhramśa past, and regional peculiarities.

The debt of the regional literatures to Sanskrit can be seen in the use of Sanskrit lexicon and imagery, of myth and story preserved in that refined language, and in frequent conformity to the ideals and values put forth in the Sanskrit texts of poetics and philogophy. The texts of the early stages of the literatures are most often mythological tales, all in poetry, drawn from the epics and purāṇas of Sanskrit. In addition to themes, the regional literatures frequently borrowed forms from Sanskrit: *The Rāmāyaṇa* of Vālmīki appears in the sixteenth-century Hindi of Tulsī-dās with the same shape, though a slightly different emphasis, as the Sanskrit. The stylized imagery and convention of Sanskrit court poetry appears again, though here too with different emphasis, in the fifteen-century Maithili (eastern Hindi) writer Vidyāpati. And the rhetorical speculations of the Sanskrit schools of poetics are used as formulas for the production of seventeenth-century Hindi court poetry.

A different type of relationship existed between regional literatures and Apabhraṁśa. Apabhraṁśa poetry employed end rhyme, a device not used in classical Sanskrit. The regional literatures too employ end rhyme. Second, there are two major poetic forms that occur in Apabhraṁśa and in the regional literatures, but not in Sanskrit: the *bāramāsa*, "twelve months," in which the beauties of a girl or of a deity might be extolled in twelve different ways, and the *cautiśā*, in which the thirty-four letters of the Devanagari alphabet are used as the initial letters of the lines of poems of thirty-four lines or stanzas. And finally, there are themes that probably came to the regional literatures from Apabhraṁśa: that of the religious hero Gopī-candra of the Nātha-yogī sect, for example, is known from Bengal to the Panjab even in the early period.

There is one other unifying factor that should be mentioned before one must begin to consider the problem of several "Indian literatures." As will be mentioned again, from the fourteenth through the seventeenth centuries, devotional religion (*bhakti*) took hold in one region after another in northern India. Not only was beautiful lyric poetry and passionate devotional song created by this movement, but in some cases, as in Bengal, serious philosophical works were for the first time written in languages other than Sanskrit. Though there is in this poetry and song much that is Sanskritic in imagery and expression, its basic character is more vital than polished, more vivid than refined.

Hindi

What is commonly known as Hindi is actually a range of languages, ranging from Maithili in the east to Rajasthani in the west. It may be said that the earliest texts in which has come to be known as the language of northern India, are those of the Muslim poet Amīr *Kh*usrau (1254–1325), who included Hindi verses among his Persian poems and romances. But of the medieval period the giant is the poet-saint Kabīr, whose *Bījak* ("Seed verses") has had its religious and literary influence since the sixteenth century. Less poetically powerful and more sectarian are two nearly contemporary poets of *bhakti*, Tulsī-dās (b. 1523) and Sūr-dās (1503–1563). Tulsī's most famous work is his version of *The Rāmāyaṇa* story, while Sūr-dās, also a bhakta, is best known for his tender poems about Kṛṣṇa the child.

Bengali

The history of Bengali literature, though somewhat longer, follows the same general contours as that of Hindi. Apart from the *caryā-padas*, the earliest texts in what is distinctively Bengali is a long poem on the Rādhā-Kṛṣṇa theme, *The Śrīkṛṣṇa-kīrtana* by Baṛu Caṇḍī-dāsa, dated by some scholars in the mid-fifteenth century. But it is certain that well before that time texts known as *maṅgal-kāvya*, eulogies of gods and goddesses, were being developed orally. But as in other parts of the subcontinent, it was the bhakti movement that established Bengali as a literary language. In the sixteenth century, not only short lyrics on the Kṛṣṇa theme but texts of biography and philosophy such as the long hagiography *Caitanya-caritāmṛta* of Kṛṣṇa-dāsa were being written. In this period also, under the stimulus of the Muslim rulers, Bengali versions of the Sanskrit epics and purāṇas were being developed. The favorite Bengali literary form of the medieval period was the *maṅgal*, and well into the nineteenth century *The Annadā-maṅgal* ("Eulogy of the food-giving goddess") of Bhārat-candra (1712–1760) was popular. But of the medieval texts, it was the devotional lyrics to Rādhā and Kṛṣṇa, known and sung even today, that mark the zenith of the literature.

Assamese

The earliest text in a language that is incontestably Assamese is *The Prahlāda-caritra* of Hēma Sarasvatī (thirteenth century), which recounts in a heavily Sanskritized style a story from *The Viṣṇu-purāṇa*. The first great Assamese poet, however, was Kavirāja Mādhava Kandalī (fourteenth century), who translated *The Rāmāyaṇa* from Sanskrit, and who wrote a long narrative on the Kṛṣṇa theme. In Assamese too the bhakti movement brought a great literary upsurge. The most famous poet of the period was Śaṅkara-deva (1489–1568), and his writing inspired such poets as Mādhava-deva (1489–1596) to write lyrics of great beauty. Among the peculiarities of Assamese are the *burañjis*, chronicles written in the prose tradition that was brought to Assam by the Ahoms of Burma, dating from the seventeenth century.

Oriya

The Mādāḷā-pāñji texts in Oriya, the chronicles of the great temple of Jagannāth in Puri, are in prose, perhaps as early as the twelfth century; these cannot yet be called literary texts in the pure sense of the term. An early literary text is the anonymous fourteenth-century *Kalasa-cautiśā*, which tells in thirty-five verses the story of Śiva and the mountain goddess Pārvatī. The fourteenth and fifteenth centuries were productive for Oriya literature, for the famous *Caṇḍī-purāṇa* of Sāraḷā-dāsa also dates from this time. But the bhakti period was again the most stimulating one. The best known Oriya poet of the medieval period is Jagannātha-dāsa, a disciple of the Bengali Vaiṣṇava saint Caitanya (1485–1533), who spent the better part of his life in Puri. Among Jagannātha-dāsa's works is a version of the Sanskrit *Bhāgavata-purāṇa*, still popular in Orissa today.

Marathi

With Bengali, Marathi is the oldest of the regional literatures, dating from about A.D. 1000. Although in the thirteenth century the two Brahmanical sects, the Mahānubhāva and the Vārākarī Panth, put forth quantities of literature, it was out of the bhakti tradition that the most famous names of early Marathi literature came: Jñāneśvara, who wrote a commentary on *The Bhagavad-gītā* in the late thirteenth century, Nāmadeva, his younger contemporary (d. 1350), and the later writer Eknāth (1548–1599), whose most famous work is a Marathi version of the eleventh book of *The Bhāgavata-purāṇa*. The most famous single name of the bhakti movement is that of Tukārām (1588–1649), whose short poems are among the most cherished possessions of Marathi literature. A unique contribution of Marathi is the tradition of *pōwāḍās*, heroic stories beloved by a martial people; there is no way of dating the earliest of these, but the tradition was particularly vital at the time of the great military leader Śivaji (b. 1627), who led his armies against the might of the Mughal emperor Aurangzeb.

Gujarati

The oldest examples of Gujarati writing are from the Jaina scholar and saint Hēmacandra (1089–1173). The language had developed fully by the late twelfth century, and from the fourteenth century there are didactic texts written by Jaina monks. The bhakti poets of the language include Narasiṁha Mahatā (1415–1481); but by far the most famous is the woman saint Mīrā Bāī, who lived in the first half of the sixteenth century. Mīrā, though married, thought of Kṛṣṇa as her true husband, and her lyrics telling of her relationship with her god and lover are among the warmest and most moving in Indian literature.

Panjabi

Panjabi developed literarily later than most of the other regional languages, and some of the earliest writings claimed by the language are in Old Hindi rather than true Panjabi. The first clearly Panjabi work is *The Janam-sākhī*, a biography of the Sikh Guru Nānak by Bālā, written in the sixteenth century. In 1605 Arjun, the fifth guru of the Sikhs, collected the poems of Nānak and others (including Kabīr) into what is certainly the most famous work to originate in the Panjab (though its language is not entirely Panjabi), *The Ādi-granth*, the sacred book of the Sikhs. In fact, writing in true Panjabi begins in the seventeenth century, and is almost entirely by Muslims. Sufis in particular, such as Bulluē Shāh (1680–1758), contributed devotional lyrics, and Sufi Islam can be said to be the main stimulus for Panjabi literature in the medieval period.

Kashmiri

The commonly accepted period for Old Kashmiri is A.D. 1200–1500, but the earliest example of literature in the language is a four-line stanza embedded in a Sanskrit philosophical work that some scholars now date as late as the fifteenth century. The verse itself is undatable. As in Gujarati, the most famous poets of the period are women. Lalla Didi (b. 1335?) wrote poems of the god Śiva; and Hubb Khātun (sixteenth century) and especially Araṇī-māl (eighteenth century) are famous for their love lyrics of haunting beauty. Despite these outstanding poets in Kashmiri, the great literary language of Kashmir in the medieval period was Persian, which was encouraged and promoted by many of the rulers of the country.

Islamic literature

While there had been an Islamic presence in India since the eighth century, the literary and cultural influence of Islam made itself felt only in the eleventh and twelfth centuries, to start flourishing in the thirteen century when there was a great influx of Muslims into India. The religious and cultural ideals of the Muslims in India found expression in various languages, Arabic, Persian, Turkish, and regional Indian languages, but increasingly in a newly transformed language, Urdu (literally "camp"), a mixture of Hindustaṇi and an overwhelming number of Persian and Arabic loan words.

The milieu of Urdu literature is that of Muslim court culture and Sufi religion, elitist and urban. The influence of court and Sufism expresses itself in two ways that were to remain central to Urdu literature. A poet would choose a teacher (*ustād*) as the Sufi student would, and the succession of gurus would be of importance to the student. The poetry would be exchanged in poetic sessions (*muša'irah*), not dissimilar to those at court. The literature began to develop in the sixteenth century around courts in Golconda and Bijapur in the Deccan, later on in Aurangabad, until in the eighteenth century it reached into Delhi itself, from where it also spread to Lucknow.

The main staple of the first three centuries was poetry; prose was not to begin until the nineteenth century. The poets pursued many genres, the *qasīda*, which are frankly encomiastic in hope of patronage, *hajw*, derogatory verse, *šahr-āshōb*, laments over a destroyed city, *marsiyah*, elegiac verse, particularly over the martyrdom of Hassan and Husayn, which were read ceremonially during the month of Muharram; but the most important genres were the *masnawī* and *ghazal*. Since the *ghazal* will be discussed in a later chapter, we limit ourselves here to the *masnawī*. This verse form was the one preferred for narrative including didactic purposes, for it is a very free verse; it consists of a series of two-line couplets, with the two lines rhyming. The more famous of the *masnawī* are by Delhi and Lucknow poets such as Mir, Mir Hasan, Daya Shankar Nasim, and Mirza Shawq. The subject matter of *masnawī* is very wide, ranging from descriptions of daily life, outings of sultans, the seasons, to autobiographical discourses. Some of the *masnawī* poets, particularly those at the Deccan courts married Hindu subject matter to the originally Persian verse form as well as the more traditional Muslim romances and utilize local Indian color. (JABvB)

The Dravidian literatures: the ancient and medieval periods

Of the four literary Dravidian languages, Tamil is the oldest recorded, followed by Kannada, Telugu, and Malayalam. Tamil literature has a classical tradition of its own, while the literatures of the other three have been more profoundly influenced by Sanskrit models.

The early classical Tamil literature (first–fourth centuries A.D.) is represented by eight anthologies of lyrics, ten long poems, and a grammar called *The Tolkāppiyam* ("Old composition"). The eight anthologies, traditionally assigned to poets of three academies or *caṅkams*, consist of love poems, poems on kings, and religious verse. The classifications and poetics of these anthologies are peculiar to the Tamil system, quite different from the Sanskritic one. The poems are classified by theme into *akam* ("interior") and *puṟam* ("exterior"). The former are highly structured love poems, the latter poems on war, death, personal virtues, the glory and ferocity of kings, and the poverty of poets. As will be seen, common to these poems is a system of "landscapes" in which a convention of highly refined symbolism enables the poet to evoke complex moods by the mention of a flower, bird, or mountain: bees making honey from kuṟiñci flowers evoke the lovers' union.

Usually dated fourth to seventh centuries are the *Patiṉeṇ-kītkkaṇakku* ("Eighteen ethical works"), in which Jainism and Buddhism are discernible. Of these *The Tirukkuṟaḷ* ("Sacred distichs"), ascribed to Tiruvaḷḷuvar, is the most famous. The work exhibits many parallels to Sanskrit works on love, social obligation, religious law, and politics.

The age of the dynasty of warrior Hindu kings, the Pallavas (A.D. 300–888) is known for its epics, the most famous of which is *The Cilappatikāram* ("The lay of the anklet"). This epic, by Iḷaṅkō Aṭikaḷ, is a fine synthesis of mood poetry in the ancient Tamil caṅkam tradition and the rhetoric of Sanskrit poetry.

In South India too the bhakti movement was a great stimulus to the production of literature, though here as early as the seventh century, much earlier than in the north. The earliest poets of bhakti were devotees of Śiva called Nāyaṉārs ("Śiva people"), whose first representative was the woman poet Kāṟaikkāl Ammaiyār. Also early in the bhakti tradition were the Āḻvārs, devotees of Viṣṇu; to the Āḻvārs, God is the light of lights, lit in the heart of the worshiper.

The period of the Cōḻa Empire (tenth-thirteenth centuries) saw the awakening of the neighboring Dravidian literatures, Kannada, Telugu, and Malayalam. The first extant work in Kannada is the ninth-century *Kavirājamārga* ("The royal road of poets"), a work of rhetoric indebted to Sanskrit works in the field but including descriptions of Kannada country, people, and dialects, with references to earlier works now lost. In this period narrative writing, partly in verse and partly in prose, gained popularity, as did renderings of the Sanskrit epics in both Kannada and Telugu.

The twelfth century also saw the emergence of one of the most famous works of Tamil literature, the poet Kampaṉ's version of *The Rāmāyaṇa*. The poem shows a felicitous blend of early caṅkam lyrics, epic poetry, and the fervent personal devotionalism of the Āḻvārs, and is a mixture of folk motifs and Sanskrit stories, meters, and poetic devices. The poem was, and is, so popular that its influence extended into the north, influencing some episodes in Tulsi-dāsa's Hindi version, and to the west into Kerala.

Previous to the fifteenth century, the influence of Tamil on Malayalam was strong, and led to the development of the *pāṭṭu* ("song"), in which Tamil meter, phonology, and poetic device are obvious. But as strong as the Tamil influence was, that of Sanskrit was stronger, in language and in literary form. There was in fact a literary dialect called *maṇipravāḷa* ("a necklace of diamonds and coral"), which was a mixture of Sanskrit and Tamil or Malayalam, and dramas, narratives, and short poems were written in it. But coexisting with this mixed language was an indigenous Malayalam literary tradition, represented mostly by folk songs and ballads.

By the twelfth century, a new genre in Kannada, the *vacaṉa* or "saying" began to emerge. These *vacaṉas* were religious poems of the Vīra-śaiva saints, expressing radical views on religion and society, rejecting both ritualism and asceticism, and breaking the bonds of caste, creed, and sexual difference.

The period of the Vijayanagar Empire (fourteenth–sixteenth centuries) saw Kannada and Telugu brought together under a single political dynasty, hospitable to influence from neighboring Muslim kingdoms. In particular, from the sixteenth century onward, beginning with the king Kṛṣṇa Dēva Rāya, royal patronage was extended to poets, and the literary arts flourished in the court. Of a literature characterized by learning, poetic virtuosity, wit, and artistry, perhaps the most famous representatives are Pingal Suranna and Tenāli Rāmakṛṣṇa. This period also produced some of the most famous popular classics in Kannada. Of these the most renowned is Gadugu's *Kumāra vyāsa*, ten cantos of *The Mahābhārata*. The work abounds in humor, passion, and memorable poetry, and is recited in assemblies as well as in the home.

The seventeenth and eighteenth centuries also saw the flourishing of Tamil court poetry—purāṇas, translations from the Sanskrit, and poems of praise, characterized more by learning than poetic genius. This was also a period of great religious activity, which gave rise to many sectarian and polemical works; even Muslims and Christians were writing epics in the Hindu purāṇic style. But probably the most impressive Tamil poetry of this period is that of the Cittars, eclectic mystics known for their radical, fierce style and everyday diction. (JABvB)

The literatures: the modern period

The "modern period" is as strictly undatable as the "medieval" one. It can be defined as beginning with the coming of the British; but Western influence on the various Indian literatures begins from different times. Overgenerally, it can be said that the influence of Western models can be discerned in the early part of the nineteenth century. The most striking result was the full-scale introduction of prose, this being assisted by the spread of printing presses and newspapers. English education and the establishment of literary clubs opened Western culture and literature to the educated elite, and after a period of translation from English writing, authors sought to imitate their models, and then to be independently creative in the new style. Prose had existed in India before the coming of the British, for purposes of disquisition, folk narrative, story, and record, but under the influence of English it came to be written with purely literary purpose. Verse also continued to be written, both in the older forms and under the influence of the new, and realism and symbolism made their appearance.

Beginning in Bengal, a new sense of national purpose gripped the subcontinent in the nineteenth century, and this became the principal motivation of much of the English as well as the regional literatures. The old traditionalism was transformed into a romanticism that looked back with pride on Indian history and sought to preserve that which was most valuable in the past. Greater social awareness on the European literary scene was reflected in the writing of the progressives, in whose works a somewhat romantic Marxism prevails. And there was a trend toward humanism. The teachings of Gandhi exerted great pressure in the early part of the twentieth century, combining social concerns with traditional ethics.

In the following paragraphs, a number of names of individual writers are mentioned. These, it is to be understood, are representative only; names of very many good writers in all the modern Indian languages have not been mentioned, for want of space.

Indian English literature

Literary activity in English began in earnest with the Bengali reformer Rām Mohan Roy, who, together with like-minded Hindus, insisted that for India to take its place among nations education in English was essential. Roy himself was a forceful writer in English among other languages. Roy was followed, in the early mid-nineteenth century in Bengal, by the poets Henry Derozio, Kāshīprasād Ghosh, and Michael Madhusudan Dutt, the last of whom wrote epic verse in English before reverting, in later life, to his native Bengali.

Far and away the most famous poet in English was Rabindranath Tagore (1861–1941), who, despite the fact that he wrote most of his vast corpus in Bengali, won the Nobel Prize for literature for his English *Gitanjali* in 1913.

The movement for the independence of India in the early part of the twentieth century gave strong impetus to the use of expository prose. Important figures in various parts of the country were Bāl Gaṅgādhar Tilak, Lālā Lajpat Rāy, Kasturi Ranga Iyengar, and T. Prakāśam. Gandhi too wrote widely in English, and edited the English-language *Young India* and *Harijan*. In writing his autobiography, *My Experiments with Truth*, Gandhi was followed by Jawaharlal Nehru, whose *Discovery of India* is justly popular.

Indian Writing in English

In the twentieth century, three novelists have produced major works. Most prolific among them has been Mulk Raj Anand, who severely criticized class and caste distinctions in a number of novels, *Untouchable* (1935), *Coolie* (1936), *Two Leaves and a Bud* (1937), and *The Big Heart* (1945). Recently he has been publishing a series of autobiographical novels: *Seven Summers* (1951), *Morning Face* (1972), *Confessions of a Lover* (1976). R. K. Narayan is perhaps more widely known because of his depiction of human folly in gently amusing and well-crafted novels about Malgudi, an imaginary place in South India. Some of his works are *Waiting for the Mahatma* (1952), *The Guide* (1958), *The Vendor of Sweets* (1967), *The Painter of Signs* (1977). Raja Rao's Vedantic worldview and unique English style with Sanskritic rhythms have attracted a wide following for his *Kanthapura* (1938) and *The Serpent and the Rope* (1960). By all accounts the single most interesting work of fiction is G. V. Desani's *All About Mr. Hatterr* (1948), about which T. S. Eliot wrote, ". . . certainly a remarkable book. In all my experience, I have not met with anything quite like it." Other popular contemporary novelists are Kamala Markandeya, Monohar Malgonkar, Anita Desai and Nayantara Sehgal.

The mid-twentieth century has seen a remarkable burst of creative effort in poetry, represented by the work of poets like Nissim Ezekiel, A. K. Ramanujan, Keki Daruwala, Kamala Das, R. Parthasarathy, Gieve Patel, Adit Jussawalla, Arun Kolatkar, Pritish Nandy.

Hindi literature

Modern Hindi writing can be said to begin with Hariścandra "Bhāratendu" (1850–1885) in poetry and drama, Mahābīr Prasād Dvivedi (1864–1938) in criticism and other forms of prose, and Prēmcand (1881–1936) in fiction. Although the second half of the nineteenth century was mainly a period of translation from Bengali, Sanskrit, and English, the growth of nationalistic and reform movements gave rise to long narrative poems, dramas, and historical novels based in the Maurya, Gupta, and Mughal empires.

Gandhi's movement inspired poets and novelists in Hindi as well as other languages. But as disillusionment with the Gandhian experiments set in, writers in the language turned increasingly to Marxism, perhaps also influenced by the growth of that philosophy on the European literary scene. In the 1930s, then, the scene was one of poets such as Mahādēvī Varmā and S. N. Pant drawing on the romantic tradition of English and Bengali poetry and the mystic tradition of medieval Hindi, opposed by Marxist poets such as Rām Vilās Shārma.

Two different trends in modern Hindi fiction, social realism and introspection, begun respectively by Prēmcand, whose *Godān* ("The gift of a cow") is still widely read, and Jainendra Kumār, have been followed to the present day. Writers like "Agñeya" (S. H. Vatsyāyan) are exploring the psychology of the individual, not always in the Indian context.

Bengali

The mid-nineteenth century in Bengal produced a spate of novels, satiric, social, and picaresque. The literary event of the period was the publication in 1865 of Baṅkimcandra Chatterji's first novel, *Durgeshnandinī*. Bankim was a tremendously influential novelist whose growing nationalism inspired his countrymen, but even more popular was Saratcandra Chatterji, whose social concerns with the family and other homely issues won him a great following. But the man who towers head and shoulders above the rest is Rabindranath Tagore. Poet, playwright, painter, novelist, essayist, musician, Rabindranath's works fill twenty-six substantial volumes. Better known for this devotional and mystical poems rather than the wit and clear thought with which his later work is filled, Tagore was the last of an era. While he looked back to the religious and political history of Bengal and of India for his inspiration, those who followed him turned more to introspection and dramatic imagery. Jibanānanda Dās (1899–1954) was the first of this new breed. Musing, melancholy, yet known for vivid and unusual imagery, Jibanānanda has had great influence on younger writers. Other poets, equally powerful, stand more apart from the mainstream. One of these was Sudhīndranāth Datta (1901–1960), a poet much like Pound in careful use of language; another is the progressive poet and novelist Buddhadeva Bose (b. 1908).

Assamese literature

Modern Assamese literature begins with the satirist and playwright Hēmchandra Baruā (*Bahiri-raṅg chang bhitare kowabhāturi*, 1861); the most outstanding, however, among modern writers was Lakṣmīnāth Bezbaroā (b. 1868), who not only founded a literary monthly, *Jōnāki*, in 1889, but infused nineteenth-century romanticism into Assamese letters. This literary point of view dominated Assamese writing well into the twentieth century. Of the modern genres, the short story particularly has flourished in the language, and most notable in the field are Maṇīchandra Borā and Halirām Dēkā.

In the 1940s the major trend of Assamese writing shifted to introspection and psychological concerns. World War II seemed to cause another shift, and since that time Assamese writers have been experimenting with new verse and novel forms.

Marathi literature

The modern period in Marathi writing is marked by the poetry of Kēshavasuta (1866–1905) who, together with his contemporaries, was influenced by British romanticism and liberalism and by the greatness of the history of Maharashtra. Kēshavasuta declared a revolt against traditional poetic forms, and started a trend, which lasted well into the twentieth century, that emphasized home and nature, the glorious past, and pure lyricisim. After the 1920s, Marathi poetry was dominated by the attitude typified by Ravikaraṇ Maṇḍal, who felt that poetry was not for the erudite and sensitive, but a matter of everyday appreciation and understanding. Again, the end of World War II marks a break with the past, and poetry since that time is subjective, personal, and colloquial.

In modern drama notable are S. K. Kōlhaṭkar (1871–1934) and R. G. Gadkarī (1885–1919). Māmā Varērkar (1883–1965) brought social realism to the stage in his attempts to interpret society's problems. In the Marathi novel too social realism is the dominant mode, beginning with Hari Nārāyaṇ Āpṭē (1864–1919). A high place in modern Marathi literature is held too by V. M. Jōshī, who explored the problem facing women (*Suśhilecā dev*, 1930), and the relationship between art and morals (*Indu Kāḷe va saralā bhole*, 1935). Important in the period following 1925 were N. S. Phaḍke, who advocated art for art's sake, and V. S. Khāṇḍekar, who countered this position with one of an idealistic art for life's sake. Noteworthy contemporaries include S. N. Peṇḍse, V. V. Shirwadkar, G. N. Dāṇḍekar, and Rañjit Desāī.

Gujarati literature

Modern Gujarati writing too begins in the middle of the nineteenth century. In 1866 the poet Narsingh Rao published a collection of lyrics called *Kusummālā*, which was deeply influenced by western literary ideals. Other poets, later in the century, such as Nanalal, were experimenting in free verse, a form previously unknown in the language; Nanalal also was the first poet to eulogize Mahatma Gandhi, himself a Gujarati. Gandhi's influence on Gujarati poetry was great; he urged the poets to write for the masses, and the result was deep poetic concern with changes in the social order. But here as elsewhere there was a reaction, and the Gandhian movement gave way eventually to a period of progressivism characterized by the class-conflict poetry of Meghani and Bhogilal Gandhi. In the period after 1947, the concerns of Gujarati writing have been subjectivism and alienation; the more traditional concerns of devotion to God and love of nature have never been fully superseded.

Social realism was also the characteristic of the early Gujarati novel, as in the *Sarasvatichandra* of Govardhanrām. The Gandhian influence is also seen in the novel, though there were some, such as Kanhaiyālāl Munshi, who spoke critically of Gandhian ideology, though he tended to preach much the same message. As in other parts of the subcontinent, the moderns have embraced existentialism, surrealism, and symbolism, and have expressed the same feeling of alienation as have the poets.

Panjabi literature

The 1860s also mark the beginning of modern Panjabi literature. In the poetry of the period, a number of trends can be discerned: there are the more traditional genres of narrative poetry, mystic verse, and love poems, to which was added poetry in a nationalist vein, in a humorous or satiric mood, and experimental verse. Among the more important of the modern poets are Bhāī Vīr Singh (b. 1872), Pūran Singh (1881–1913), Amrita Pritam (b. 1919), and Bābā Balwant (b. 1915).

Modern prose is represented by the novelists Bhai Vir Singh, Charana Singh, and Nanak Singh, and the short-story writers Gurbhaksh Singh and Devendra Satyarathi. Among playwrights mention may be made of I. C. Nanda, Harcharan Singh, and Santa Singh Sekhon.

Urdu literature

The modern period in Urdu literature coincides with the emergence of a middle class that saw in Western thought and science a means of needed social reform within the Muslim society. Under the impetus of the movement led by Saiyad Ahmad Khan (d. 1898) were produced the novels of Nazir Ahmad (d. 1911), the poetry and literary criticism of Altaf Husain Hali (d. 1914), and the scholarly treatises of Shibli Nomani (d. 1914).

The greatest modern poet in Urdu is Muhammad Iqbal (d. 1938), whose activist philosophy won him the admiration of his fellow Muslims at a time when a general sense of national purpose and independence was sweeping the subcontinent. In prose, it was Premchand (d. 1936) who produced during the same period the single most important corpus of long and short fiction in Urdu.

A period of literary progressivism followed, when attempts were made to make literature an arm of social revolution. The major writers identified with the Progressive Writers' Association are Faiz Ahmad Faiz (poetry), Krishna Chandra (fiction), and Sirdar Jafri (poetry). But more influential were the contributions of Miraji and N. M. Rashid in poetry and Saadat Hasan Manto and Rajendra Singh Bedi in prose, their commitment being more to the aesthetics of their craft and their personal world views than to any ideology.

Two major novels highlight the period since 1947. Qurratul Ain Hyder's *Aag Ka Dariya* and Abdulla Husain's *Udaas Naslen* both deal with the plight of the individual caught in the maelstrom of large-scale sociopolitical changes. In poetry, one most significant event has been the resurgence of the *ghazal*, the new *ghazal* being more imagistic and more far-ranging in its themes.

Tamil Literature

Out of the contacts of Western culture and a long-standing classical Tamil culture, modern Tamil prose, poetry, and criticism were born. The struggle of Arunachala Kavirayar (18th c.) to bring together the spoken and the written languages was continued in the realistic, humorous early novels of Vedanayagam Pillai (*Pratāpa Mudaliyār*, 1879) and Rajam Iyer

(*Kamalāmbāl,* 1893–95), in popular novelists like Kalki, and in the poetry of Bharati in the 20th century. The journal *Maṇikkoḍi* of the '30's gave rise to a new movement in which the social critic and short-story writer Putumaippittan stood out. The fine fiction of Mauni, Piccamurti, and the younger trio Janakiraman, Ramamrutam, and Jeyakantan, the new stories of Ramasami and Asokamitran, as well as the critical writings of K. N. Subramanyam and C. S. Chellappa (and his influential journal *Eḻuttu*) must be mentioned. After Bharati's rousing, ranging poetry, the low-profile experimental verse of New Poets like Vaittheeswaran, Jnanakkoottan, and Shanmuka Subbaiya is significant.

Malayalam

Beginning in the early 20th century with the erotic and religious verse of Asan, the classicism of Ulloor, and the romantic many-sided Vallattol, modern Malayalam literature reflects the concerns of a spirited, highly literate, politically conscious people. Of the older poets, Sankara Kurup and Balamani Amma are notable. Chandu Menon's *Indulēkha* (1889) was the first significant novel; today, there are many outstanding writers of realistic fiction: Thakazhi (*Chemmīn,* 1957), Kesava Das, Basheer, Pottekad, Kuttikrishnan, O. V. Vijayan. The earlier Ibsenesque plays of Krishna Pillai and the new poetry of poets like M. Govindan and Ayyappa Panikkar are good examples of the vigor of modern Malayalam.

Telugu

Modern Telugu literature begins with the prolific reformist writings of Kandukuri Veerasalingam, which were followed by Gurajada Appa Rao's play *Bride Price* and Rayaprolu Subba Rao's "romantic" poetry. Sri Sri in the next generation led a "progressive" movement, Marxist and radical. Viswanatha Sathyanarayana was a revivalist and classicist who wrote a *Rāmāyaṇa.* An angry, leftist, anti-establishment poetry was written by a younger group, Digambarakavulu ("the Naked Poets"). Novelists like Kutumba Rao and Viswanatha Sastri were also politically involved, while Muppala Ranganayakamma devoted her novels to the depiction of women's lives. (V. Narayana Rao)

Kannada

As in other Indian literatures, the spirit of national purpose and the forms of Western literature (lyric, novel, short story, etc.) have informed modern Kannada. The translations of B. M. Srikantayya in the '20's; the poetry of Bendre and Puttappa; the New Poetry of Adiga (in the '50's) the prolific novels of Karanta and the short stories of Srinivasa; the plays of Kailasam, Sriranga, and Karnad; and more recently the fiction of Anantamurthy, Lankesh, and Bhairappa and the folk-plays of Kambar make modern Kannada literature rich and outstanding.

Written texts and their preservation

Early Indian books were copied by hand. And their only mode of duplication was by recopying. No manuscript can ever hope to be entirely perfect, and over the centuries mistakes, copied several times and at other times more or less "corrected," would undoubtedly produce final versions that deviated significantly from the author's original text. Furthermore, remarks were made upon the margins by users of the manuscript. These marginal notes might subsequently intrude upon the text like footnotes embodied in the page face. But there is just so much that can be written even in very wide margins, and lengthy comments and additions might again have to be made on extra pages.

Theoretically, an original Indian book would most easily be defined as the number of pages it had in the beginning. But this implies that pages were bound together as a single book. In fact, the materials available for writing, usually birchbark or palm leaf, did not allow any such manipulation. The best that could be done would be to cut the leaves to roughly the same size and tie a cord around them. To protect the first and last sheets a wooden board would sometimes be placed at both ends. If the possession was highly prized, the endboards might be made of metal or silver, encrusted with gems, illuminated with pictures. But in spite of decorations and care, boards and cord could never adequately keep the book together. A book was only as secure as the cord that tied it. For additional security a hole was sometimes pierced through the middle of the leaves of the book, and the cord run through that. But cords would break, and whole chapters be lost.

Besides, a book was the personal property of the one who owned it, perhaps because he had inherited it, or had transcribed it with his own hands, or had it copied by a scribe whose fee he paid. He was not restrained by laws of copyright from making his own additions, any more than people of later ages have been restrained from marking printed books with exclamation points, scribbled references, or marginal criticisms. One might even go so far as to insert loose leaflets between pages that particularly incite one's interest. Similarly, the Indian might well have found it in him at the time of copying to correct the corrupt readings that he found, or to embroider upon a felicitous turn of phrase he encountered. If any statement, of fact, of rule, or of sentiment, struck him as not universally valid, he might well decide to point out its limitations, the better to bring out the undoubted meaning of the ancient wise author. Just because the book that came to the reader was obviously the product of many copying hands before him, it did, in a way, lack credibility as the original document. Until this day, paṇḍits go on correcting automatically the manuscripts they are transcribing.

Sometimes the very excellence of the work before him might inspire the reader to emulate it. To one fine verse, another fine verse might be added by the proud owner of the manuscript. But the copyist of that manuscript would have no way of knowing what was original and what was added, and incorporate both equally. Thus there is the paradoxical fact that transmitted by oral tradition the text of the *Ṛg-veda* is better preserved than texts transmitted in writing. The written tradition has not preserved any of the works of the great Sanskrit author Kālidāsa in their original form.

The pages between two boards, then, could become the beginning of a modest library. It was like an expanding folder: nothing was easier than to insert at the appropriate leaf a number of other leaves cut to the same size and covered with texts that expanded on the original, made exceptions, and added further illustrations. This is, as will be seen, the way in which the great epic *The Mahābhārata* must be viewed. It is a book that was expandable almost to the size of a library. And it is at this point that the scholar's casual dating of *The Mahābhārata* between 400 B.C. and A.D. 400 makes sense. For a book, a dating over eight centuries makes none. For a library, it does: one may date a library between its founding and the time when no new acquisitions were made. (JABvB)

The principal sources of literary activity

Except for The Songs of Solomon, The Book of Psalms, Ecclesiastes, and a few more easily identifiable passages, the Bible is thought of by many as literature only because of the abiding beauty of the great English translation called the King James Version. On the other hand, apart from this translation, the Bible is unquestionably one of the major sources of European literature. It is a store of tales, allusions, and situations that provides a common intellectual and literary repertory for a fair proportion of the Western world. A poet within the Western tradition can draw upon this store with the assurance that his imagery and metaphor will be understood by readers also within it, and that certain psychological configurations can be assumed, and others drawn. Archibald Macleish's play *J.B.*, as has been suggested, is able to take much for granted: that its audience knows and understands both intellectually and emotionally the point as well as the story of The Book of Job. The other major source of European literature comprises the Greek myths and drama and the prototypal persons put boldly forth in them: Oedipus, for example. Oedipus and his fellows name and make visible for Westerners characteristics of Western thought and perceptions of themselves and their world; and to that very considerable extent they have shaped Western literature.

It is easier to compare the epic *Mahābhārata* with the Old Testament than with the more narrowly purposive New Testament: *The Mahābhārata* and, it might be added, the later *Purāṇas*, are compendia of stories and tales and sayings that document the thoughts, the religious attitudes, and the perceptions of self and world of the Indian peoples. Though few people read the complete *Mahābhārata* (as, indeed, few people read the Encyclopaedia Britannica from cover to cover, and the parallel is not too far-fetched), all know many of the stories in it. As was suggested, Kālidāsa can write his *Śakuntalā*, as Macleish his *J.B.*, knowing that his audience is familiar with the story and that therefore he can concentrate on his poetry and the delicacy of its presentation. Thus a modern poet writing in Kashmiri, let us say, can write a poem on this same theme and at the same time as a modern Malayalam poet is writing one, and both can draw upon the same imagistic and psychological repertory presented by *The Mahābhārata* and bejeweled by Kālidāsa. The epic source is diffused through both time and space. Or take the situation of the religious lyrics of the Vaiṣṇavas of Bengal—worshipers of Kṛṣṇa and participants in the bhakti movement of medieval times.[1] Although most of these lyrics were written between the sixteenth and the eighteenth centuries, they have considerable literary stature today, and one of the first books of poetry by Rabindranath Tagore, *Bhānusiṁha ṭhākurer padāvalī*[2] ("The collection of poems of Bhānusiṁha"), used their unique imagery and language. These lyricists assumed that the reader or listener knew the story of Kṛṣṇa. They further assumed that he knew that within Bengal, from the twelfth century, the doctrinal and poetic emphasis of the Vaiṣṇavas was on the allegorical love relationship of Kṛṣṇa to the Gopīs, the cowherd girls, and particularly to Rādhā. The Indian writer assumed a knowledge both of the all-India tradition and of the regional tradition on the part of his audience.

The first of these types of knowledge offers a common literary repertory. The Indian poet can assume that his readers will know the puranic story, also told by Kālidāsa, of how Kāma the love god was burned by fire from the wrathful eye of Śiva for trying to tempt that great god from his meditation. Thus the poet can make references to "the bodiless one," and play with the notion of the god reborn or embodied in the mind or the imagination, and his readers will understand and appreciate the extent of his subtlety.

The second assumption that can be made is that the Indian writer is writing primarily for a particular audience of Indians, most of whom will have a certain common core of experience. If everybody knows that the rainy season is the time for lovers to be together, a poet can arouse a whole chain of associations by the mere mention of the first rain cloud appearing on the horizon. Whether this reaction is conditioned by natural experience or by literary or other conceits is not here significant. It is a literary fact.

In this, as in all areas, it is impossible to discuss the unity of Indian culture from any point of view without hastily redressing the balance with a statement of its diversity. The variety of languages has been treated, and it remains only to remark that although the old Sanskrit metaphor of the relationship between full moon and beautiful face may persist, the form in which it is stated must change. Although Hindi is derived from Sanskrit, the linguistic necessities and possibilities of Sanskrit are quite different from those of Hindi, just as those of Hindi are different from those of Tamil and even from those of the much more closely related Bengali.

Again, for whatever historical or social or psychological reasons, certain religious and sectarian traditions seem to have found the soil of one part of the subcontinent more congenial than that of another, and emphases vary. Yet, although in modern Indian literature a secular bent may prevail, even modern literature draws upon the fund of the religious literature of the past. And while there is even in older times secular didactic writing, and history with the merest of puranic veneers, and war poetry, and secular folk song and story, it must be said again that the bulk of the old and medieval literature in the regional languages was religious. God is deeply imbedded in Indian soil. And God has many forms.

Thus, the *vacanas*, hymns in the Kannada language (from A.D. 1100), are lyrics that celebrate, with power and precision, the great god Śiva, the moon-crested one. The poems of Tulsīdās (fifteen century) in Hindi speak of the noble and divine Rāma, conqueror of demons, and of his consort Sītā, prototype in beauty and in loyalty of the Indian woman. But in Bengal, Śiva is prone to sleep, as the puranic story tells, while the Goddess in her form as Chaṇḍī or Durgā or Kālī dances wildly on his chest, in her lust for the blood of demons; and Rāma is largely ignored.

And each of the forms of God has many forms. The cult of Kṛṣṇa is popular in much of India. The Tamil Aḷvārs, before the end of the first millenium A.D., sang of him, and so did the princess Mīrābāī in Rajasthan, and Sūrdās in northern India, and so did the Vaiṣṇavas in Bengal. Yet to Mīrābāī he was husband, as Christ was husband to Saint Catherine; and to her he was, at the same time, the all-pervading, infinite, and mighty God. In Bengal, Kṛṣṇa is the gentle lover of the Gopīs, who in giving up their homes and husbands and honor to go to him demonstrate the proper attitude of man toward God; and God returns their love.

In such ways the ancient puranic stream diffused. And in medieval times it was joined by another: the traditions and literature of Islam. In one sense, the Muslims in India, conquerors and rulers, kept themselves aloof from their new Indian surroundings, "preserving," as Peter Hardy puts it, "their religious and cultural identity."[3] The great tradition of Persian literature was preserved and promoted in Urdu and Persian in the courts of Delhi and elsewhere. If this were all, it would be possible to treat the Urdu and Persian tradition as separate from that of "Hindu" India. In fact, this is impossible. For while on one level some Muslim scholars and idealists like Dārā Shikōh and Akbar the Great Mughal himself were concerning themselves with Hindu texts and traditions, on another level those ecstatic poets of divine love, the Sufis, were spreading over northern and central India, preaching, in beautiful metaphor, a doctrine also propounded by the Hindu devotees of the bhakti movement. It was largely through these Sufis that the Hindu and Muslim literary streams met and blended, and the nightingale in the Shirazi garden of the great fourteenth-century Persian Ḥāfiẓ became the bird trapped in the ribcage of the body of the mendicant singer, the Bāul, of Bengal:

> He comes and goes within his cage, that unknown bird.
> If only I could catch him, I would keep him fettered
> with the irons of my mind.
> My whole life I have nourished that bird,
> but still he evades me.
> I have given you bananas
> and the milk of my breast,
> O bird,
> and still you ignore my coaxing.[4]

And the same image turns up again in the poetry of Rabindranath Tagore:

> The bird of the forest flies away,
> and with him my heart's joy.[5]

Likewise, the medieval Hindi poet Kabīr could draw on the traditions and the religious and literary repertory of both Hindus and Muslims, often approving of the externalities of neither, and castigating both:

> If Allah lives in a mosque,
> who inhabits the rest of the world?
> Hindus say that he lives in the idol;
> both deceive themselves.
> O Allah-Rām, it is for you that I live,
> O master, have mercy on me.
>
> One says that Hari lives in the south,
> and that Allah resides in the west:
> search for him in your heart, search for him in every heart.
> There is his dwelling and his residence.[6]

In a sense, Indian literature, like the rest of Indian culture, can be thought of as infinitely fragmented, and in another sense as forming a single universe of discourse. Like the local goddess who, although she has her own personality and her own dominion, is at the same time an aspect of the Great Goddess, Indian literature can be viewed in a variety of ways. There are, running through all the literatures of India, certain abiding forms, shapes, and above all a more or less constant view of the nature of the universe and man's relation to it.

It has often been recognized that Indian philosophical and religious thought seems to be based on the premise that there is nothing new under the sun. Truth, like the eternal Veda, is there, waiting to be discovered; it has been revealed, and needs only amplification. Whole systems of philosophy and ritual are built upon the exposition of each of the four great Vedas. And in other areas, such as grammar, the truth, codified by one such as Pāṇini, stated in aphorisms called *sūtras*, is expanded into schools of thought by meticulously careful commentary on their implications.

This style explains several things about Indian literature. First, the relationship of commentary to *sūtra* is also the relationship of literature to its usually religious source. From this point of view, the dramatist Kālidāsa's *Śakuntalā* is an elaborate exposition of a simple story from *The Mahābhārata*. The whole great corpus of the Vaiṣṇava lyrics of Bengal is an amplification of the notion of God as lover. And in the second place, such a view of the progressive discovery of revealed truth relates the distant past to the present in a way that might seem strange to the Western mind. The modern poet, like the Vedic one, may be viewed by his society, and sometimes by himself, in the privacy of his own mind, as the instrument that brings into expression the word, Vāk, the Vedic goddess who is just as powerful and awe-inspiring now as she was three thousand years ago.

This view means that nothing is ever really created completely. The implications of this, for the older literature and even for that much smaller portion of modern literature that is oriented toward the traditional view, are two. The first is that given such a view there will be less personal pride of authorship, and the discovery of the authorship of an older text is often a major scholarly accomplishment. Implied also is the explanation of why, to some Westerners, Indian literature sometimes seems saline and exhausted, as if too many crops have been grown on the same soil. To say something new, to be unique, is, from this point of view, impossible. The business of the writer is to uncover, in a way that employs to their best advantage the many facets of his art, in a way that both edifies and gives pleasure, a corner of revelation that might previously have been perceived, though sometimes dimly. It may also be in reaction to this traditional view that some modern writing is so taken with experimentation; uniqueness takes on a value of its own. Traditional attitudes may change with time and external influence; they change their shape. But sometimes even seeming opposites, as Freud has pointed out, have their origin in unity. (ECD)

The persistence of attitudes

It has been stated in a variety of ways that if one wants to recognize change, one must recognize the norm. Also, in order to understand the literature of an unfamiliar culture, it is necessary to understand some extraliterary detail. There are key concepts that both shape and reflect the culture's attitude toward things. An understanding of some of these will not explain Indian literature, but it will help to place the various literatures in their environment. Some of the concepts are pan-Indian; others are regional. One that is pan-Indian though perhaps having regional variations and that might be taken as illustrative, is that of *dharma*.

Dharma is a term that must be translated in a variety of ways, depending on its context: it can be "law," or "righteousness," or "property," or "that which is proper," or "fate." But none of these is quite accurate, for *dharma* has to do with the notion that man and the universe are somehow one, that the order of man's life and that of the universe are intimately related. Thus, when it is worked out on the personal and psychological, rather than the metaphysical, level, the term comes to mean something like "role:" a physical, worldly role that is metaphysically determined. The idea of role is familiar everywhere: people play roles as husband, wife, student, teacher, parent, and so on. And each of these roles is defined, as Kenneth Burke would say, by "scene": a man's role and the way it is played depends on the situation in which he finds himself. It is often the physical scene that is the determining factor;

for the rest, it is a matter of one's own reaction to that environment and to the people in it. But Indian thought is not entirely satisfied with that. For in the Indian tradition, role is determined not only physically, but metaphysically. Such a determination is not entirely unfamiliar to the West. For example, in one episode of John Steinbeck's play *Burning Bright* the clown makes a moving speech, after finding that his wife will not be able to bear him children, to the effect that if he is unable to continue his line, if there are no more clowns in his family, somehow the proper order of the universe will be upset; somehow, disaster will result.

In the West, role is largely a matter of the person who fills it. It is the individual who is important. If a particular individual were not playing his role as son, the role would be empty; there is no one else who could play it. To Indian thought, the role seems more important than the individual. The role is there, and it must be played. Every Indian family must have a son: the son must touch the fire to the dead lips of his parents. If this role is not filled, if a family has no son, it is not only a misfortune: it is an indication that the family is at odds with the moral order of the universe.

On the other hand, if things are properly attuned—if a king performs properly the duties of a king, or if a wife acts well the part of wife, or a student the student—everything must, in this ordered universe, turn out well. If one is in harmony with the moral order, the wheels turn smoothly and inexorably, the world revolves in its well-oiled sockets. One way in which Premendra Mitra's short story "Where the River Meets the Sea"[7] might be read is against this background of *dharma*. The story frame is this:

A high-caste Brahman widow is on a pilgrimage to the holy place at the mouth of the Ganges. On the boat on which she is traveling she finds herself thrown together with a party of prostitutes, including one who has a daughter, a little girl of eight or nine. At first the Brahman woman shuns the girl, horrified at the necessity of being in the same boat with these unclean women; she refuses to eat and bathes constantly. But a storm overtakes and wrecks the boat, and the woman and the little girl find themselves clinging to the same bit of flotsam. At first the woman, giving way to an uncontrollable impulse, shoves the little girl off the piece of wood. But then, equally uncontrollably, she dives under and saves the girl at the risk of her own life. They are picked up by some fishermen, who think that they are mother and daughter: who but a mother, they say, would have risked her own life to save the girl? The Brahman woman cannot persuade them otherwise.

Gradually, of course, the two come to love and depend on one another, and after a series of fallings-out and reconciliations they reach the place of pilgrimage. The Brahman woman is tormented by the thought of having to choose either to bring the unclean girl home to her aristocratic family, or to abandon her to an orphanage. Her choice is made easy, however. The girl catches pneumonia and dies. The Brahman woman's words, when the hospital attendant asks the name of the child's father, are: "How can you expect me to speak my husband's name? Give me some paper. I'll write it down."[8]

The question that the story asks, of course, is what happens when the woman's *dharma* as Brahman—to preserve her family purity and honor, for one thing—comes into conflict with her *dharma* as woman, to protect and preserve children, however much impurity they may have inherited. Whether the author intended it or not, the woman is saved from committing herself to one path or other. *Dharma* is operative on both characters and on the author. Neither is the question a new one, for it is the very problem with which the ancient *Bhagavad-gītā*, the famous religious discourse (ca. 100 B.C.) now embedded in *The Mahābhārata*, begins: should Arjuna obey his *dharma* as warrior, or his *dharma* as a relative of those against whom he is about to do battle? Mitra's story is stylized in other ways as well. It is as in a masque: expressions on faces do not change, and actions depend less upon inner passions and desires and longings than they do upon outside forces.

Given a strong, inflexible standard, all deviations are frighteningly obvious, and if other outside pressures on the characters, such as societal ones, are recognized, frighteningly predictable. What then gives the Mitra story its effect is not the inner psychology of the two principals —these are neither stated nor suggested—but the very fact that both are, and ought to be, predictable. How predictable they are, and therefore how effective the story is, depends upon the reader's grasp of the Indian context. Neither of the principals in the story is, therefore, a "self," in the sense that self is an independent and therefore "real" entity. The woman and the girl react to one another; they do not interact with one another. They are role-players. They do not examine themselves, they do not ask why they do what they do. This will be seen as a constant in much Indian literature. The characters do not intrude themselves upon the reader; the writer also does not attempt to shape fate: things work themselves out by the law of *dharma*. It is true that the Mitra story has been used as an illustration because it fits the point that ancient and pervasive values persist even in modern writing. It is also true that different modern writers use their tradition differently, and that the same writer uses it differently in different stories. But in one way or another, most do use it.

To understand Indian literature, then, one must understand its context; and one must define Indian literature not only in terms of its quality, but also in terms of its sometimes unique aims. If one is to speak of Kālidāsa's dramas, Shakespeare's aims are irrelevant. If one is to judge *The Rāmāyaṇa*, *The Odyssey* should be far from one's mind. Western approaches to literature may not only be passively irrelevant to one's appreciation of the Indian tradition, but may actually foster and encourage principles of criticism that make unintelligible the literature one wishes to study.

This book, then, attempts to do three things. It attempts to present in some depth studies of representative genres and pieces of writing. It attempts to provide as much of the contextual, nonliterary background of those genres and pieces of writing as may be necessary to understand them. And, in the chapter on poetics, it attempts to provide the non-Indian reader with the critical context by which judgment might be made from within the tradition itself. It is admittedly difficult for a Westerner to approach an exotic literature from a critical point of view that is itself alien to Western habits and principles of literary judgment. It might even be questioned whether such an approach, even if possible, would yield the immediately relevant and sympathetic understanding of Indian literary works that is one of the important ends of any criticism. The difficulties are obvious, but the attempt must be made. (ECD)

The subject matter of the book

Apart from such cultural concepts as *dharma*, in an overview of Indian literature there are immediately evident two continuous traditions that run on two distinguishable levels of concern: that of the epic and that of the story. While they are distinguishable, the two are hardly separable, since the epical literature has absorbed a great deal of folktale material, while the story literature was deeply influenced by the epics. Nevertheless, the concerns of the two traditions can be distinguished: one might be described as moralistic and the other as secular. It seems that a good story never dies, and the same anecdotes that circulated in antiquity about the Phoenicians are, with the merest change of names, told about the Scots; and these again are hard to distinguish from the stories told of certain modern Brahmans of the Indian state of Maharashtra. Apart from local color, the story literature has less that is characteristically Indian than any other genre; but its role in the totality of Indian literatures has been very important. It has been treated toward the end of the book, first because it is of all ages, and second, to provide some contrast to the prevailingly religious tone of most of the other literature.

The epic will be discussed first, because it stands practically at the beginning of Indian literary traditions, because it makes statements about India that are as general as it is possible for statements about India to be, and because it is presupposed by all other genres of literature. Before any Hindu child and many a Muslim child can write he knows much of the content of the epics. From time immemorial this has been universal subject matter, the common reservoir from which all Indian writers have drawn. It is partly for this reason that *The Rāmāyaṇa* has tempted later writers to imitation, translation, and new creations on the theme, and thus through it different styles, emphases, and selectiveness of the various Indian literatures can be illustrated. Further, *The Rāmāyaṇa* has become a part of folklore, and grand performances of the Rāma story take place annually in most parts of India, in the "Play of Rāma," *The Rām-līlā*. The tremendous popularity of the epic proves that, however distinguished its poetry may be, it is essentially a folk book. But just as the epic is popular, so it can be enacted on a high level of literary sophistication.

By starting off with the Indian epic, the entire ancient literature of the Vedas is consciously excluded. For however important Vedic tradition may have been in the religious and cultural development of India, its influence on the evolution of Indian literature per se has been remarkably limited. The Vedic texts—not only the "Four Vedas," but the prose disquisitions of *The Brāhmaṇas* and *Āraṇyakas*, and the dense speculations of *The Upaniṣads*—very soon became the property of the priestly classes, manuals for practical religious purposes; their literary influence was tenuously indirect.

The drastic excision of that group of texts through which many Westerners know India best indicates the trend of the treatment of Indian literature in this book. Its principal concern is with abiding themes and forms in Indian literature, and with certain expressions of such themes, even if their influence on later history was restricted, as in the case of the Sanskrit drama. These continuing themes and forms will lead from language to language and from age to age; they will allow a range and greater fairness to periods such as the medieval one (arbitrarily defined here as between A.D. 1200 and 1700), that are usually overlooked equally by the classicist and the observer of the contemporary scene, both in India and in the West. An attempt will be made to bring out the peculiar Indian character of some of these themes, some of which still inspire modern literary genres, though forms in modern times may be borrowed from the West. But even forms have a way of perpetuating themselves: behind the novel we discern the novella. If modern Indian literature is worthwhile, it must be read at least in part in the light of its history. The shades and shadows of a modern Bengali or Kannada poem are more clearly seen in the light of their traditions.

Are theme and form enough to define Indian literature? For the epic, the *purpose* must also be considered. Certainly one aspect of the purpose of literature is the giving of instruction. Edification is far more agreeable to the Indian, and perhaps always has been, than it is to modern Western man. Wisdom of any kind is, and has been, loved. The Indian has enjoyed hearing endlessly about his God, whether that God is formless and transcendent, or wears a cobra, or plays a flute. Edification, wisdom, moral lessons have a pleasurable quality that an earlier age in the West enjoyed in homiletics. And on the other hand, the Indian has never been pleasurably attracted, as Western man has been, by psychological variety, individualistic introspection, and moral ambiguity. If the story literature differs significantly from the epic, it is probably in the sharp distinction it draws between pleasure and edification.

If this general approach is accepted, always bearing in mind the increased complexities of modern India that may make some modification necessary, the usual genre classifications of Indian literary history can be done without. Another massive body of texts, *The Purāṇas*, the "ancient lore," which, like the Vedas, have influenced Indian literature in a restricted and definable way, can be left aside. Although they provide an indispensable and seemingly inexhaustible source of information for and about the legends and attitudes of the Indian people, *The Purāṇas* can be treated adequately in terms of the Hindu epic, especially *The Mahābhārata*, as long as we know what the Hindu epic really was. The epics are compendia of the same type of lore as is found in the Purāṇas, and their bulk is tremendous—100,000 couplets in *The Mahābhārata*, 25,000 in *The Rāmāyaṇa*. *The Rāmāyaṇa* will be treated in detail, rather than *The Mahābhārata*, for a number of reasons. The most important of these is that *The Rāmāyaṇa* is the more unified of the two, and the typical features of the Indian epic can therefore be more clearly seen.

Partly because of chronology, and partly because it provides a natural transition, the chapter on the epic is followed by one on the classical theater. While almost universally based on popular themes, epical and otherwise, the theater deliberately limits its audience to the educated and refined, using old and well-known stories to rouse in the audience a symphony of moods beyond the uneducated sensibilities of the uncultured. It does so with a unique combination of great poetry, acting, mime, ballet, song, and music. The Sanskrit theater is the stage of all the performing arts.

In art, theory follows practice; and the experts on dramaturgy and poetics follow the playwrights and the actors. In this work too a discussion of poetics follows here, because of its intrinsic interest as well as its importance for the later development of poetry, and because it provides a critical stance from which poetry can be viewed from within the tradition. And the poetics, presupposed by many of the later authors, leads naturally to a discussion of the short poem. The first section of this chapter deals with Sanskrit verse, thus remaining within the limits set by the previous two: the Great Tradition overlaying many smaller ones. But soon this tradition develops into a variety of other and newer forms. In theme and style, the Bengali lyrics for a while lean heavily on the Sanskrit, but with a muscle and character all their own. And in the meantime the Islamic culture was introducing its own forms, from Arabic and Persian, unlike anything India had seen earlier. Thus Urdu poetry, illustrated by its favorite form, the *ghazal*, offers a proud contrast and a complement to other Indian literatures. And an equally proud contrast is offered by the Tamil anthology verses, not now from outside but from within the Indian cultural tradition. And at this point, when Indian literature seems to have broken up into a variety of traditions, it is necessary to bring in the story literature, which on various levels of culture through time provide once more a continuity of letters. It also affords the opportunity to bring in values and themes that the concerns of other genres have neglected, values and themes that recur in modern writing as well—success, material well-being, worldmanship, and human love.

And finally, there is modern literature itself, product of a period in which yet another culture, that of Britain and the West impinges on India. The attitudes of writers have changed. Their forms, and sometimes even their language, are those of the West. More universal education and the printing press have changed their audience. And yet, in a variety of ways, the voice keeps speaking with that characteristically Indian tone that had been prepared and polished by traditions of nearly three thousand years. (JABvB)

1 The Indian Epic

The formation of The Mahābhārata

It is not exaggerated to say that just as *The Iliad* stands at the beginning of Greek literature, so at the beginning of Indian literature stands *The Mahābhārata.* This statement of course has to be qualified at once by the remark that, while no Greek literary works are extant from the period before Homer, the entire Vedic corpus preceded the Indian epics; as has been said, however, in spite of the occasionally distinguished poetry of the Veda, the primary influence of that great body of texts has been in terms of religion and ritual. It is fair to say that after the Vedic period, Indian literature seems to start anew.

The sacred quality of the Veda prevents it from being considered, in the Indian tradition, as literature. To the ritualists, even the poetry of *The Ṛg-veda* and *The Atharva-veda* was reduced to mere recitation, where sound was more important than meaning. The Veda is considered *mantra*: lines that at particular sacrifices have to be recited in this way or that by certain priests whose hereditary business it is to know which lines to recite and when—and not to know what they mean. The Vedic corpora became the property of certain priestly classes, who were more interested in the niceties of pronunciation, in the gods to whom the hymns were addressed, in the meter, and in the seer first associated with these hymns than in the interpretation of their meaning. The professional priest-to-be went through the most rigorous training imaginable, achieving the virtuosity of being able to recite the verses both forward and backward, leapfrogging lines, handling with ease the complicated shifts of euphonics, mastering litanies that might last for three hours without reference to a written text; but he was hardly educated in the literary beauty, or in the sense, of what he knew so perfectly by heart.

Nor had the Vedic poets made it very easy for later generations to follow their meaning. They delighted in obscure vocabulary, complicated grammatical forms, antique modes of expression, and above all elliptical references to ancient myths and names that in time had been forgotten. Moreover, as time went on, attention shifted away from the direct invocative or evocative powers of the hymns to the context in which their recitation took place. The sacrifice itself became the focus of interpretative acumen. Concern was no longer with what the lines meant, but rather with what was going on ritually and cosmically as they were spoken, and as the oblations were offered into the fire. The priestly handbooks, *The Brāhmanas* (ca. 1000–800 B.C.) do not even trouble to spell out the lines, but content themselves with indicating first words, which trigger the rest of the line in the prodigious memory of the specialist. For the rest, those manuals speculate on the meaning hidden in the number of lines spoken at this or that occasion, the use of this rather than that special meter, or the significance of the myth lying behind the rite. Very rarely do they speculate on the meaning of the verse; if they do, the correctness of the literal meaning is too frequently sacrificed to esoteric speculation.

Furthermore, if the Vedas were known only in a limited sense to those whose business it was to know them, to outsiders they were known not at all. The Vedas were never generally available to the population. Except for a small number of auspicious verses they were not recited in public, but only at sacrificial sessions not accessible to everyone; while for those who might attend, the virtuoso's speed at recitation, whenever indeed the recitation was loud enough to be heard, would hardly make the lines intelligible.

But if the Vedas were not public, other genres that existed side by side with them were. In the more recent texts of the Vedas there are references to *itihāsapurāṇam*, which, after the four Vedas, is enumerated as a fifth erudition. The word *itihāsa* can be translated literally as "that is how it was," and, as will be recalled, *purāṇa* means "ancient lore." One can only guess, from later examples, what the contents of this literature were, but it is certain that they comprised not only mythological lore but also bardic accounts of great exploits of individual chiefs, their families and dynasties, how battles were won and cattle raids averted, how one tribe achieved paramountcy over another, how new land was created by burning down forests—the epoch-making feats of the not-so-numerous invaders who spread themselves within five hundred years over an area the size of Europe. In the Veda itself are mentioned "praises of heroes"; in these, perhaps, there are the beginnings of an epic. They would not have constituted a coherent, edited, and polished account, but they would have been the ballads and tales, describing individual heroic achievements, out of which epics are built. And different professional reciters would have had different repertoires of these.

Such a reciter would have been the close companion of the person about whose family the ballads were sung. One of his names is *sūta*—"Charioteer"—the lieutenant or friend who drove the chariot for the warrior, as Patroclus did for Achilles in *The Iliad* or Kṛṣṇa for Arjuna in *The Mahābhārata*. Both indispensable companion and witness to the warrior's feats, the sūta would urge him on in battle by recalling the bravery of his ancestors, or gratify him at the victory feast with a ballad of his fighting. History would be edited into legend, and legend into history, the stories of "how it was" would be passed on to son and to son's son, by the clan or tribe to further generations, until a desultory repertory had grown that waited only to be woven together.

The frame on which many of the ballads and lore were hung was the ancient story of the internecine warfare of the Bhāratas. The basic story was of how two branches of the same family, the Kauravas and Pāṇḍavas, fought over a disputed patrimony. But the form that the "original" epic had is not known. Other stories became interwoven with it; it is probable that several accounts of the war survived, and that these several became intertwined and mixed with accounts of other warlike incidents. It is difficult to trace all this in precise detail, but a few examples may indicate the process. When the two opposing parties are drawn up for battle, the hero Arjuna faces the prospect of killing his kinsmen. He sits down, dejected and uncertain as to what he should do; and at this point his charioteer, Kṛṣṇa, admonishes him. Out of his admonitions grow the eighteen chapters of *The Bhagavad-gītā*. Or again, the hero Bhīṣma, great warlord and sage, is dying; a moralistic discourse is put into his mouth, and this discourse grows to hundreds of chapters. And another hero laments his misfortune: "Can anyone have been more unfortunate than I?" Whereupon a sage replies: "I shall tell you the story of King Nala," and the famous Nala episode, a book in its own right, is inserted. In the end, the main story of the epic comprises only one half of the text.

There are two ways of looking at *The Mahābhārata*: as a repertory and as a book. As a repertory it was the collective possession of generations of bards, some belonging to certain courts or tribes, others probably wandering from court to court as Phemios in Homer. The repertory of a bard might include the story of the Bhārata war; but it would include far more. If his road were to lead him to a religious festival, he would draw on his store of myth and legend, some his own and some borrowed. Moral examples and edifying tales, folk stories and fables, would be woven through the main recitation, where interest demanded it or entertainment was called for. Thus *The Bhagavadgītā*, hardly critical to the central story, finds itself included when the epic is finally written down.

For the second way of looking at the epic is as a book, a single entity. It is quite impossible to tell under what circumstances the bardic recitations were written down. Although, apart from the writing on the seals of the Indus valley civilization, the earliest inscriptions in India date only from the third century B.C., it is safe to assume that writing was known much earlier. But the historical picture is confused by the fact that in India "books" were not necessarily recorded on bark or palmleaf, but quite frequently were committed to memory. Schooling was—and often is—by rote, and the teacher gave individual care to each of his students. Where a doctrine or a story was especially prized by a certain group, or where specialized knowledge involving complete accuracy went with a vocation, transmission of the text would have been by the oral means. It may be assumed that this was the case with the recitations of the bards.

But at some fairly early time the repertory of recitations must have been recorded. It may have been a prince who ordered the recording for his own purposes, or it may have been that an entire community of learned scholars decided at some point that the epic should be noted down. The increasing tomes of the Buddhists, whose canon is significantly called *Tipiṭaka* ("three baskets" of manuscripts—an indication that the Buddhist texts were written down early), might have inspired a similar response on the part of these who proudly claimed a book tradition of their own. But this remains uncertain.

In a way that might seem paradoxical, it was the physical availability and accessibility of *The Bhārata* or *Mahābhārata* as a book that laid it open to almost infinite expansion. *The Mahābhārata* is usually dated between 400 B.C. and A.D. 400, a span of eight centuries. No civilization, even the so-called unchangeable ones, can reasonably be expected to put eight centuries of itself into a single "book." And it has been seen what a book was in the Indian context of the time.

No summary of the story of the epic, then, is meaningful, any more than a summary of all the books in a library is meaningful, or in fact possible in limited pages. The character of the epic in its present form lies more in the stories that have accreted around its basic core than in the core itself. And these stories have become so interwoven with the core that scholars can agree only on a minimum definition of what that core might have been. But while reading the subject catalogue of a library may be neither particularly edifying or exciting, some idea must be given of what the general frame of the epic is.

The epic as we now have it consists of eighteen books. In addition to these eighteen there is a final book in three parts, called *The Harivaṃśa*, or "Dynasty of Hari (i.e., Kṛṣṇa)," which most agree is a later addition to the text. The first book of the epic, an introductory book, deals with origins in general, and in particular with the origins and childhoods of the heroes of *The Mahābhārata.* Dhṛtarāṣṭra and Pāṇḍu were brothers, and were educated together by their uncle Bhīṣma. When it was time, Dhṛtarāṣṭra married a woman named Gāndhārī, who had one hundred sons called the Kauravas, and Pāṇḍu married two wives. The first of these died, but the second, named Pṛthā or Kuntī, survived her husband to bring up his five sons. These sons were really sons of the gods, whom she had invoked. They were Yudhiṣṭhira, son of Dharma, Bhīma, son of the Wind, Arjuna, son of Indra and the main hero of the epic, and the twins Nakula and Sahadeva, who were sons of the Aśvins.

The epic proper begins in the second book. The scene is a gaming hall at the court of the Kauravas at Hāstinapura (which on present-day maps is about sixty miles west of Delhi). The sons of Pāṇḍu, the Pāṇḍavas, had been invited there from their own city of Indraprastha, for the Kauravas, jealous of the growing power of the Pāṇḍavas, intended to cheat them of their wealth and their kingdom in a game of dice. Yudhiṣṭhira indeed did gamble away all their wealth, and finally gambled away himself, his brothers, and even their common wife Draupadī. On an all or nothing throw, with years of exile wagered against restoration of all that had been lost, Yudhiṣṭhira again lost, and the five brothers and their wife went into exile in the forest.

The book that describes the exile, the "Forest Book," is full of stories told to relieve the tedium of life in the forest, and these include the famous story of Savitri, the prototype of the faithful wife, and the power of her chastity, and that of Nala and Damayantī. The brothers finally allied themselves to a king called Virāṭa, who lends his name to the fourth book of the epic; with him, at the end of twelve years of exile, they fought against the attacking Kauravas. The fifth book is called "The Preparation for War"; by this time, Kṛṣṇa had been enlisted by the Pāṇḍavas, the alliance taking place because Arjuna had married his sister. The next four books describe the war with asides: *The Bhagavadgītā* is inserted into "The Book of Bhīṣma." The encounters and tales of battle in these books are far too numerous even to hint at; in one of the most famous ones Karṇa, son of the sun god, and half-brother of the Pāṇḍavas but fighting against them because of an insult, was slain by Arjuna.

Finally, most of the Kauravas were routed or slain, sometimes through treachery. But in the tenth book those remaining mounted a night attack in which the army of the Pāṇḍavas was defeated and killed; only the five brothers themselves remained. The book following is that of the lamentation of the women over the slain warriors.

The war was over. But somehow Bhīṣma survived to preach, in the next two books, long sermons on ethics and philosophy. And the basic story itself comes to an end in the fourteenth book, in which Yudiṣṭhira was finally crowned emperor, and proceeded to perform the horse sacrifice, symbolizing the stabilization of his power. The next books tell of a variety of events, some related only marginally to what had gone before. For example, "The Book of the Club Battle" relates the story of the deaths of Kṛṣṇa and his brother Baladeva: Kṛṣṇa's family, the Yādavas, had been cursed by a brahman, and destroy each other. The last two books, before *The Harivaṃśa,* recount the story of the Pāṇḍavas giving up their kingdom and ascending into heaven.

The epic lay open to insertions and interpolations on two scores. As a conglomerate of bardic stories, legends, and lore, it did not have the inner and formal integrity that a planned poem would have. Even when these clustered around the core of the story of the war between the Kauravas and Pāṇḍavas, the general structure remained loose. Unlike *The Iliad,* it is not for all time an epic sung by one poet. The Sanskrit lines abound in such phrases as "exactly like before," "just as it was told," and "precisely as it happened"; yet the epic is not a one-time creation, reasonably unchanged through time, the authentic work of perhaps a mythical but identifiable author.

While Plato, somewhat pedantically, can refer to Homer's lies, and Horace, more urbanely, reflect that even Homer may doze at times, these criticisms reflect a conception of authenticity that never bothered the Indian. A Vyāsa is named as "author" of *The Mahābhārata*; but he is also named as author of the eighteen major *Purāṇas,* and as the compiler of the four Vedas. The name is of course merely symbolic. And this, while unsatisfactory to a Western mode of thinking that needs historical order, is significant. The truth is more important than the individual who gives it voice. In fact it is held by later schools of ritualism and philosophy, the Mīmāṃsā and Vedānta, that no person, human or divine, can be the author of the scriptures. They are not dictated by God, as the Qur'ān was, or inspired by the Holy Spirit as the Bible, nor hieratically oracled by a sage like Confucius. They are simply there; the popular myth has it that at the beginning of creation the Vedas were waiting to be "seen" again in order to inspire the creation that was about to unfold. But at the same time, in the fact of the composition of *The Mahābhārata* there can be seen an increasing frustration with the Veda. It is held that creation was parceled out in several eons of increasing deterioration. A "Golden Age," or, in Sanskrit terms, the "Best Throw of the Dice," is followed by increasingly worse throws, until we now find ourselves living in the worst Throw of all, the Kali Yuga, the Age of

Nought. In these four successive eons even the quantity of the Veda varies. The first Age had the Veda complete, but the last and final Age, the present one, has only a very incomplete Veda left. The benighted world needs further instruction.

This then is how later generations looked at the epic: as a second round, so to speak, in revelation. But although the epic was virtually as anonymous as the Veda, it was so much less closely intertwined with standard Brahminic erudition and ritual practice that it could never achieve the Veda's sanctity. The epic is called the "fifth Veda," but it is classified as *smṛti*, "tradition," "that which is remembered," and not, like the Veda, *śruti*, "revelation," or "that which one has sacramentally heard."

How, it may be reasonably asked, could a loose collection of epical cycles ever attain this high, though ambiguous, position? The answer is that *The Mahābhārata* became the founding library of Brahmin-Indian civilization. It is necessary to understand the epic as an encyclopedia of that civilization: it includes the basic story of *Śakuntalā*, so beautifully embroidered by Kālidāsa in his drama of that name, as well as the basic story of *The Rāmāyaṇa*, which in the poetic voice of Vālmīki is itself the second great Indian epic. It includes history, legend, edification; religion and art; drama and morality. If an analogy were to be made to western culture, one would have to imagine something like the following: an *Iliad*, rather less tightly structured than it now is, incorporating an abbreviated version of *The Odyssey*, quite a bit of Hesiod, some adapted sequences from Herodotus, assimilated and distorted pre-Socratic fragments, Socrates by way of Plato by way of Plotinus, a fair proportion of the Gospels by way of moralizing stories, with the whole complex of 200,000 lines worked over, edited, polished, and versified in hexameters by successive waves of anonymous church fathers. In the Western tradition this seems incredible. In the Indian civilization *The Mahābhārata* is a fact.

From one point of view, then, the great epic is a record of the warlike past. From another, it is a record of the self-view of the dominant Brahmanical tradition. For the future it will be revelation of a kind, anonymous like the Veda, complementary to the Veda, embodying the sum total of beliefs and practices that somehow never found expression in the Veda but were religiously remembered from the time when the Veda was. In its eight centuries of formation it was to become the principal library of all texts that were written in the verse form called *śloka*, in the Sanskrit language, and in conformity with a growing Brahmanistic consensus. It is the massive effort of generations, nameless as generations, and gray like the consensus of generations.

But what has been said must now be qualified. Not everything written in *ślokas* was predestined to become absorbed into *The Mahābhārata* or be lost forever. For between the time when *The Mahābhārata* library was founded and when it was finished, *The Rāmāyaṇa* was created. (JABvB)

The Rāmāyaṇa of Vālmīki

It is not easy to compare *The Rāmāyaṇa* and *The Mahābhārata*. For one thing, *The Rāmāyaṇa* is only about a quarter as long, and it is not the compendium *The Mahābhārata* is. For another, it is not anonymous, but bears the name of a single author. It is not as old: its substance is a morality tale of a single hero living in a settled society, protesting for a settled society, not the warfare of contending tribes yet embattled for a place in the sun. On the other hand, it is not as young: in it, rules for conduct are still being formulated by practice, not quoted from immemorial custom.

Nor is it easy to describe the difference in the type of influence that the two books have exerted on later Indian literature. *The Mahābhārata*, however great at times its poetic power, is not carefully and consciously unified and wrought. Yet it was the well from which later authors continued to draw their substance as well as inspiration. *The Rāmāyaṇa*, on the other hand, is consciously literary. And while Vālmīki basically tells one story, *The Mahābhārata* tells hundreds. If Vālmīki's materials are folktale, the form in which he cast them permits consideration of *The Rāmāyaṇa* as his own creation.

This unitary character of Vālmīki's *Rāmāyaṇa* and its clear plot, which has a beginning, a middle, and an end, lent themselves more to imitation and restatement than did the chaotic bulk of *The Mahābhārata*. Its great hero, Rāma, soon came to be considered as an incarnation of the great god Viṣṇu, and this opened the feats of the hero to religious interpretation. And at the same time Rāma remained a folk hero, and *The Rām-līlā* was—and is still—annually reenacted to the delight of the countryside. The moral and social arbiters of the Hindu tradition found in Rāma the king the epitome of dharma, and in the Rāmarājya, the kingdom of Rāma, the mirror of the ideal society. All such elements and more are present in *The Mahābhārata*, but in that epic they are spread over a great number of characters and an enormous number of stories.

The Rāmāyaṇa is a consciously literary work, and Vālmīki is the First Poet, the *ādikavi*, even though by later standards his composition might be found to be lacking in poetic power, refinement, and precision. In fact, many of his concerns are reflected in later classical court poetry. He excels in leisurely description of natural scenery, the beauties of palaces, the grandeur of the forest; he delights in poetic elegies and laments, and he has a poet's sense of a woman's heart.

Since the contents of *The Rāmāyaṇa* are known throughout India, some knowledge of the basic story is necessary. In oversimplified terms it can be described as an Indian "Labors of Hercules," set in the romance of an exiled prince questing for his abducted princess. In its present form, its 25,000 couplets are divided into seven books. The first and last of these seven are held to be added later by unknown religionists: they glorify Rāma as God. In the other five books Rāma is still a human hero.

There need be no doubt that the author was actually called Vālmīki and that he came from the eastern part of central India. To him is attributed the invention of the śloka, a meter so popular that a word or two might not be out of place here. Almost the whole of *The Mahābhārata* is composed in this meter, as are the eighteen major Purāṇas and a vast popular literature of edification. Its wide usage is certainly due to its simplicity. Like Greek and Latin poetry, Sanskrit verse is scanned by long and short syllables. A single stanza consists of two identical halves, each divided into two quarters, or *pādas*. The word *pāda* also translates as "foot," which is misleading, since it has nothing to do with the foot of classical European prosody; in Sanskrit it simply means one quarter of a complete stanza. The full śloka consists of thirty-two syllables, and is a couplet, each line being made up of sixteen syllables. The fact that it is a mixture of free and bound verse makes the śloka particularly suited to extended works. The first quarter begins with four syllables that are indifferent as to quantity, followed by four that obey rules of quantity, followed again by four that are indifferent and four that are metrical. The other half repeats the same pattern. As an example, here is the first śloka ever sung, when Vālmīki saw a fowler kill a heron drake lamented by his mate:

> mā niṣāda pratiṣṭhāṃ tvam agamaḥ śāśvatīḥ samāḥ/
> yat krauñcamithunād ekam avadhīḥ kāmamohitam//

> "May you fail to find rest, O Fowler, for all eternity,
> as you have killed, of a couple of herons, the infatuated male."

In Sanskrit open syllables with the long vowels ā, ī, ū, ṝ, e, o, ai, and au are long by nature, while short vowels followed by any cluster of two or more consonants form a syllable that is long by position. The above śloka therefore scans:

> long short long long *short long long short* (or long)
> short short long long *short long short long*;

long long short short *short long long short,*
short short long long *short long short long/short.*

or in schematic form:

⏓ ⏓ ⏓ ⏓ ⏑ – – ⏓, ⏓ ⏓ ⏓ ⏓ ⏑ – ⏑ ⏓/

⏓ ⏓ ⏓ ⏓ ⏑ – – ⏓, ⏓ ⏓ ⏓ ⏓ ⏑ – ⏑ ⏑//

The result is a very fluid meter, only half dictated, and thus allowing the poet a very great freedom of expression. (JAVBvB)

The Rāmāyaṇa story

Once Nārada, the divine sage, eternal messenger between gods and men, was relating to Vālmīki, himself a sage, the adventures of the life of Rāma. Profoundly intrigued, Vālmīki was pondering these matters as he went to bathe in the Ganges. Close to where he was bathing two beautiful herons were sporting among the trees on the river bank; suddenly one of them was shot down by the arrow of an unseen fowler. The other hovered frightened about his dead companion, crying out in anguish. Greatly moved by pity, Vālmīki gave voice to his anger and compassion, and found that his words had arranged themselves in a metrical fashion appropriate for musical accompaniment. Then Brahmā, the Creator-god, appeared in Vālmīki's hermitage and revealed to the poet that the *śloka* had manifested itself so that he might write in this meter the account of Rāma's life. Thus *The Rāmāyaṇa* was born, out of anger, pity, and poetry.

In the country of Kosala, on the bank of the river Sarāyu, stood the fortress city of Ayodhyā, "the impregnable one." The country it commanded was perfect—rich, abundant in food and learned Brahmans, and protected by warriors from the envy of its enemies. The king of this country was Daśaratha, old, wise, and unchallenged; but he was haunted by one grief: that he had no children. To assuage this grief and accomplish his desire, he followed the advice of his Brahmans and offered a Horse Sacrifice. Many animals were killed, but the sacred horse itself was released by Dasaratha's first wife Kausalyā. The gods, recipients of the oblations, appeared to collect what was due them, and promised the king four sons by his three wives.

Meanwhile a race of Giants, Rākṣasas, under the leadership of the awesome Rāvaṇa who had ten heads and twenty arms, was threatening gods and men. Rāvaṇa had subjected himself to great austerities and, made powerful thereby, had wrested from Brahmā a boon that he could not be slain by the gods. That he might be slain by a man had never occurred to him.

The gods approached Brahmā for succor, and he in turn approached Viṣṇu. Viṣṇu, the Protector-God, consented to be born as the four sons of Daśaratha to stop Rāvaṇa, and he now appeared in the sacred fire, black, red-faced, and with disheveled hair. In his hands he held a golden pitcher filled with nectar; of this he bade the king make his queens drink. The nectar was distributed among them, but unequally, the first wife Kausalyā receiving the major share. And so were born, in time, Rāma, Lakṣmaṇa, Bharata, and Śatrughna.

The universe of *The Rāmāyaṇa* is one of strong contrasts: there are a few resplendent fortified cities, where all manner of luxury and enjoyment is for the taking, and in between them desert, jungle, and forest, inhabited only by sages and recluses, forever haunted by demons. These demons tend to belong to packs and families, and although the imagination of Indian writers has pictured their monstrosity in exquisite detail, they have some traits in common. They are not men, but they behave in many ways much like men, with family pieties and bonds, with a class system, with a propensity for asceticism shared by men and gods alike, with great cities and vast armies. They are Protean, capable of changing their shapes and sizes at will, which is one of their great strengths in battle. They come in two sexes, the demonesses at times importuning men, and the demons abducting women. They are particularly bent upon disturbing the sacrifices of Brahmans and the austerities of Brahman ascetics; they haunt the bleak wasteland of desert and jungle, and are not seen in cities. They are antigods, and the gods often need the protection of men against them.

The sages they like to haunt are powerful ascetics, to whom age and time mean nothing. The great Viśvāmitra once performed the yogic feat of holding his breath for a thousand years, upon which smoke rose from his head. The same sage once created a rival universe of stars and galaxies to spite the gods. But whenever the asceticism of these sages tends to produce powers equal to those of the gods, Indra, the old king of the pantheon, is apt to dispatch one of his dancing girls to seduce them, for chastity is the basis of their ascetic power.

It was the great sage Viśvāmitra who came to Ayodhyā to enlist Rāma's aid against the demons who were disrupting his mortifications. And reluctantly the king Daśaratha let his sixteen-year-old son go. Accompanying Rāma, as he would for the rest of his life, was his younger brother Lakṣmaṇa.

Viśvāmitra, in gratitude for Rāma's help against the demoness Tāṭakā, who bothered him particularly, bestowed on him a number of magical weapons, which were in effect genii at Rāma's beck and call, like the weapons that Vulcan fashioned for the gods. Rāma's favorite weapon was the bow, and his marksmanship was so perfect that he could shoot down the arrow of an enemy in full flight with his own. Trees, mountain peaks, or dust thrown at him were shot away, and his arrows sowed panic even in the ocean deep.

After their labors for Viśvāmitra, which were to set the pattern of their lives, Rāma and Lakṣmaṇa made their way to the court of King Janaka of Videha, whose daughter Sītā was of marriageable age. This girl had been miraculously born. Once when her father the king had performed a ritual ploughing of the earth in order to beget offspring, Sītā had sprung from the furrow. And now that she was to be married, only a hero could become her husband. The qualifying task was to stretch the bow of Śiva, with which that powerful god had once menaced the pantheon. The bow was huge: it was transported on a four-axled wagon that could scarcely be budged by five thousand able-bodied men. No one of Sītā's suitors had been able to bend the bow. Then came Rāma, with his brother Lakṣmaṇa, and Viśvāmitra. And not only did Rāma bend the bow, he broke it, the thunderous crack knocking all those present to the ground.

Rāma's father and his other two brothers came to Janaka's court for the wedding, and all four boys were married at one grand occasion; with the sacred fire as his witness, Rāma married Sītā; the others also found brides at Janaka's court. Afterward, Viśvāmitra repaired to the Himālayas, while the court of Ayodhayā returned to their own city.

Rāma, because he was the first born, was destined to become king; not only was he the son of the present king's first wife, but his virtues were those of a king. But though Rāma's mother Kausalya had the privilege of rank, Queen Kaikeyī, mother of Bharata, had the privilege of the old king's love; and in the weakness of his passion Daśaratha had once promised her the boon of any two wishes she might ask of him. While the preparations for Rāma's installation as Young King proceeded, a deformed slave-woman, Mantharā, maliciously planted jealousy and rancor in Kaikeyī's heart, and that lady demanded that the king make her son Bharata his successor. The complications that polygamy creates for the legitimacy of succession are well illustrated by history; in *The Rāmāyaṇa* it changes everyone's life and brings disaster to the kingdom.

The king protested, but Kaikeyī remained adamant and demanded the fulfillment of her two wishes: that Bharata be elevated to the throne and that Rāma be banished to the forests for fourteen years.

A promise made under the sway of passion might well be considered less than binding; but one's pledged word, especially when it involved the *dharma* of a royal personage, could not be dishonored. Rāma himself implored his father not to break his promise, and with the greatest reluctance Daśaratha canceled the arrangements for his favorite son's elevation. In loyalty to his father and his father's word, Rāma accepted the exile. Nor would Sītā be left behind; she preferred the privations of the forest to the solitary comforts of the city. Rāma's loyal lieutenant Lakṣmaṇa also decided to follow his brother into exile. Kaikeyī, triumphant, rushed to provide the three with the crude bark clothing suitable to those who have lost everything and must live apart from men.[1]

(JABvB)

2.23.1 Taking leave of Kausalyā, Rāma set off for the wood,
blessed by his mother, and fixed in his righteous path.
2 The Prince embellished the royal road and moved
the hearts of the crowding throng with his splendor.
3 His virtuous wife, meanwhile, knew nothing of this,
her thoughts delighting in the royal installation.
4 She did her daily worship, gave thanks, and, glad,
awaited her royal husband, mindful of her royal duties.
5 Rāma then entered his beautiful house as his
servants rejoiced—but his face was cast down in shame.
6 Trembling Sītā rose and looked upon her husband
afflicted with grief, his mind distracted with thoughts.
7 Sensing his pain, and seeing his pale and sweaty,
impatient face, she said "My Lord, what is this now?"
8 "Was not Bṛhaspati's royal chariot today by Brahmins
commanded to be yoked? Why then be sad?
9 "Your lovely face is covered by shadow and does not shine,
as by a hundred-ribbed parasol, the color of sea foam.
10 "Your face and its lotus eyes are not fanned by fans
whose beauty is that of the moon and the swan!
11 "I see no happy bards, no heralds or poets praising you
today with eloquent and auspicious words;
12 "No Veda-knowing Brahmins bathe your oft-anointed
head with ghee and honey according to the ancient rite;
13 "No loyal subjects form a waiting line, nor do citizens
in proper dress seek to follow you about.
14 "Why is your great chariot not here in front of you
with its four speedy steeds, gold adorned?
15 "Why no decorated elephant, auspiciously adorned
like a great mountain or black rain cloud, promising a
tranquil journey?
16 "I see no golden palanquin, nor throne
honorably preceding you, my handsome one!

17 "The consecration is about to start! Why now this
strange unusual cast of face? Joy would better fit!"
18 Rāma then replied to the grieving girl
"Oh Sītā, the king himself has sent me to the forest.
19 "Listen how this has come to pass for me,
you who are born in a great and pious family!
20 "My royal father Daśaratha, always faithful,
once gave to Kaikeyī two boons, for he was pleased.
21 "It is she who seizes on this advantage
now that my consecration nears.
22 "I must live for fourteen years in the forest of Daṇḍaka
and Bharata is now appointed to the throne
so I have come to see you on my way to exile.
23 "You must never mention me to Bharata,
for those who prosper will not hear another's praise,
and no qualities of mine should be related either.
24 "Nor must you depend on him in any way;
ways will be found for you to live agreeably
25 "And I must keep my promise to my father,
and go today into the forest; be brave, wise woman!
26 "And while I'm gone into the sages' wood
it is your task to fast and keep fidelity, my faultless one.
27 "Arise at dawn and honor gods according to the rite
and praise my father Daśaratha, lord of men.
28 "My old mother Kausalyā, wasting away in grief,
also deserves your honor; you must put dharma first.
29 "And her sisters also deserve your love
for they are like my mother in my affections.
30 "My brother's sons must be looked to specially
by you, for they are dearer than life to me.
31 "Nothing displeasing to Bharata must ever be done
for he is King and Lord of the country and our house.
32 "And Kings who are pleased by efforts and by virtue
please in return, and anger otherwise.
33 "Lords of the Earth cast off their sons who do no good;
they gather to their heart the subject who does well.
34 "I go now to the forest, love; remain here while I'm gone.
As you would do no falsehood to any man, so live.
This is my word."

2.24.1 The Princess of Videha, lovely, speaking her love
was angered by his trust, and thus replied:

2 "The noble Prince must know that each of us
father, mother, brother, son—accumulates his merits and
enjoys a proper fate.
3 A wife though has no destiny but her husband's very own:
thus your command should be: "Live in the forest with me."
4 "My father, son, myself, my mother or my friends
provide no refuge; my man alone is my resort.
5 "If today you go to the wild forest land
I go before you, smoothing paths through the wild grasses
6 "Anger and envy will leave me; I drink only water you've
left; take me, O hero, in trust; there is no sin in me!
7 "The shadow of her husband's feet is there in every place:
upon the palace roofs, in carriages, in swift horse race.
8 "My mother and father told me often, in every circumstance
so to conduct myself that I need never be taught good
conduct.
9 "Happily will I live in the forest, as in my father's house
meditating not on heaven, thinking only of my husband's
vow.
10 "In the fragrant forests I will love you more:
obedient, forever modest, as virgin as a student.
11 "You, my Lord, will give protection in the wild
and none here can do the same; you are my guardian of
honor!
12 "Doubt not, I'll live till death on food of fruits and roots,
and cause no unhappiness, dwelling at your side.
13 "I thirst to see the streams, the hills, the shady groves
and have no fear, for you my wise resourceful Lord are
there.
14 "Happily with you I'd glance upon the lotus pools
in full flower and filled with ducks and swans,
15 "And there I'd flirt and play with you, my wide-eyed one,
for a hundred or a thousand years, if only you be there.
16 "Were I to live without you, even in paradise
the pleasures of eternity themselves would vanish.
17 "None can keep me from that frightful forest
dangerous with elephants and deer and monkeys;
I will there as in my father's house,
embracing your feet alone, and thus requited.
18 "Oh lead me with you! I die in separation—
my soul is yours, my mind knows no other life.
Grant my wish! I'll be no burden as your wife."

19 But the king desired not to lead his wife away,
conscious of his duty, though she spoke such words;
and he told her of the painful forest life
and more, in hope to turn her mind away.

In 25 Rāma describes the horrors of forest life.
In 26 Sītā refutes Rāma, citing śāstric parallels and her own horoscope, but he does not relent. She threatens suicide, and cries.

2.27.1 The daughter of Janaka, Princess of Mithilā, determined
to live in the forest, belittled her husband's reluctance;
2 In utter distraction, from affection and from honor,
Sita thus reviled the wide-eyed Rāghava:
3 "Why did my father, Mithila-lord, King of Videha, rejoice in
you as his son-in-law?—you a woman in the shape of a man!
4 "Yes, the world speaks falsely for it knows you not:
there is no glory in Rāma like the blazing of the sun!
5 "What have you done to despair? Of what are you afraid—
that you will forsake me, weak and without refuge?
6 "Do not you see in me another Sāvitrī, following her
Satyavant?
I live only that your will can take effect!
7 "I would not look, nor think on any man but you, unlike
others who disgrace their families; I would go with you.
8 Will you now give me to another, like a pimp,
your Sītā, your wife, your princess, your eternal companion?
9 "You cannot leave this place without me; I care not
whether the forest be a penance or paradise itself,
10 "And I will never tire in the forest paths,
or in eating or in sleeping, so long as I can follow you.
11 "The thorny trees, the reeds, the thistles and the grass
will be as cotton and as silk, if you are there beside.
12 "And the dust that you scatter on me stirred by the gusty
winds will be sandal paste itself, of greatest price, my love!
13 "I will lie on mats of thorny grass on grassy places,
beyond the forest even will my mind dwell in it; what is
more pleasant?
14 "Whatever you give me, or however much—a leaf, a root,
a fruit—I'll eat what you despise, thinking it nectar.
15 "I'll use the fruits in season, and the flowers,
and never pine for father, or my mother, or my home.
16 "No trouble will you ever have because of me
I will never be a grief nor hard to bear.

17 "Where you are will be my heaven, your absence be my hell;
go then with me, and know that my affection has no bound.
18 "But if you will not take me, who am determined, to the
forest—I'll take poison! I'll never bow before my enemies!
19 "For later on, the pain will make my life a curse
and death is my only friend if you abandon me.
20 "I cannot bear such sorrow for a moment more—
can you expect my grief to last for fourteen years?"
21 And so the sorrow-stricken woman moaned, and pleaded
with her pitying husband, and embraced him much and
often.
22 She was pierced by his many words like an elephant by
poisoned darts and her pent-up tears gushed forth like fire
from the rubbing sticks.
23 And the grief-born tears like crystal drops fell
from her eyes like morning dew from lotus petals.
24 Then Rāma spoke these words to comfort her,
taking in his arms the swooning, suffering girl:
25 "Even heaven would not please me, if I gained it by your
pain; nor have I fear of anything, like Svayambhū himself.
26 "I did not know the measure of your trust, sweet-smiling
one, and so did not approve your forest life, though none
could guard you better.
27 "Since you're created along with me for the pleasures of the
wild I cannot abandon you; none can leave behind his
reputation.
28 "The dharma has guided the path of the just through the
ages; I follow it today like Splendor [his wife's name] does
the Sun!
29 "And my dharma now is the will of my father and mother;
I could not bear to live disrespecting their command.
30 "As my father commands me, firm planted in the path of
truth, so I desire to do; this is the ancient dharma,
follow me, fear not, be my companion in my duty.
31 "Give your jewels to the Brahmins and food to the beggars
who call for it; do not tarry, hurry!"
32 When she knew that her company pleased her husband,
the queen was overjoyed and rushed to give her goods away.
33 Pleased, her wishes filled, the glorious wife
obeyed her husband's words,
Began to give away her monies, and her jewels—
most honorable among the wives of kings! (EG)

The parting was pathetic, and the people of Ayodhyā grieved. And Sītā, who as a virtuous wife had always lived in such seclusion that even the spirits that walk the skies had never set eyes upon her, was now exposed to the stares of all that walk the road. At night, while the camp slept, Rāma, Sītā, and Lakṣmaṇa slipped away into the wasteland of the Daṇḍaka forest.

The three settled down close to Prayāga (the present Allahabad) at the confluence of the sacred rivers Ganges and Yamunā and the invisible Sarasvatī. Meanwhile the old king succumbed to his sorrows and died. His sons Bharata and Śatrughna, who had been absent during all this, hurried to the capital. They were shocked and indignant to hear what happened. Bharata reproached his mother and, in Rāma's absence, performed the last rites for his father. Bharata assiduously refused to accept the throne and led the whole court, in spectacular royal procession, to the forest where Rāma was.

Rāma was finally found at Mount Citraketu and informed of his father's death; he fell unconscious, and upon revival performed the obsequies in the simple manner befitting a forest dweller. He steadfastly declined the throne in order to honor his father's instructions that, however reluctantly wrested from him, remained his commands. Bharata obtained Rāma's sandals, and with these as the visible presence of Rāma, returned to Ayodhyā. He resolved to act as regent for Rāma until the years of exile were past.

In his description of Rāma's sojourn in the forest the poet indulges both his feeling for the quiet idyll of the hermitage and for the fantastically gruesome. The "forest" means any tract of land that is not under active cultivation; it may indeed be a forest, but it may also be wilderness in general. In it live all who are not part of the ordered society of village and town: anchorites who have retired from social life to devote themselves to mystical introspection, great ascetics whose aeons of austerities have created in them incredible powers, and also monsters of every conceivable description, bent on disturbing the meditations and mortifications of the hermits and ascetics. Nature changes its aspect according to the aspects of those who people it. It provides the scenic surroundings of fruit-bearing trees, blossoming vines, clear and tranquil ponds covered with lotuses and water-lilies. It also provides the lairs of unspeakable horrors that emerge from the stark bleak wasteland of sheer mountain drops, impenetrable rain forest, and barren desert.

Rāma and Lakṣmaṇa had meanwhile returned to their task of clearing the forest of demons; soon they were set upon by a horribly ugly demoness, who begged the brothers for their favors. Lakṣmaṇa disfigured her even more by cutting off her nose, a punishment reserved for unchaste women. She thereupon roused a vast army of demons, and fourteen thousand of them assailed Rāma. They were all overcome, but one brought the news of the defeat to King Rāvaṇa in his island fortress in Lankā, identified by tradition with present day Ceylon. The disfigured giantess was Rāvaṇa's sister; she tried to exhort him to do battle with Rāma, but excited his interest only when she described the beauty of Sītā.

Rāvaṇa then resolved upon Sītā's abduction, and for that purpose he arranged for a silver-dappled golden antelope with sapphire belly and jeweled horns. When Sītā saw the animal she became entranced, and Rāma took off in pursuit of it, as Sītā asked. The deer took Rāma far away. When Sītā seemed to hear Rāma cry out for help, she sent Lakṣmaṇa after him, upbraiding him for his reluctance. She suspected that the younger brother himself had dishonorable designs upon her.

Rāvaṇa then appeared before Sītā as a kindly mendicant, and was so overcome by her beauty that he indulged in a description of it:

> "Who art thou, golden woman, clad in yellow silks, wearing like a lotus pond the bright garland of lotuses? Are you Modesty, Beauty, Fame, the Good Goddess of Luck, a celestial Nymph, oh bright-faced woman? Or Prosperity, my large-buttocked one, or Lust that freely rambles? Your teeth are even and pointed and smooth and white, your eyes are wide and clear, tinged with red at the ends and black in the pupils! Your buttocks are broad and firm, your thighs tapering like the trunk of an elephant. And these prosperous breasts, round, firm, bouncing, their tips firm and erect, lovable and smooth, like cocoa nuts! They glow with the jewelry of the choicest of gems. . . . With your charming smile, your charming teeth, your charming eyes, oh playful woman, you take my mind away, my love, as the water wears down the river bank. Your waist can be spanned by the hand, your hair is glossy, and your breasts are firm. Never have I seen on earth such a woman, neither Goddess, nor Nymph, nor Fairy, nor Elf. Yours is the finest shape in all the worlds, the greatest delicacy, the most beautiful maturity; and your garment in this very jungle drives my mind to madness. Fortune be yours, you should not make your dwelling here. This is the haunt of gruesome ogres who can change their shape at will. Only the roof terraces of palaces and delightful city gardens, wealthy and fragrant, are fit for you to walk. The choicest garlands, the choicest foods, the choicest robes, oh radiant one, and the choicest husband, oh dark-eyed one, are worthy of you. Who are

> you? With your beautiful hips you seem to me a goddess of Rudras, Maruts, or Vasus! No celestial musicians will ever come here, or gods and spirits. This is the realm of the ogres—why have you come here?" . . .[2]

But when Sītā did not give in even to such blandishments, Rāvaṇa assumed his real twenty-armed, ten-headed shape, and, seizing her by the head and legs, carried her off in his donkey-drawn airborne chariot. Sītā's cries awakened the great bird Jaṭāyus to the last vigor of his lifetime of sixty thousand years, and a terrible battle followed between the huge vulture and the flailing giant, which lasted till the bird was killed. Rāvaṇa then continued to carry Sītā through the sky to the island Lankā. There he tried to persuade Sītā to become the queen of all his queens, to accept wealth and power, to give herself to him. Sītā refused. Rāvaṇa was angered, but because of his love for her did not force his will upon her.

And while she was immersed in grief, wretched and powerless, the king of the Rākṣasas forcibly showed her his mansion, which was like the palace of a god, built up with terraces and pavilions and crowded with thousands of women, sought out by swarms of all manner of birds and filled with all manner of jewelry. It rested on columns of ivory and gold, quartz and silver, and on pillars of beryl and diamond wondrous to behold. Celestial drums reverberated through the halls, the gate towers were fashioned from purified gold; and the king ascended with Sītā the golden stairs.

Rāvaṇa's approach was a direct one:

> "Whether among gods or spirits, the celestial musicians or sages, I see no one in all the worlds who equals me in might. What use is Rāma to you now, deprived of his kingdom, a wretched, miserable peon, a mere human of little power? Do not set your mind on seeing him again, beautiful one. What power has he to come here, Sītā, even if he desires? The mind-fast wind cannot be tied by fetters in the sky, and the pure crest of a flaming fire cannot be seized by the hand. I cannot find in all three worlds a single one who could forcefully lead you away while you are guarded by my arms. Rule over this mighty kingdom of Lankā, and all Rākṣasas like me, even gods and all that moves and stands still will be your servitors. . . . Love me, Sītā, and I shall be your husband, and, my timid one, together we shall enjoy for certain our youth."[3]

And thus addressed, Sītā, as though discarding a straw, replied fearlessly:

> "There is a king Daśaratha, like the unshakable dam of *dharma*, true to his pledged word and famous—and Rāma is his son. Rāma indeed is famed in the three worlds for his virtue of *dharma*; his arms are long, his eyes are wide and by divine behest he is my husband!"[4]

When he discovered that Sītā had been abducted, Rāma was beside himself with anger, fear, and grief; only with difficulty did Lakṣmaṇa persuade him to restrain himself. Now single-mindedly bent on recovering his wife, Rāma entered into an alliance with a king of Apes, named Sugrīva, who was himself in more or less the same predicament as Rāma: he had been expelled from his kingdom by a brother who had also taken possession of his wife. Rāma agreed to help the Ape recover the throne, while the Ape agreed to locate Sītā and help slay the enemy. At the Ape's city of Kiskindhā, Sugrīva on Rāma's suggestion challenged the usurper to single combat, and when Sugrīva was losing, Rāma killed his opponent from ambush, self-righteously defending this breach of chivalry.

After the monsoon, the Apes assembled in their billions and spread out to search the world. They failed. Then the great Ape general sent word from the South: Hanumān, the Son of the Wind, had discovered that Sītā was being held in Lankā. The allies massed on the shore of the ocean, and Hanumān undertook to jump the water barrier that separated Lankā from the mainland. The Ape who, like the ogres, was able to increase or decrease his size, grew to mountainous stature and leaped. While he was flying through the air he was met by the Mother of the Serpents, who assured him from her gaping mouth that he had to pass through it. Hanumān made himself larger; the serpent's mouth became larger still. Suddenly Hanumān reduced his size to that of a thumb and leaped in and out of the snake's mouth. But his trials were not yet over. A dragoness grabbed his shadow as it flew over the surface of the water, and slowed his pace. But Hanumān once more reduced his size, jumped into her mouth and killed her from within.

Having disposed of these impediments, Hanumān landed safely in Lankā. Dwelling for a while on the wealth and beauty of Rāvaṇa's island palace, Hanumān found Sītā in an idyllic *aśoka* grove within the spacious compound of the demon king's fastness. Sītā was surrounded by horrendous ogresses that guarded her. While Hanumān watched, Rāvaṇa arrived in state and wooed her, and Sītā, with scorn and pride, rejected him:

> "Turn your thoughts away from me, rather set your mind on your own kind. You do not deserve to propose to me, criminal,

> any more than to propose to success. I am a wife who lives for her husband, and I shall not commit a despicable crime: I was born in a great dynasty and wedded to a holy one!"[5]

She was firm in her rejection, although the demon threatened to kill her and feast upon her flesh. And Hanumān watched Rāvaṇa retire, leaving the guardian demonesses to continue the persuasion at which they equally failed.

This is in a sense the climax of the story. The scene convinced the Ape, and Vālmīki's audience, that the conduct of Sītā in captivity was fully irreproachable, that it was the conduct of a truly chaste woman who honored her marriage vows. Rāma however was unaware of this; when the fortunes of war made women change hands with the rest of the loot, capture was tantamount to infidelity. And lest one sympathize with Rāvaṇa for his gentlemanly consideration, Vālmīki quickly points out that Rāvaṇa was not inspired by chivalry but by fear. He had once raped a celestial nymph, and at that time Brahman had cautioned him that if it happened again, he would be torn to pieces.

The Ape finally spoke to Sītā, in flawless Sanskrit, comforting her with the prospect of rescue and an offer to carry her off. Sītā refused. She would not allow her body to be touched by any male but Rāma. So Hanumān departed. But on his way back to Rāma, he was lassoed and brought down before Rāvaṇa. In a rage, Rāvaṇa ordered him to be killed. But then he realized that Hanumān was an envoy, and thereby sacrosanct, and he changed his mind. But Hanumān was to be humiliated. A torch of cloth dipped in oil was tied to his tail, while Sītā prayed to the fire not to harm her ally. But Hanumān, leaping through Lankā, set fire to the city. Finally he returned to the waiting armies and reported to Rāma.

As the armies of the Apes were encamped on the shore, they were joined by the demon Vibhīṣaṇa, who had fled from the wrath of his brother Rāvaṇa, to whom he had counseled moderation. It was resolved to attack Lankā. But the ocean was too wide and deep to cross, even though Rāma released his shafts upon it, shaking it to its innermost depths. Then the king of the ocean appeared, and advised the Ape architect Nala to build a bridge. The bridge was built, and the Apes swarmed across. Meanwhile Rāvaṇa had tried a desperate device to win Sītā's favors: he had a replica of Rāma's head fashioned by a wizard, and showed it to the woman as proof of her lord's death. The suffering Sītā was deceived, but when Rāvaṇa was called away, a servant betrayed the stratagem to her.

A titanic battle ensued between ogres and Apes. One of the greatest of the demon warriors was Rāvana's brother Kumbhakarṇa, who lived on a diet of a thousand human beings a day. To save the earth from swift depopulation, Brahmā had decreed that this cannibal should sleep for six months at a stretch and wake up for only one day. This was Kumbhakarṇa's day. His appetite whetted, he began to feast on thousands of Apes, some of whom were able to make good their escape through his nose and ears, until finally he fell under one of Rāma's magical arrows. Sugrīva launched a night assault on Lankā and set the entire city on fire.

The next day Rāvaṇa sallied out with a hundred and fifty million chariots, three hundred million elephants, and twelve hundred million horses and donkeys. The battle between Rāma and Rāvaṇa was unparalleled:

> As the ocean compares with the sky and the sky compares with the ocean, so the battle of Rāma and Rāvaṇa was only like the battle of Rāma and Rāvaṇa.

Rāvaṇa, in the end, was felled, and the battle won.

Sītā was then brought before Rāma, discreetly veiled from the glances of the Apes, but Rāma ordered her to walk unveiled so that his allies could see her: Rāma's presence was protection enough. But the reunion was a bitter one. Rāma, whose laments at her loss had torn the skies, now coolly rejected Sītā: her captivity had surely spoiled her fidelity. In a pathetic scene Sītā recalled his erstwhile love: "Hath my lord forgotten?" Sorely aggrieved and indignant, she ordered the ever-faithful Lakṣmaṇa to build a funeral pyre, and he did so, while Rāma looked silently on. Sītā threw herself on the pyre and was enveloped by the flames.

At this point, Brahmā and the multitude of gods appeared, revealing that Rāma was really Viṣṇu, while the Fire-god raised Sītā from the flames and announced the queen's fire-tried purity. With joy Rāma took his wife to his heart.

On his return to Ayodhyā Rāma assumed the government of the country and his rule was law incarnate. But the people, always quick to suspect the great, laughed at Rāma for keeping a wife who had been so long in another man's captivity; and when the harvest failed, they saw in this the result of Rāma's flouting the moral law. Sītā at this time was with child, and she voiced a desire to visit the holy hermitages. Rāma consented, and sent Lakṣmaṇa to conduct her there, with instructions to abandon her in the jungles of Daṇḍaka. Abandoned, roofless, and without a protector, she roamed the wilderness until finally she was found by Vālmīki. In his hermitage she gave birth to twin sons. These sons later became bards at Rāma's court. Recognizing and acknowledging them, Rāma invited Sītā to return and assert her innocence.

Sītā sadly rebelled at this. In her red robe she beseeched Mother Earth:

> "If it is true that even in thought I have never wavered from Rāma, so may the goddess of the earth grant me refuge."

The earth opened, a golden throne arose from the chasm, borne by splendid serpents, on which Mother Earth was seated. She placed Sītā beside her, and while they descended, a shower of flowers fell from heaven.

The Rāmāyaṇa is a romance; but it is also a popular book whose influence is still very strong in India. The question is, what are the reasons for this? No doubt in the first place it is popular because it is a romance, involving the fortunes of the great of the land, with the glamor of royal courts, the awesome fascination of great exploits in terrifying forests, the sanctity of incredibly powerful sages and ascetics, the irresistible attraction of the monkey Hanumān, still today one of the most popular of helpful gods, and in the end the massive defeat of the demons who had come close to vanquishing the world. The forces of good had triumphed, and civilization had been saved.

It is the particular quality of this civilization that for the Indian listener lifted the epic above mere romance. For it is the civilization of *dharma*, that world order based on superhuman Law that transcends all who live in it. Ayodhyā, the capital of Daśaratha, is a microcosm of the world. King Daśaratha is a good king who becomes inadvertently trapped in an intrigue from which he can escape only by breaking his word. But such a breach of faith would strike at the root of *dharma* itself, which is the endlessly reiterated pledge of man to his ordained duty. By insisting that Daśaratha remain true to his word, regardless of the circumstances under which it was pledged, Rāma becomes the very symbol of *dharma*.

But in the hands of Vālmīki, this *dharma* is not a bleak law that oppresses the obedient observer, for he has charged it with love, and even more than that, with compassion; this underlying theme, complementing and orchestrating the leitmotif of *dharma*, probably contributes, even more importantly, to having made the story accessible to the hearts and imaginations of generations of Indians. It is certainly not by accident that Vālmīki is said to have "discovered" both *rasa* and poetry (as well as bad puns) when he turned the grief (śoka) of the *krauñca* bird into the first verse (śloka), and thus began his poem. Almost all forms of love are illustrated in his poem. There is the filial piety that Rāma bears to his father, the piety that affirms the bonds of family that will secure the line for generations past and present. And Daśaratha, in all his unwilling weakness, responds to this piety with a sorrowful paternal love to which in the end he succumbs. Lakṣmaṇa, the selfless follower who never demands anything in return for his devotion, is the epitome of all the qualities of a good subject to his king as well as those of a self-effacing, devoted friend. But the great love is between Rāma and Sītā, illustrated in the famous lament of Sītā, translated earlier. As is proper, Rāma's love is the more remote love of the virtuous husband that is more likely to find expression when the beloved wife has disappeared than when she is comfortably around. While it is by no means his *dharma* to be faithful to his wife, he resolves to retrieve her from Rāvaṇa. That he does this instead, as would have been more usual, of simply accepting the situation, was perhaps itself edifying. Western romantic notions might suggest that his deep love would weaken his *dharma*. But this would be a misunderstanding. Not only must Caesar's wife be above suspicion; Sītā's purity is part of Rāma's own *dharma*, and Rāma's own loyalty to his *dharma* secures the *dharma* of his kingdom. It was firmly believed that a breach of *dharma* would upset the precarious equilibrium of the good society, so that it could indeed result in famine and pestilence for his people. As husband, Rāma always acts the king.

It is Sītā's role to be the wife, the eternally devoted one for whom the husband is a god. She is queen only to the extent that Rāma acts like a king, and the inherent tragedy of Rāma's final rejection of Sītā is to a large extent alleviated by the necessity of *dharma*. Sītā in the end has to be sacrificed to the well-being of the king's subjects. She thus becomes the idealized prototype of the wife who must share in her husband's misfortunes, but cannot always share in his fortunes. For the Indian, Sītā accepting her fate made her a heroine of the greatest nobility, to be respected, emulated, and loved.

Even today, among pious Vaiṣṇavas of South India, the compassionate parable of Sītā's love, which adversity only strengthens, is taken as a model of everyman's relationship to his dharmic God, who may indeed be Rāma deified. Sītā, much like Rādhā in the Kṛṣṇa legends, becomes a symbol of the human soul, but her passion for God is not exhausted in weak sentimentality; against the background of inflexible *dharma*, her love, indeed her suffering, seems not only more real, but by that fact, more pathetic, and more pertinently expressive of the compassion we all must feel for our fellow man caught in the web of this life and far from the God who even in saving us casts us off. (JABvB)

Variations on the theme

The Rāma story is as popular as any in India, and Vālmīki's version of it is graceful, detailed, and in many ways to be considered the authoritative version. Why then are there so many other *Rāmāyaṇas*, written in so many different Indian languages, not all of them remaining close to Vālmīki? One answer might be that the Vālmīki *Rāmāyaṇa* is only one among several ancient recensions, though the only one that has come down to us, and that variations are not necessarily deviations from Vālmīki, but that they represent variant traditions. But apart from this possibility, certain things do seem clear.

First, the Rāma theme, because it embodied royal grandeur, human love and *dharma*, edification and war, so many things dear to the hearts and imaginations of people, seems long to have been the poetic theme par excellence: writing the story of Rāma and Sītā was a test of the poet's powers, and writers in many languages submitted themselves to it.

Second, as time went on and the Sanskrit language gave way more and more to the regional languages, the poetry of Vālmīki became further removed from the people at large. The story itself might have been the product of a national consciousness, but it was eventually necessary to restate that story in language that the people could understand.

Finally, and related to the previous point, if *The Rāmāyaṇa* is a kind of morality tale, with Rāma the epitome of kingly virtues and Sītā those of womanhood, and with the inevitable conquest of the demonic forces of the world by those of justice and uprightness, the theme, putting forward as it does so many of the ideals and so much of the taste of Indian readers, would be bound to reassert itself in many times and places. And since, unlike the Veda, the Rāma story is not canonical Brahmanical literature, it might vary slightly or even greatly, with time and place.

Of the numerous *Rāmāyaṇa* versions, among the most popular in their own regions are the Kamban *Rāmāyaṇa*, a Tamil version of the eleventh or twelfth centuries A.D., *The Rāmcaritmānas* ("The Holy Lake of the Acts of Rāma") of the sixteenth-century Hindi poet Tulsīdās, and the Bengali version of Kṛttivāsa, which scholars place somewhere between fourteenth and late sixteenth centuries. These later versions, and others, demonstrate various tendencies in Indian literary and social history. They show changes in religion and morality through time. And they show synchronic variation as well: regional versions of the epic took on the characteristics of the developing subcultures of the subcontinent and of a new literary sensitivity.

Both Hindi and Bengali writers pay their respects to Vālmīki (as indeed most Bengali writers of *Rāmāyaṇas* after Kṛttivāsa do to Tulsīdās as well); and both, following the finally accepted "Vālmīki" text, divide the epic into seven chapters. The seventh is not present in Kamban. Both follow fairly closely Vālmīki's story line. But while Kṛittivāsa is in the Sanskritic tradition in his usage of lush imagery, Tulsīdās was too much of a religious devotee to indulge in such sensuality as that found in Vālmīki's description of the beauty of Sītā. Still, it is in terms of content, rather than of language or form, that the most instructive contrasts can be found.

Rāma, in the later texts, is far more than a hero. Following the suggestions of Rāma's divinity in the apocryphal first and last books of Vālmīki, the later writers strongly stress the point that Rāma is an *avatāra* (incarnation) of the great god Vishnu. The Vālmīki *Rāmāyaṇa* begins with a conversation between the sage Nārada and the poet. Vālmīki, describing Rāma's qualities, asks:

> Who is there in the world today so endowed with excellent and heroic virtues, versed in all the duties of life, grateful, truthful, pledged to his vows, who takes many parts, benevolent to all creatures, learned, eloquent, handsome, patient, slow to anger, and truly great; who is free from envy, but when excited to wrath can strike terror into the hearts of the gods themselves?[6]

Vālmīki's Rāma is a hero whose arms were "hard as iron bars" to draw the bow of war. But Kṛittivāsa's Rāma, an *avatāra,* comes to earth a merciful being, to save the world, who as a child "wandered in the garden with a bow made of flowers," a gentle god. Tulsīdās's Rāma is even more so, and that writer begins his story with homage to Rāma and Sītā, the cause of creation, preservation, and destruction, destroyer of pain and source of all blessings:

> Be homage paid to Lord Hari, Rāma, to whose power of illusion the whole universe, Brahmā, and all the gods and demons are subject! Because of his true being all this unreal world only *seems* true, like the snake which is only a rope. His feet are the only boat for those who would cross the sea of birth and death. He is the first cause beyond all other causes.[7]

Such a supposition of the divinity of Rāma obviously necessitates some changes in the internal logic of the story. A man, in Vālmīki, Rāma can go chasing after the golden deer merely because Sītā covets it, thus quite straightforwardly setting the scene for Sītā's abduction by Rāvaṇa. But in Kamban's version, for example, because Rāma is divine he knows that the golden deer is there because of Rāvaṇa's illicit purpose. He pursues it anyway, aware that only in this way will the drama be able to work itself out and he be able to conquer the demons and establish the kingdom of truth, as is his goal and destiny. The ultimate reduction of this is in a late *Rāmāyaṇa* in which Sītā asks Rāma to take her with him to the forest; Rāma refuses, and she returns the argument: "Countless *Rāmāyaṇas* have been sung in countless ages. Tell me, in what *Rāmāyaṇa* did Rāma go to the forest without his Sītā?"

As Rāma becomes less human and more divine, so Sītā also becomes less of a woman. In Vālmīki she is proud and dignified, and answers, when Rāma unjustly accuses her of unchastity: "Prince, why do you act a vulgar man? Why do you speak so rudely that you shock my ears?" In Kṛittivāsa much of this pride is lost, and she becomes a whining woman who replies to her accuser: "Even when I was a child, I never even touched a boy child." In Vālmīki, when Lakṣhmaṇa refuses to go to Rāma when she thinks she hears his cry for help, she says:

> You wretch of evil heart, disgrace of your family! You delight in Rāma's misfortune! A scoundrel like you will talk like this from foul motives in the hour of Rāma's distress. Faithless man, you came here to the forest with Rāma to lust after me, a traitor disguised as a friend![8]

Less strong, though still strong enough, are her words in Kṛittivāsa:

> Your half-brother could never be your own! . . . Bhārata took his kingdom, and now you take his wife! You are in league with Bhārata! Will you ignore Rāma, despite my wish? If my heart were to go to another man, I would take my life with a hook in my throat.[9]

She is in Kṛittivāsa less of a woman than is Vālmīki's Sītā, but still is flesh and blood. But in Tulsīdās, she becomes the *śakti*, divine power seen as female, inseparable from the male god. And in this text, before Rāma goes off to chase the deer, he puts the real Sītā into a fire to await developments, and replaces her with an unreal facsimile. All that happens afterward in no way affects her purity.

Thus it is too when Rāvaṇa comes to Sītā when she is sitting alone in the forest awaiting the return of Rāma. He tries to persuade her to become his queen, offering her riches and power beyond belief. In Vālmīki, angered at her chaste refusal, Rāvaṇa reveals his true demonic nature and, seizing her by the hair and thighs, throws her into his chariot and carries her off to Laṅka. Kṛittivāsa, close to Vālmīki's spirit, describes the scene in this way:

> So Rāvaṇa, in the guise of an ascetic, came to Sītā, an alms-bag over his shoulder, an umbrella in his hand. . . . He was enchanted

> as he saw her extraordinary beauty, heard her sweet voice. Gently he spoke to her, "Lady, what is your family? In which country do you live? Whose daughter are you, and whose beloved? You cannot be human, my lady, you are a golden goddess. But in this wild forest ferocious tigers live; by what strange circumstance do you stay here alone, O beautiful one? . . .[10]

Sītā then tells who she is and Rāvaṇa replies:

> My name is Rāvaṇa, so the sages know; seeing you I fell in love. For a long time have I lived in this forest, meditating and mortifying myself. . . . Give me alms, and I shall return to my own place. Then Sītā said: O Brahman, there are fruits in my house—I pray you, eat them![11]

But Rāvaṇa says that he cannot enter a habitation because he is an ascetic, and tries to persuade Sītā to bring the food to him: if she does not do so she will break the laws of hospitality. Finally,

> with the fruits in her hand, Sītā came out. The evil Rāvaṇa pretended to take them, and grabbed her hand instead. "What is this foul thing you do?" She said "Get away from me, you miserable evil man! For touching me you will die, with all your kin." Then Rāvaṇa said: "Sītā, listen to me. I am Rāvaṇa, king of the Rakṣasas. My home is Laṅka. I have twenty arms, and twenty eyes, and ten heads. I came to this forest disguised as an ascetic. Be kind to me, and I shall be your slave. My city of Laṅka is greater than Indra's city of Amarāvati. You will see a rare world, my beautiful one—for I have fallen in love with your beauty. Many queens will be your slaves, I shall make you queen over them all. . . . Your throne will be golden and studded with jewels. You serve Rāma now, and your life passes in misery. Serve me instead, and live in happiness and joy ever after. For the three worlds tremble before my arrows, while Rāma is but a mere man—I count him a worm. His life is short, his knowledge small; but I—I live from age to age. O Sītā, you are beautiful, in grace and in dress, and I desire you."[12]

Enraged at these words, Sītā cursed him with all the curses that came to her mind, and said: "This is an unjust, vile, and wicked thing you do; Rāma will kill you, and all your people. Rāma is a lion, and you a jackal. By what strange courage dare you speak of him? He is an incarnation of Viṣṇu, and you are a vile thing that stalks the night. . . ." Here too,

Rāvaṇa physically picks up the weeping Sītā and puts here in his chariot, which was "like lightning glittering on a cloud."

Kamban cannot bear to have Rāvaṇa touch Sītā at all. He harks back to Brahmā's curse on Rāvaṇa because of his rape of a celestial nymph, that if he ever again tried to take a woman forcibly his head would split into a thousand pieces. As a result, Kamban has Rāvaṇa dig into the earth around the place where Sītā is sitting, lift the whole affair in his two hands and place it in the chariot. Tulsīdās also allows Sītā—the false Sītā—to be abducted; but Rāvaṇa, who "found delight in the adoration of her feet," could "scarcely drive the chariot for fear" of his holy burden.

By the time of Kṛittivāsa and Tulsīdās, the *bhakti* movement of devotional worship to a monotheistic god was in full swing in northern India and in Bengal. In northern India, Rāma as an incarnation of Viṣṇu was himself an object of devotion, and *The Rāmāyaṇa* came to be a sacred text in those parts. The changes that intense religious devotionalism wrought upon the Rāma story are profound. We have seen that in Vālmīki the demon Vibhīṣaṇa, brother of Rāvaṇa, deserted to Rāma's side. Tulsīdās makes much of this. In his version of the story, Vibhīṣaṇa comes to Rāma and says, in effect, "I do evil because my body happens to be a demon's; but in my heart I am a *bhakta*, a devotee of Rāma";[13] whereupon Rāma embraces him and calls him the best of his devotees. The basic story is the same, but Tulsīdās's way of looking at it is quite different. To Tulsīdās, even Rāvaṇa was a devotee, fallen into a demon's body and struggling for the release that he finally found in Rāma's belligerent presence.

In Bengal, where devotion is more directed to Kṛṣṇa than Rāma, the results were equally strange. One author nicely understates the case:

> It is certainly a marvel that the battlefields, in the hands of the poets, were transformed into pulpits and the raksasas reformed Vaiṣṇavas of the Gaudiya (i.e., Bengal) order.[14]

A case in point is that of the Rāksasa called Atikāya. Like Rāvana himself in Tulsīdās, this demon is basically a worshiper of Rāma:

> Seeing the five heroes fallen, Atikāya entered the battle, bow in hand. He reflected to himself, "O son of Kaushalyā, give me a place at your feet. If you do not have mercy on me because I am a son of Rāvaṇa, there will be a stain on the name of the all-merciful Rāma.[15]

Even more interesting is the case of a Rāksasa called Taranīsena, son of the apostate demon Vibhīṣaṇa. Rāvaṇa is on the verge of despair, for all his bravest followers have now fallen in battle. Taraṇīsena volunteers to lead the next charge. He goes to his mother, who has already lost a hundred thousand sons in the fight, and says:

> Mother, at your feet I pray. The king has ordered me to battle. I shall see the god Nārāyaṇa, Rāma who is the full Brahmā with my own eyes. Seeing Rāma will purify my body. Give me your leave, mother, let me go and fight!

His mother replies:

> What are you saying, my son! My heart trembles at your words. I shall not let you fight the armies of monkeys and men; I shall take you away from here, to some far place. . . . Let the kingdom go! Let the king of Laṅka protect his realm! Everyone knows your father was a good man, that he left the ways of sin and took refuge at Rāma's feet. Go, bow instead to Rāma's feet; Rāma is not a man: He is lord of Goloka, who has come to earth to kill the evil-doing Rāksasas and all their kinsmen. Viṣṇu has come to earth at Rāma in the house of Daśaratha. I had a hundred thousand sons, and not one remains. . . . Your father understood, and went to Rāma's side. You too are wise and clever. You know all of this, why do you want to go to war?

Taraṇīsena's reply is illuminating:

> I know well that Rāma is Viṣṇu come to earth. That is why I make war on him. For if I die by the hand of Rāma, I shall go to Goloka. . . . Mother, why are you distressed? Who can kill whom? Who is whose enemy? Viṣṇu alone fills the universe, in different bodies. And, in time, the world will finally be dissolved. . . . Why, mother do you unreasonably fear death?[16]

He goes to battle, with the name of Rāma written all over his body "and on the four sides of his chariot."

It is a tenet of many worshipers of Visnu and his incarnations that even hostility to the deity can lead to rapid salvation: enmity is a powerful emotion, and any kind of powerful emotion, when directed toward the deity, is efficacious. In Kṛittivāsa's text, the pious interloper Vibhīṣaṇa laments:

> Atikāya and others have already been saved by fighting you and being killed at your hands. What profit have I gained by being loyal, O lord?[17]

In Tulsīdās, Rāvaṇa, the true devotee, struggles to find release from his demon body. His way is to fight against Rāma, knowing that in the end he will be killed, and thus attain salvation.

The ultimate in such developments, it would seem, is in a version of the story in Kannada, in which Rāvaṇa is no longer killed by Rāma but by his brother Lakṣmaṇa: Rāma, gentle deity that he is, can no more kill anyone.

In later versions these tendencies became even more pronounced. In an eighteenth-century version by a Bengali writer called Raghunandana, whose text is named *Rāma-rasāyaṇa*, Rāma's character is that of Kṛṣṇa. The scene of the gathering of the cowherds' wives to see Kṛṣṇa enter the city, popular in Bengali poetry of many periods, is easily transformed into the gathering of women to witness Rāma's triumphal entry:

> Hearing that Rāma had come, young women ran, forgetting their husbands and elders and all their household duties. Some had only one foot dyed with lac, some had only one anklet on, some wore jeweled necklaces around their wrists, others had put their waistbands around their necks, some had kohl on one eye only; thus the girls, and faithful wives, ran, with swelling hearts.[18]

Compare, of numerous possible passages, this section of a lyric by an earlier Vaiṣṇava poet named Vaṁśī-vadana, which describes Rādhā's agitation:

> As Rādhā was dressing, she heard the sound of his flute. She did not finish tying up her hair. What should be done, what should not be done—all was forgotten. . . . She tied the garland of flowers on her foot, put her anklet on her wrist, her waistband on her throat, her necklace around her hips. . . .[19]

It would seem that the various regions of India reflected *The Rāmāyaṇa* according to the ways of the times. Writers of later versions added to their model lines or even full stories that changed the interpretation of the whole to one congenial to the dominant sectarian, moral, or social climate of a particular part of the subcontinent. In some places, partisans of entirely different religious traditions appropriated the story to bolster their own points of view. Where writer-devotees gave precedence to the Kṛṣṇa-avatāra of Viṣṇu over the Rāma-avatāra, the story still remained within the domain of Viṣṇu. But some later Bengali writers, worshipers of the mother-goddess, go so far as to hold that the story demonstrates the greatness of the Mother: the tide of the battle in Laṅka changes only because the Goddess switches her allegiance from Rāvaṇa to Rāma. And in some Tamil versions the conflict between Rāvaṇa and Rāma becomes an allegory of the relationship between the philosophical pair *aram* and *maram*. Aram is righteousness, *dharma*, and maram is everything that is not aram—material welfare and earthly power. The allegory is obvious: Laṅka, the realm of the demon king, is infinite in its pomp and the majesty of material wealth and power; the kingdom of Rāma is the place where all is harmony, where rich and poor are alike where perfect peace and justice prevail.

An epic can be defined in a variety of ways. One is that it is what a culture thinks of itself. What India thinks of itself varies with time and place. New values, such as religious ones, induce reformulations, and thus new interpretations of the epic. But reformulation is not always tantamount to change. There is change, as when, in a modern version of the Rāma story from nineteenth-century Bengal, Rāvaṇa becomes the noble and chivalrous warrior hero: perhaps romantic ideals got from the West did not allow Brahmā's curse as the explanation for Rāvaṇa's courteous behavior. But it is possible to make too much of regional and temporal variations. Much remained constant. Sītā, who is at least the second most important and impressive figure in the epic story, is the prototype of the Indian wife. She is spiritual sister to the proverbial Sāvitrī, who because of her chastity and devotion had the power to snatch her husband from the jaws of death. She is sister to the medieval Bengali Behulā, who, as the story is told in *The Manasā-maṅgal*, a long eulogistic poem reciting the myth of the snake goddess Manasā, conquered by chastity and devotion that fierce goddess who had taken her husband's life, and brought about his resuscitation. She is sister also to the famous Rajput princesses, the *satī* (Suttee), "true wives," who leaped onto the funeral pyres of their husbands rather than risk dishonor at the hands of their conquerors. The complexities of life in modern India sometimes obscure the ancient ideals, but they are never lost. Sītā is *pativratā*, a chaste woman, true to the vows she made to her husband.

The Rāmāyaṇa remains popular. In a room of a university hostel in Allahabad where Rāma and Sītā once sojourned, a group of girls chants the tale according to Tulsīdās, and in minutes the doorway and the hall beyond are crowded with people listening. In a remote village in Bengal, in the deep of night, an old man sits on a veranda chanting the story according to Kṛittivāsa, perhaps reading by the light of a kerosene lamp, perhaps reciting from his memory; and young people and old sit before him, as entranced by the tale as they were centuries ago. And its popularity persists not only through chanted and literary versions. Groups of strolling players come to villages and act, with tinsel crowns and wooden swords, the titanic struggle of gods and demons, the conquest of Lanka. In the south, puppet plays and temple plays and *kathakali* dancing reproduce, for amusement and for edification, to the recitation of the Kamban *Rāmāyaṇa*, thirty-two of the dramatic incidents of the story. Stories from the epics, unchanging views of how-things-ought-to-be, personified by heroes, never wear thin. And most popular of all is *The Rām-līlā* of north India, the "Play of Rāma," in which, to the recitation of the lines of Tulsīdās and the cries of delighted children, actors play out episodes from the epic, culminating in the pyrotechnic end of a ten-headed, papier-mâché Rāvaṇa: it is the annual defeat of hostile forces, and the reestablishment of goodness on the earth. The story of Rāma retains its capacity to support different religious and social doctrines; to this the recent satirical version of the story by Aubrey Menon bears ample witness. (ECD)

2 The Classical Drama

Background and types

The Rāmāyaṇa presents a continuity and development of theme and form that spans many centuries of literary activity in India, whatever the region or the language. A genre that has not left such a legacy and that must be studied within the context of classical culture alone is the drama. Despite the fact that the drama did not provide a basis for development in time and space, it is of interest not only because as an art form it has an intrinsic fascination and because such plays as *Śakuntalā* delight people even today; but as example the drama provided the estheticians with the materials for their systematic objectification of Indian literary values.

Attempts have been made to link the origin of the classical Indian theater to the Greeks.[1] In principle, the possibilities of such influence cannot be ignored. The history of Indian art bears sufficient witness to the influence that Hellenistic art had upon the sculpture of the Gandhara region of the north western part of the subcontinent. Besides, such influence could have been mediated not only by the Indo-Greek kingdoms, but also by the flourishing trade between India and the Roman Empire in the last century B.C. and the early centuries A.D. Indian astronomy shows distinct influences from outside, while Indian geometry found its way into the Middle East. In short, strong cultural influences from beyond the northwest border of the subcontinent could have impinged upon the attention of the literate.

Not only that, but at the beginning of the first millenmium A.D., Indian culture had grown cosmopolitan. A class of educated and highly literate courtiers and sophisticates had formed around the courts of cities that thrived on trade with the West, the Far East, and Southeast Asia. And although differences between Hindus and Buddhists might have been felt strongly where matters of doctrine were at issue, there were no differences in matters of literary taste; also, the paintings of

Ajantā give a striking picture of the variety of races and dresses at the courts of the rulers. Such variety might well indicate a possibility of deeper contacts between cultures and their literary genres.

However, no Hellenistic influence has yet been discovered as the source of the classical Indian theater. Its roots are obscure. As so frequently happens with high Sanskrit literature, the Indian drama first appears as an accomplished fact. The fine examples of the genre that are the earliest known show little of the long process of development through which it must have gone. It would not in any case be wise to look for any single origin, in dialogue hymns of *Thr Ṛg-veda*, or in mystery plays of the conquest of demons by a locally popular god, or in the conversations of the epics. All of these may well have contributed to the drama; but essentially it emerged as a genre *sui generis*.

The mere name "classical drama" calls to mind the European classics; but comparison of the Indian classical theater, with for instance, the Greek stage, would be deceptive. The three unities of place, time, and action so familiar to the structure of the Greek play do not apply to the Indian one. And the most obvious distinction in categorizing Greek drama, and all Western drama since the Greeks, that between tragedy and comedy, has no relevance whatever in the Indian context. Western critics often note and sometimes deplore the absence of tragedy in the Indian drama. But the Indian drama, like all Indian literary forms, must be seen in context; and the underlying climate of Indian thought was not conducive to the development of what the West calls tragedy. Those who deplore its absence take for granted that tragedy is an almost natural expression of any culture, and that India is unnatural and deficient for not having it. One may, conversely, argue that Greek tragedy does not constitute the rule, and that it presupposes—apart from the religious pageantry in which it developed—a very specific notion of *moira*, fate, that is peculiarly Greek. The hero who demanded more than his share became the victim of the Fates, who had set for him so much and no more and exacted excessive repayment. The guilt thus incurred, or incurred by heinous crimes that flaunted civil and divine law, could be visited on later generations, until an entire great dynasty was brought to doom and final destruction. The hero or heroine might achieve a brief grandeur, defying what is ordained by the Fates, but they would be brought down in the end by the guardians of the impossible.

In comparison with this view of the human condition, Indian thought might well be said to have forfeited any view. Its governing doctrine that each individual has a continuing series of lives, with conditions in each one changing as a result of activities in previous ones, makes any single life merely an episode in the longer chain. No single life makes ultimate sense in itself, but the chain of lives does; and this chain, in turn, is contrasted to a higher condition of release from it all, to a reality outside it. Yet it is not entirely out of such high thought that the untragical character of the Indian drama is to be explained, but also out of a more direct view of life.

Indian practice has always been capable of making sharp distinctions between the ethics of living in the present life and the ethic of eventual release from the chain of lives: between *dharma* and *saṃnyāsa*, between the moral law and the renunciation of society and the world. And although examples of *saṃnyāsa* are not lacking in individual pieces, Indian drama as a whole is concerned with the realm of dharma and this world.

This *dharma*, as has been seen, is both the whole system of Law, moral and legal, that has its foundation in the transcendant order, and the specific system of rules and regulations under which a given individual lives. The world is seen as a hierarchically ordered society in which individuals have their being. These individuals are not regarded as unique, self-identical, irreplaceable human beings, of one time and of one place, but as incumbents of positions that survive them. The textbooks on Law, *The Dharmaśāstras*, operate with a simple pattern of "class' and "stage of life." There are four classes: Brahmin, ritual specialist, teacher, arbiter of conduct: Kṣatriya, ruler, protector of the oppressed, avenger of the injured; Vaiśya, artisan, maker of vessels, and plougher of soil; and Śūdra, servant, hewer of wood, and carrier of water. And for the first three of these, the so-called twice-born, there are four stages of life: *brahmacarya*, when one is a student of the Veda; *gṛhastha*, the stage of the family man; *vanaprastha*, when one retires to the forest; and *saṃnyāsa*, when one has renounced the world. Each of the classes and stages defines the scope of the individual's life. And likewise, the drama sees the character in the first place as the incumbent of a *dharma* role. A king is at all times king, with the dharmic as well as the folkloristic character that kings have: they are noble, protective, impetuous, and just; they like women, horses, and hunts. Similarly, a forest recluse is an aged man with a white beard, his long hair braided in a particular knot, who is bent on profound thoughts while he continues the ancient fire-rites in the company of his fellow sages; he is also likely to succumb to the wiles of loose women. Housewives are faithful, self-effacing, honoring their husbands even under the most tragic circumstances, and likely to be beguiled by parasitic priests and soothsayers. Courtesans, on the other hand, are faithless, greedy, sophisticated, and artistic, but sometimes irresistibly carried away by a love that may never be theirs.

Such characters are only to a certain extent the stereotypes of the Greek or any other traditional theater; primarily they are theatrical reflections of dharmic stereotypes. The theater, in other words, does not create its characters out of the inexhaustible supply of human individuals, but out of the hieratic roles of the dharmic society. It is true that the stong conviction that the hieratic role as it were preexists before its human incumbent is correlated with the doctrine of transmigration: no conception of divine justice can account for the inequality of human beings, and their present estate can only be the end result of the sum of acts they did or failed to do in a previous existence. Man finding himself in the world has already created his fate. But it is of his own making, depending upon his actions in his previous existence, and therefore it can in principle be transcended by effects inspired by his own free will; it cannot be affected by outside forces.

Thus the Indian is content with his role in the structure of things, relative to other roles, though he may, and will, complain about the inequities of life in general. The playwright sets his play in the known world, and the known world, even if it happens to be supernatural at times, has its own immemorial rules. Thus too, no distinct notion of a protagonist and antagonist is found, as in the Greek plays with their inbuilt struggle, but rather a *nāyaka*, a "leader" or hero, and a *nāyikā*, a heroine, around whom the story unfolds.

It is this same acceptance of the hierarchically ordered society that introduces into the classical play a distinctive characteristic: it is multilingual. A character speaks the language of his birth or of his choice. The language of his choice is Sanskrit, the language par excellence, the "tongue perfected"; and when Sanskrit is spoken, it reflects status, or education, or wisdom. Entitled by status to speak Sanskrit are the Brahmin and the king; but Sanskrit comes naturally to no one, and it reflects not only status, but also rigorous education. The child of a Sanskrit speaker will not yet be able to speak the language, and speaks instead his mother-tongue. A woman, though she might be of brahminic or royal status, is not supposed to speak Sanskrit, which is the privilege of men (with the exception of female ascetics, who are in any case not really feminine). A king addressing his queen or his son will find his Sanskrit understood—he tends to be simpler in this context than when addressing his fellow-Sanskritists—but he will be answered in Prākrit (the "natural" language). These Prākrits too, and there are several, reflect social differentiation. The character who speaks the Prākrit of the western part of the subcontinent can be identified as a "nice" person; he who speaks that of the east is an undesirable. And the lowliest characters, such as outcast executioners, speak a language that cannot even be dignified by the term "natural"; their language is qualified as *apabhraṣṭa*, "corrupt."

It is quite obvious that it was not only the actual linguistic differentiation of society that caused the playwrights to use different languages. The character's knowledge of Sanskrit, though often bespeaking status, and always bespeaking education does not necessarily bespeak moral character. However reluctantly, even the dharmic society allows voice to its urban demimonde. There are those who may have fallen on evil times, and, though educated, may be thieves or gamblers; yet education will tell—even these will be specialists in their craft, poets of the inconstancy of luck. They appear in the plays without the tidy background of family and upbringing that alone demonstrates status. They are on their own, living by their wits and exploiting their education. And here the theater has made a type of the urban sophisticate unaccounted for in *The Dharmaśastras*. He is the literate sponger and *bon vivant* for whom *The Kāmaśāstra*, the "Textbook of Pleasure," was written, equally at home among staid pillars of society, in the assembly of a king, and among addicts of gambling dens and the more refined connoisseurs of the better brothels. He has no trade, though perhaps a small patrimony, and his way of life is to be a *nāgarika*, a "city man." Poet, wit, universally informed and always at loose ends, he naturally gravitates to the society of a wealthy but less sophisticated patron. As a Roman noble would travel with his Greek philosopher for the consolations of the wisdom and the status that the philosopher supposedly provided to his retinue, so his Indian opposite would have his sophisticate, to instruct and to amuse.

And to this cast must be added the character of the uneducated Brahman, often a parody of the fat *purohit*, priest, who is a glutton for sweetmeats, likes to play the buffoon, who knows no Sanskrit, and is always at the side of his hero, dispensing comic relief as well as faithful advice.

So we find in the classical drama a curious intermixture of the simplicities of dharmic life and the complexities of courtly or urban life, the first often involving a heroic theme, the latter an erotic one. King and Brahmin may appear in their ancient roles of protector and teacher respectively; and the same two may appear again in their no doubt more contemporary characters of gay dog and literary wit. There is a conscious cultivation of simplicity, which goes side by side with an acceptance of all the gorgeous trappings of power. In *The Minister's Seal* (*Mudrārākṣasa*), a chamberlain is deputed to the house of the prime minister Kautilya, and on seeing the simple dwelling, he exclaims:

> A broken stone to break up cowdung cakes;
> A mound of sacred grass his students brought;
> And kindling sticks laid out to dry that bend
> The roof skirts of a cottage near collapse![2]

And in the same play, the king Candragupta consciously thinks of himself as Kauṭilya's pupil, to such an extent that even feigning a quarrel with his teacher upsets him emotionally. In *Śakuntalā*, by Kālidāsa, the king Duḥṣanta wanders from his royal palace into a hermitage, which is an oasis of antiquity. He marries the maiden Śakuntalā in the most simple fashion imaginable, then returns to the magnificence of his estate. This most interesting tension between the ideal and the actual is typically illustrated in that type of high drama called *nāṭaka*. This "heroic drama" draws on traditional lore and deals with ancient themes in new forms, and in it the old verities and virtues find expression.

It is out of this *dharma*-oriented world view that the absence of tragedy in the Indian classical theater can be explained. The playwright does not pit his character against a force that is bent on his defeat; he places him in a facsimile of the dharmic society and sets him on his way. The way is not a solitary one. It takes for granted the constant presence of other characters who likewise have their conscious places in life. What conflict ensues is essentially *minor* conflict, adventitious to the proper order of things, and ultimately resolvable according to this proper order. No doubt life has its crises, and chance a way of playing foul with even the most letter-perfect readers of their social roles. But this does not affect the ultimate correctness of the society that is, in all perpetuity, based on the eternal Veda.

Hence, not fate but chance becomes an important factor in the Indian play. And the Indian mind, which abhors a lack of causes, is reluctant to look upon chance as pure and blind coincidence of character and situation. In *Śakuntalā*, which tradition acclaims as Kālidāsa's finest play, much of the dramatic conflict centers on the king's absentmindedness. Having been out on a hunt and having stumbled on the hermitage in which the young girl Śakuntalā is being brought up, the king falls in love with her, marries her on the spot, and returns to his city, asking his new bride to join him later. He gives her a ring to remind him. On her way to the city she loses the ring, and the king does not know her. But she has conceived a son; she gives birth and passes from the scene. It happens that the ring was swallowed by a fish. The fish is caught, and the ring found and returned to the king. He then remembers Śakuntalā, and a reconciliation is effected.

All this coincidence does not go unexplained. Once, when Śakuntalā was day-dreaming about the king, she had failed to do proper homage to an irascible ascetic. He cursed her for it, saying that she would be forgotten by the king, and that he would remember her only when he recognized a ring that he had given her as a keepsake. It was a minor bit of misconduct that was to wreck her life.

Another illustration of the role of chance can be taken from *The Little Clay Cart*. An impoverished merchant, Cārudatta, and a popular courtesan, Vasantasenā, have fallen in love. Pursued by a villainous wooer, she takes refuge in the merchant's house, and on leaving entrusts a golden box to Carudatta's care; A burglar breaks in and steals it. But the burglar himself has an eye on one of the inmates of Vasantasenā's house, and eventually the box is recovered, unbeknownst to Cārudatta, who is despondent. He looks upon the box as a sacred pledge that he has forfeited, and he replaces it with a priceless necklace, offered him indirectly by his lawful wife. Meanwhile, the unsuccessful wooer, who happens to be related to the king, has sworn to revenge himself on Cārudatta. On leaving the merchant's house, Vasantasenā is to take a coach to meet her lover in the park. The villain is walking in that same park, waiting to be picked up by his own coach. In a traffic jam at Cārudatta's door the girl takes the wrong coach, the villain's, and is taken to the park. The villain importunes her, and when she remains adamant, almost strangles her. Cārudatta is accused, and only the timely appearance of the girl, who had only been unconscious, saves him from death. An equally timely palace revolution in the end restores his fortune.

While many of these coincidences are only that, the villain exploits them and makes them serve his ends, thus giving them a causal reality. There is a further stage in the matter, in which coincidence is deliberately engineered, and what looks like pure chance to the uninformed is in reality the judicious move of a master strategist. This is best illustrated by *The Minister's Seal*, in which the great politician Kauṭilya, locked in a battle of wits with an enemy minister, engineers a logical series of coincidences that bring him eventual victory.

Chance therefore is at best ambivalent, and the suspicion is always there that what looks like chance is in fact a plot of men or gods. But it is not the same kind of chance that made Oedipus face his father Laius in a hollow road or unknowingly marry his mother. The Indian stage could never allow a son to fail to know his father or mother, for such a failure would be simply unimaginable in the dharmic society; it can however permit a king to fail to recognize an incidental wife, who once irritated a sage, or a flustered mistress to mistake a coach.

The Indian theater thus takes the final view that in spite of all its apparent capriciousness, the world makes sense. The world as the characters in the play know it is not the best of all possible worlds; it is the only possible one, the present product of all the interacting destinies created by people through innumerable lives. It is a world full of chance, which affords ample opportunity for all sorts of minor mistakes that have their varied consequences. And it is a sensible world in which harmony finally prevails. Virtue necessarily triumphs over evil. The hero is necessarily better than his opponent. The outcome is never in doubt; the art of the playwright is to present the chain of events that leads in its own deceptively arbitrary way to this outcome.

Of the various kinds of dramatic presentation, playwrights as well as theorists prefer the *nāṭaka*, which, in its oldest definition by the poetician Bhārata, is "the imitation of things done in former times by gods and men, by kings and the great ones of the world." For his subject matter the author of the *nāṭaka* draws upon the epics and the purāṇas. From one point of view this drawing from a well of traditional lore diminishes the scope of the author's inventiveness; and no doubt it does. But this is his deliberate choice, since he also has available to him a second alternative, the type of drama known as *prakaraṇa*, the theme and plot of which may be entirely of his own invention. His choice is dictated by his view of his art, and his view is often that his art is essentially the perfection of words. Although it is always perilous to compare genres between cultures, it is tempting to seize, not on the play, but on the opera as a Western parallel. The composer of opera chooses his grand themes just because they are grand, and because thus they enable him to use his musical art with greater effectiveness. His concerns are not with the uncertain shades of emotion, with the inchoate actions and half-finished thoughts of everyday life, but with certain manifestations of emotion, where love is love, hatred is hatred, and jealousy just that. The composer of operas can not only afford, he must *court* simplicities. His story should be one known from tradition—from the Bible, history, or mythology, lest an undesirable narrative suspense interfere with the far more important suspense of the audience's roused emotion.

It would not do to extend the parallel too far: the clearly tragical bent of opera makes it a Western phenomenon. But the concern of the Sanskrit playwright was to write that language as the composer writes music. The Indian playwright's mastery is that of language—of many languages, but above all of Sanskrit. Like opera, the themes of the Indian play are grand and eternal, its technique learned and complex, its execution that of the virtuoso. The declamation of a perfectly turned

Sanskrit stanza may inspire the same pathos as a well-executed aria, and thus the playwright misses no opportunity for poetry in his libretto.

The place of poetry in the drama is extremely important. When a situation calls for the expression of a truth, the evocation of a sentiment, the recollection of a significant event, it calls for poetry. The stanza may be at once narrative and self-contained, but it is always the climax of an episode, however minor. On occasion, the poetry may run away with the play, as it does in *The Little Clay Cart* when Vasantasenā and the libertine engage in a kind of contest to best describe the impending monsoon:

LIBERTINE:

Packed round the mountain peaks the looming clouds are groaning
As though of lonely wives to echo the low moaning,
And at the din the peacocks suddenly dart out
And with their jeweled feathers fan the air about!

Their faces damp with mud the rain-blown frogs drink deep,
The peacock cries its love, the nipa glows in bloom,
As scoundrels selflessness, do clouds obscure the moon
While lightning streaks like whores to their perdition leap.

VASANTASENĀ:

With the roaring thunder Night wants me to stay:
"Blind woman, what are you if on my breast
Of full round clouds your man seeks love and rest!"
And like a rival in a fury blocks my way.

LIBERTINE: So it is indeed. But then, take her to task!

VASANTASENĀ: But why take one to task, Master, who is so ignorant of a woman's heart?

Let clouds hurl thunderbolts, or rain, or growl,
A woman yearning for her love counts fair nor foul!

LIBERTINE:

Racing wildly with the wind, shooting shafts of rain,
Beating the drums of thunder, fire-flags flying high—
A king invading a weak enemy's domain—
It robs moon's silver from the fortress of the sky!

VASANTASENĀ:

But if the roaring clouds—gray elephants that flaunt
Their lightning banners—have already stabbed my heart,
Must then the heron sound the drum of death to haunt
My tardy lover, still ajourney and now doomed,
And cry of rain! rain! casting caustic in my wound?

LIBERTINE:

And heaven's gloomy bulk, with cranes that pleat
White headdresses on it, and lightning flying
Like yak-tail plumes atop, seems bent on trying
To imitate an elephant in heat!

VASANTASENĀ:

Between the dark *tamāla* leaves of clouds blooms pale the sun—
Like arrow-showered elephants the ant-hills sink and fall—
A golden torch, the lightning roams on castle roof and wall—
And clouds abduct the daylight like a wife whose man is gone.

LIBERTINE:

Brightly caparisoned with lightning flashes,
A battle line of elephants that clashes,
The javelin-throwing clouds at Indra's word
Rescue the world as on a silver cord.

The storm-blown clouds, dark as a herd of buffalo,
That rage like seething seas and speed on lightning-wings,
Into the fragrant earth their diamond arrows throw
Until the dying grass into lush verdure springs!

VASANTASENĀ:

Welcomed by shrilly screeching peacocks: "Here! Come here!"
While cranes take wing to catch him in their fond embrace,
And swans, leaving their lotuses, piqued upward peer,
Appears the Cloud that casts collyrium on space!

LIBERTINE:

The world now seems to sleep in day nor night,
Staring with the blank eyes of lotus-ponds,
Its dark sky-face lit up by sudden light—
To sleep unmoved below a thatch of clouds,
Within a house of clouds that holds it tight.

VASANTASENĀ:

The cloud is rising, falling, raining, roaring, darkling,
And like a new-rich man in a thousand splendors sparkling.

LIBERTINE: So it is, and behold the sky—

Blushing with lightning and smiling with hundreds of cranes,
Skipping rope with the rainbow that scatters a shower of arrows,
Roaring with thunder and whirling along with the wind,
And perfuming the spaces with serpentine indigo clouds!

VASANTASENĀ:

Have you no shame, you cloud, to rail me
While I am speeding to my love

With your great voice and from above
With you wet hands yet to assail me?

Ah, Indra!

Have you then been in love with me before
That you should roar at me to stay me?
And while I yearn for him ought you to pour
Your showers in my path and dare delay me?

If you once for Ahalyā's sake
Lied you were Gautama, then pray,
God Indra, pity me and take
The cloud that bars my road away![3]

But the poetry may also itself become a factor in the action, as when, in *The Minister's Seal*, the court poet Stanakalaśa—"one for whom pitchers are breasts," one of the most common comparisons in Sanskrit poetry—excites King Candragupta to apparent rebellion against his minister:

Sire, kings of your mettle
By the creator created
As vessels of valor,
Lords of all world,
Who defeat with their might
Enemy elephants
Streaming with rut,
Will no more than a lion
Suffers the breaking
Of his powerful teeth,
Suffer the breaking
Of any commandment
At any occasion,
But prove their contempt
For the other's conceit.[4]

Prose merely tells what is going on; poetry suggests that what is going on matters.

Nor did the traditional lore limit or inhibit the author in a significant fashion. The stock of stories in the epics and purāṇas is truly enormous; and even minor episodes could be built into major plays. In his treatment of a story the author was bound by little more than the general outline. And the myths and legends were far from being sacrosanct: these are *smṛti*, tradition, and not revealed truth; they are intended to edify and exemplify, not to lay down the law. There were variants of these stories current at all time, and the playwright had as much right to his variant as did any of the purāṇic authors. Besides, the playwright's virtuosity in wielding language could bring out hidden meanings to which the specifically Hindu purāṇic or epic sources often did not do justice. In his choice of subject and in his poetry, the playwright found himself trammeled in nothing but his own limitations.

The theater could well be only one of several interests of the author. A good example of the versatility of the Indian author is provided by Kālidāsa. This writer, undoubtedly the most inventive and refined of all Sanskrit poets and dramatists, not only composed three famous plays, *Mālavikā and Agnimitra* (*Mālavikāgnimitra*), *Urvaśī Held by Courage* (*Vikramorvaśīya*), and *Śakuntalā and the Ring* (*Abhijñānaśakuntala*), but also two lyrical epics, *The Dynasty of Raghu* (*Raghuvaṃśa*) and *The Birth of the War God* (*Kumārasambhava*); he also composed a long lyrical evocation of nature intertwined with a love lament, *The Cloud as Envoy* or *The Cloud Messenger* (*Meghadūta*), and an anthology of short poems on love and the change of seasons, *The Seasons* (*Ṛtu-saṃhāra*). Some authors are known solely as playwrights. But often, as in the case of Bhavabhūti, plays might be primarily a convenient vehicle for poetry.

The staging of the drama

A poet's composition was not primarily meant to be read, but to be heard. Although it may seem incredible that some of the involuted poetry of the more recherché authors could be comprehensible at first hearing, the author recited his compositions to an audience. It was this same audience that would attend his play, at which the poetry was not only heard, but set in the context of dramatic action.

What distinguishes the play from other genres is primarily the author's dependence upon others for its execution. In other respects, the boundaries between literary genres in Sanskrit are not too sharply drawn, and if it were not for the staging, Kālidāsa's *Urvaśī Held by Courage* might conceivably have become another *sargabandha*, or lyrical epic.

It was usual for the director to recite the introduction to the play; sometimes this took the form of a conscious humility, as when Kālidāsa somewhat diffidently lists great predecessors in the field, and sometimes of a haughty self-assurance, as when Bhavabhūti remarks that "somewhere, sometime, someone will appreciate me." This introduction also had the function of a signature to the play, which might well become part of the repertory of a troupe that would take it to distant courts or festivals where the author's name was unknown or manuscripts unavailable.

The theater itself would be a simple affair: a pavilion or a raised platform with four pillars at the corners supporting a marquee, with a curtain in the rear that was split in the middle. On this simple stage all kinds of variations could be made, but the bare floor provided all that a play essentially needed. The color of the back curtain was important: it would indicate to the audience what mood might be expected. Behind it was a backstage area, from which the characters might enter solemnly, the curtain being drawn apart by two beautiful women, or perhaps might enter impetuously, without it being drawn at all. Props were not really needed, though on occasion they might be provided. The pride of the actor was to *show* what he was doing, by elegant gesticulation. But great importance was attached to dress and the manner of its being worn, which, as it always does in India (though sometimes not to the untutored eye), identified a person. Here, too, colors played an important role in conveying immediately to the audience the nature of the character, or his mood: the color red, for example of the curtain, suggested violence; white was suggestive of the erotic mood, dark or gray the pathetic, and black the tragic or the marvelous.

Such a simple stage might be erected anywhere at a moment's notice. Generally the occasion would be a grand one, worthy of being celebrated by a dramatic pageant, and likely to attract a sufficient number of the learned and cultured for an audience to be formed. It might be a special occasion at a court, or a wedding in the mansion of a rich man, or a religious festival presided over by a local arrangements committee, or an assembly of the learned who might desire appropriate recreation. Although nothing definite is known, these facts, and the prologues to many of the dramas themselves, suggest that dramas were composed for such occasions. Many royal patrons retained stables of poets and playwrights, whose job was eulogy of the king, and the following of their craft. The audience for the play was equally courtly and highly qualified by inclination and by training, being made up of "men with heart" (*sahṛdaya*), whose "minds have become lucidly receptive like a mirror, through effort and constant practice of poetry." Westerners are inclined to expect dramatic performances in the evening; the Indian drama would often be performed early in the morning, when cultural and religious events are apt to start.

Players traditionally enjoyed a very poor reputation. They inhabited a demimonde of courtesans and their entourage—which indeed recalls the world of actresses at the time of Alfred de Musset. In many parts of the world, the line between a courtesan and an actress has never been very clear. In India, where dour views were (and are) held about the constancy of women, an unmarried female adult was almost by definition loose.

Literature records the palatial establishments of the great courtesans of the city, who counted among their many accomplishments—perhaps their most lucrative one—the ability to act and to dance. A woman might well play a man's part and an actor the actress's. And, not unfamiliarly, members of the profession might well belong to a somewhat illicit in-group, the best actresses being the mistresses of kings and the great of the land, while the minor retainers, against all *dharmaśāstra*, did the procuring.

Acting and dancing were interwoven. Acting was not an imitation of actual behavior, but was made up of hieratic gestures. There grew up a complete repertory of gesticulation that gave a highly stylized form to normal gesture and accompanied the speaking of the lines. A glance could betray modesty or freshness, a hand the plucking of a lotus or the killing of a man. Vestiges of this art linger with the representatives of the ancient *bhāratanāṭyam* school of dancing, who can tell a story by gesture, without giving voice to a word. So in the drama: bits of dancing weave effortlessly in and out of the action. Music was never very distant: dance, music, and acting belonged to a single establishment, and love songs in particular must actually have been sung.

Thus the performance of a play could become a great spectacle in which all the arts were combined. And all the arts in combination created a particular mood that would communicate itself to the audience. The notion of *rasa*, the state of esthetic appreciation into which the audience was put, is more fully discussed in the following chapter on poetics; here it suffices to note that this *rasa* found its fullest manifestation in the performance of a play.

The audience before whom all this unfolded was highly critical. Not only could one not write, but one could not adequately follow, a play, unless he had undergone a classical education. There were few educated people who had not learned by heart, at the age of eight, the *Eight Chapters* of Pāṇini's Sanskrit grammar, the commentaries thereon, and the discussions thereof. And all educated men would have, securely lodged in their prodigious memories, hundreds and thousands of stanzas against which the playwright's poetry could be weighed. A faulty accusative case in grammar would offend such a man, unless, to his erudite delight, he found it obedient to some more obscure rule. And later in time, everyone would know, probably by heart, the major manuals on poetics, and a daring conceit would surprise less by its novelty than by the fact that novelty was still possible. All of them were able to retain in their minds an adjective that came at the beginning of a stanza, until it was finally wedded to its noun at the end of it. In other words, the pleasure felt by a member of the audience at a play was as much in his own erudition that made him capable of following it as it was in the play itself.

The great age of the drama was the Age of the Guptas (fourth–fifth centuries A.D.), and one of its important centers was the city of Ujjayinī. Here Kālidāsa must have lived for some time; it was a city that Śūdraka, the reputed author of *The Little Clay Cart*, knew quite well; and Viśākhadatta, the author of *The Minister's Seal*, was clearly a courtier of Candra Gupta II Vikramāditya, who made Ujjayinī his second residence after Pāṭaliputra.

These three plays, which will be compared, are practically anonymous; we know little about their authors but their names. They probably did not live very far apart in either time or space, and a study of a play of each of them will give us a notion of the scope of Sanskrit drama. Each is a master in his own way and each had quite a different conception of a play. Kālidāsa is a mythographer, Śūdraka a social satirist, and Viśākhadatta a political scientist. All three give a different treatment to their heroes and heroines and to the quality of love.

Both Kālidāsa's *Śakuntalā* and Viśākhadatta's *The Minister's Seal* are officially described as *nāṭaka*, plays whose themes are traditional, while Śūdraka's *The Little Clay Cart* is a *prakaraṇa*, a play with a theme born in the imagination of the author. How unsatisfactory this distinction ultimately is, is shown by the fact that the first two, though both *nāṭakas*, have nothing in common except that they both deal with famous men. *Śakuntalā*, universally considered Kālidāsa's best play, is based on a story found in *The Mahābhārata*, the outlines of which have been given. As a lyricist Kālidāsa is the great poet of love-in-separation, which has been an abiding theme in Indian poetry. *The Little Clay Cart* is a romance also based on earlier literature—this time a play by Bhāsa (second–third centuries A.D.) or perhaps on that story from which Bhāsa also got his inspiration. Quite unlike *Śakuntalā*, which moves between earth and heaven, it is set in the middle of the romantic city of Ujjayinī, with its great squares, gambling dens, courtesans, parks, and halls of justice. It is a rambunctious comedy of errors with *commedia dell'arte* overtones, of dire treachery and happy rescues, all strung on a tale of love between a merchant and a courtesan. There is none of the mythology that, with its heavens, divine voices, and gratuitous demons and sages, gives a universal validity and traditional propriety to the vicissitudes and emotions of *Śakuntalā*.

The Minister's Seal, in contrast, is a political drama set at the time when Kauṭilya, the historical author of the political and administrative handbook the *Arthaśāstra*, guided Candragupta Maurya in the establishment of his empire. This king is a historical person who, in the wake of the upsets that Alexander the Great's foray into the Panjab seems to have caused, started to carve out a kingdom from the eastern principalities. He may have been a bastard son of a ruling prince, as Viśākhadatta, and indeed the name "Maurya," suggests. Traditionally, his ascent to power marked the defeat of the old warrior class, the Kṣatriyas, who claimed in their lines the great heroes of *The Mahābhārata* and *Rāmāyaṇa*, and who were so beloved of Kālidāsa. The new aristocracy was not the god-given one of birth, with its necessities of protection and succor, and virtues of courage and strength. It was a man-made aristocracy that could be overthrown by men, and would be, were it not constantly on the alert. In the play, the Maurya's kingship is the kingship of diplomacy as well as war, of administration as well as raiding parties, of hard ministers as well as faithful companions. And Viśākhadatta's imagination sees in this historical setting a battle of merciless wits between two opposing ministers, and the triumph of loyalty. While *Śakuntalā* deals with love, in the *Seal* friendship takes the place of love.

These plays proceed through an unequal number of acts. They all open with a benediction, often addressed to Śiva, who, dancer among the gods, had become patron of the theater. But none of the plays are religious in the strict sense of the word. The setting of *Śakuntalā* is the mythical world of *The Mahābhārata*, where the terrestrial continues unbroken into celestial, where there are gods such as Indra, divine messengers, demons to be defeated, and sages to be placated. The world of *The Cart* is the urban world of Ujjayinī; that of *The Seal* is the stern world of power politics.

Synopses of three plays

Śakuntalā

Of all classical Indian dramas, the best known, and most beloved, is the *Śakuntalā* of Kālidāsa. It is a play in which many of the favorite emotions and conditions come into conjunction: heroics, love, the sadness of love in separation, and in which these culminate in recognition of the truth, in reunion with a wife, and the recovery of a son. And this ancient theme is ornamented by the exquisite poetry of Kālidāsa. It is said that of all drama, *Śakuntalā* is the best, that of the acts of the play, the fourth is the best, and that of all the ślokas of that act, four are the best. One of them goes as follows:

> Śakuntalā is going now, touching my heart
> With a new longing; tears within choke up
> My voice, and worries obfuscate my sight.
> This weakness of my mind I own, for love

Affects, alas, the hermits of the woods—
How then must fathers, heads of families,
Suffer the novel pangs that separation brings
When daughters are about to leave for good?[5]

Śakuntalā opens with King Duḥṣanta hunting. In pursuit of an antelope he happens upon a hermitage. Descending from his chariot (by Kālidāsa's time surely an antique vehicle), he expresses his wish to pay his respects to Kaṇva, the *guru* of the hermitage, and is told that he is absent. But Kaṇva's foster-daughter Śakuntalā, the offspring of the great sage Viśvāmitra and Menakā (the latter being a nymph sent by Indra to seduce the sage, whose austerities were threatening his throne), is there. About this time she is chased by a bee, which is attracted by her blossom-like eyes. The king, whose *dharma* is the protection of all, chivalrously rescues her. Duḥṣanta falls in love, and Kālidāsa's poetry delicately traces the budding of reciprocal love in Śakuntalā. But then the king is called away: a wild elephant menaces the tranquillity of the hermitage.

The second act opens with the Fool, a remnant of the popular stage, whose vulgarity and gluttony point up the nobility of the royal hero. The Fool complains that the king's hunting is bringing all sorts of trouble and discomfort. The king enters to cancel the hunt, for Śakuntalā's sake. He tells the Fool of his love, but gets no sympathy. The ascetics of the hermitage, meanwhile, beseech the king to protect their place from attacks by demons, and he is honored to comply. He packs the Fool off to his capital, assuring him that the tales of his love for Śakuntalā were not serious. The king thus wards off complications at home, but causes them for Śakuntalā.

An entr'acte follows, in which a young Brahman praises the exploits of King Duḥṣanta, recounting how Śakuntalā is pining for him: her companions are worried for her life, which is the very life of Kaṇva.

Act three shows Śakuntalā deeply in love; at her friends' urging she writes the king a letter. The king, who had been eavesdropping, enters, and they confess their mutual love. A female ascetic comes to take Śakuntalā away.

Another entr'acte follows. The king has married the girl and departed for his capital. Meanwhile Kaṇva, who knows nothing of all that had happened during his absence, is about to return. But there is a sudden outcry: the notoriously irascible sage Durvāsas had arrived, and Śakuntalā, deep in lovelorn thought, had failed to receive him properly. As epical sages are apt to do, he curses her on the spot: she will be forgotten by her husband. Only slightly mollified by the supplications of her friends, Durvāsas tempers his curse by saying that it will come to an end when the king recognizes the ring that he gave her as a keepsake.

This curse, which might seem a silly diabolus ex machina—if epical surroundings and the mortal terror that ascetics can inspire even today are forgotten—now becomes itself an actor in the play. From now on a mood of sad expectancy is all-pervasive.

The fourth act finds Kaṇva informed by a celestial voice that Śakuntalā has been properly married and is now with child—a divine mediation that holds out hope of an eventual solution of the tragedy that is sure to follow. But the mood of sadness is deepened by the pathos of Śakuntalā's leave-taking, as she prepares to depart from the hermitage for her husband's house.

The departure of a young bride from her father's house is one of the most poignant scenes in real Indian life, and perhaps never in Indian literature has the grievousness of this scene been so movingly told as by Kālidāsa. For this reason Indian tradition, extolling the *nāṭaka* above all other genres of literature, and *Śakuntalā* above all other *nāṭakas*, extols this act as the greatest.

In deliberate contrast, Act five shows the king immersed in his royal affairs: he is no witless roué, but a conscientious ruler, equally under the ascetic's curse. The hermits who have accompanied Śakuntalā to the capital now announce themselves, and simultaneously we hear the king's queen lamenting his unfaithfulness. The king dispatches the Fool to comfort her, and awaits the hermits. He does not recognize Śakuntalā, and refuses to receive her. But the hermits reproachfully insist on leaving her with her husband, and finally the king's priest offers her refuge in his house until the child is born. Then a divine maiden appears and carries Śakuntalā away, leaving the king astounded but still unrecognizing.

All now depends upon the ring. Śakuntalā had lost it while bathing. An entr'acte shows a sketch of constables maltreating a lowly fisherman who is accused of stealing a ring belonging to the king: he has found it in the belly of a fish he had caught.

Act six treats of the king's awakening, after the recovery of the ring. He is plunged into grief, staring at Śakuntalā's portrait. His melancholy is interrupted first by a concubine and then by a minister, who asks him for a decision on a case of succession. This reminds the king that he himself still has no sons. The shouts of his Fool, who is being manhandled by the charioteer of Indra, bring the king back to a consciousness of his public duties: the gods need his help in a battle against the demons.

The last act shows the king as victor; he travels in Indra's chariot through the sky to Mount Hemakūṭa, where the sage Marīca and his wife live. There he discovers Śakuntalā, who is living as an ascetic, and his son. They are reunited, as the sage explains that the king is not to be blamed for the grief that Śakuntalā has suffered.

Throughout the play there is no doubt a tension between public duty—Śakuntalā's receiving a guest, the king's protecting the oppressed and judging cases of law—and the private sentiments of love. But principally it is a dramatic representation, with all its baroque battles fought between acts, of Śakuntalā's love as a young girl and her frustration in marriage. The greater tension is between passion, and its corollary sorrow, and the dispassionate tranquillity of the hermitages of Kaṇva and Marīca. The curse is the very power of *karma*, the automatic retribution for past deeds, which may at any time take effect in anyone's present life. The grandiose setting of the play—hermitages where the ancient sacrificial fires still smolder, royal palaces, aerial chariots, gold-peaked mountains—only point up the simplicity of the basic issue: love first reciprocated, then forgotten, the woman in virtual exile while the busy lives of others go on. Thus Kālidāsa appealed both to the fascination that the spectacular has for the Indian mind, and to the deep awareness in the Indian heart of the simple values on which all the spectacle must eventually rest.

The Little Clay Cart

The second play is of a different kind. The hero Cārudatta is an impoverished merchant. His governing virtue is that of generosity: it pervades the entire play and his relations with everyone except his wife. He had been a rich man, but has now fallen on hard times, because he has doled out all his wealth to various parasites and solicitors. His constant companion is a sublimated Fool, who is, in reality, the only friend that has stayed with him. The play opens with Maitreya, the Fool, bringing Cārudatta a present from a rich acquaintance: a sad reversal of roles for the once-liberal Cārudatta, who describes his poverty as "the deadly sin they forgot to count." It is evening. Suddenly the focus is upon a wild chase scene that is occurring close to Cārudatta's house: the courtesan Vasantasenā is being pursued by the Śakāra, the villainous brother-in-law of the king. Vasantasenā stumbles through a door into Cārudatta's house to safety (there have been intimations that the two are in love), and before leaving she deposits a golden box with Cārudatta for safekeeping.

The second act is a series of sketches, illustrating the lowly but fascinating life that flows around a courtesan's establishment. While Vasantasenā is musing lovingly, a barber-masseur comes seeking refuge: he has run away from a game that he had lost, has been pursued by the winners, a banker and gambler, to a temple where he imitated the statue of the god, and has finally been lured out and chased to the courtesan's door. This barber-masseur proves to be one of Cārudatta's old retainers; Vasantasenā pays his debt—unheard of generosity in a courtesan, a member of a group proverbial for their greed. In a fit of disgust the barber decides to take the Buddhist cloth, and immediately gets embroiled with an elephant, which he hoped to tame with his monastic serenity, as the Buddha once did. A retainer of Vasantasenā rescues him, in reward for which a stranger, seeing the rescuer's chest to be devoid of jewels, throws him his cloak. The beneficent stranger was Cārudatta.

Act three introduces a learned, Sanskrit-speaking burglar, who gives a running erudite commentary on his craft:

Enter ŚARVILAKA

ŚARVILAKA: Erudition and energy opened a hole that allowed easy ingress, and thereby the way to easy success! And now I crawl through, groveling in the gravel like a snake wriggling out of its old skin. (*He studies the sky; pleased.*) Ha! The moon is down. And Night, obscuring the Stars behind a Veil of Clouds, covers like a mother the world's greatest Hero whose nocturnal sallies, when he is bent on the Plunder of his Neighbors, moves the King's Constabulary to panic! Now I have breached the garden fence, and lo! I am in the middle grounds. There remains the house itself now to be violated. Onward! Let people decry our handiwork that flourishes during sleep, let them protest that a confidence trickster is a robber, not a clobber—but if we have a bad name, at least, it is better to be free than to kneel to a Master; and besides, Aśvatthāman has set the example by the Massacre of the Sleeping Kings.

Now in what precise location do I make the breach? Where is the wall weakened by seeping water? Where will the noise go unheard? Where do I risk no gaping holes that demand to be noticed? Where is the mansion's clay emaciated by the corroding effect of saltpeter? Where may I avoid casting my gaze upon womenfolk? There indeed shall lie my success. (*He feels the wall.*) Here the ground is eaten away by perpetual exposure to the sun and the leaking of water—and also corroded by saltpeter. And a mousehole! To be sure, success is mine! This is the first sign of a burglar's success. First stage: I must now create a hole. But what kind of hole? The Lord of the Golden Lance has addressed himself to this problem and suggests four methods, to wit: baked bricks are to be pried out, unbaked bricks are to be broken, clay elements are to be watered, wooden elements are to be hacked.

Here we have an instance of baked bricks—the bricks are to be pried out. Next point: the nature of the hole. Lotus Cup? Sun-shaped? Crescent? Oval? Cross? Conic Pitcher? What spot is most suitable to exhibit my craftsmanship and astonish on the morrow the staring citizenry? It is a baked-brick wall, therefore the Conic Pitcher looks best. Which I now create. Indeed, on all occasions when I opened at night walls that had been affected by saltpeter and embarked on difficultous operations, the neighbors would congregate in the morning to discuss my craftsmanship, noting errors as well as marking dexterity. (*He prays.*)

I bow to thee, Granter of Wishes, Kumāra Kārttikeya!
I bow to thee, God of the Golden Lance, Subrahmaṇya,
That art vowed to the Gods,
I bow to thee, Son of the Sun!
I bow to thee, Master of Magic whose first pupil I am!

The God has graciously granted my prayer and given me the Unguent of Invisibility! When I have applied it, the constables will not detect me, and swords, if they strike me, will not hurt me. (*He rubs himself with an ointment.*) Oh bother, I forgot my measuring tape! (*He thinks.*) No matter, my Brahmin's thread will replace it. Indeed a Brahmin's thread is a tool of many uses for a Brahmin, especially for one like me. If one makes a professional hole in the wall, one can use it to measure with. If one wants to lift a jewel off a body, one can use it as a lasso. If one wants to open a bolted cage, one can use it to pull the bolt. If one's bitten by an insect or a snake, one can use it as a tourniquet.—Now to measure and on with the work! (*He starts working and stops to study his progress.*) One more brick and the opening is made. Ouch, a snake has bitten me! (*He ties his Brahmin's thread around his finger and shows signs of severe pain. He applies some salve.*) I am well again. (*He finishes the hole and looks through.*) Ah, there's a lamp burning.

The flame traces a golden line,
Piercing the hole, onto the ground:
Slight beam amid the dark around,
As on a touchstone a golden shine.

(*He continues working.*) The hole is finished. Good. I'll enter now. Or rather I will not enter, but introduce my dummy. (*So he does.*) Fine, nobody. Thank you, Kārttikeya! (*He enters and looks about.*) Ah, two men sleeping. Very good, I'll open the door just in case, so that I can save myself.—Why, the house is so old that the door squeaks. I shall have to get water. Now where do I find water? (*He looks right and left, finds water, and pours it over the door with great care.*) I must not let the water splash on the floor. So far so good. Now I must see if they

> are really sleeping or just pretending. (*He tickles them and watches for reactions.*) Splendid, they must be really asleep. Their breathing is unsuspecting, it is very clear and rhythmic. The eyes are shut tightly, both of them, and no movements behind the lids. The joints of the body are relaxed and stray limbs stick out of the bed. And no one will bear light in his face unless he is sleeping. (*He reconnoiters the surroundings.*) Ah, a drum? And a flute. And a tambourine. And here is a vīṇā too! And reeds. Books over there. Have I broken into the house of a music and dance teacher? But I came to burgle because I had the impression it was a *decent* home! Now, is he really so poor, or does he keep his treasures buried, not to have them taxed or stolen? Anything buried is mine! Very well, I'll throw some witching grain around. (*He does so.*) The seed is sown, but nothing shows up. He is really poor. All right, I'm off.[6]

This burglar enters the house and steals the golden box that had been entrusted to Cārudatta. On waking up, the generous victim is saddened that the thief had had to leave empty-handed, until it dawns on him that the box has been stolen. This was a sacred trust, and he fears that his poverty will make people think that he is a thief. In a very touching scene, Cārudatta's wife, the mother of his son, gives the Fool a pearl necklace, her sole remaining property and incomparably more valuable than Vasantasenā's box, to give to Cārudatta.

The thief, however, is in love with one of Vasantasenā's handmaidens. He wants to buy her freedom with his plunder. Though at first she is uncertain as to Cārudatta's safety, Vasantasenā, who, in a favorite dramatic device, has been eavesdropping, learns the truth and generously sets the handmaiden free. With a sudden switch, departing from the play that was his model, Śūdraka now introduces a political plot: Āryaka, a pretender to the throne, has been jailed. The thief suddenly decides to join his party, leaving behind his newly married bride. Meanwhile, the Fool arrives with the necklace to replace the box, which Cārudatta pretends he lost gambling—thereby avoiding naming the thief; Vasantasenā accepts, so that she may once more return to Cārudatta.

Act five finds the libertine, who has been previously introduced as a companion of the Śakāra, the villain, conducting Vasantasenā to Cārudatta's house; he has been sent as an envoy on his master's behalf to request the courtesan's favors. The monsoon is about to break (and the coming of the monsoon, when travelers rejoined their wives, was ever the time for love-making), and libertine and courtesan, as we have seen, engage in a veritable duet of poetry. Finally the courtesan reaches Cārudatta's house, where she spends the night.

The sixth act finds Vasantasenā trying to return the necklace to Cārudatta's wife, who declines. The merchant's little son enters, crying that he has only a little toy clay cart to play with; Vasantasenā stuffs it with pearls, so that he may buy a cart of gold. This little cart—from which, of course, the play has its name—thus becomes the sudden symbol of Cārudatta's poverty and of the generosity of both his wife and mistress (the latter of whom might be expected to consider the pearls as payment for services rendered). Confusion at once ensues. The courtesan is to join her lover in a park. Meanwhile the pretender Āryaka has escaped and is abroad. In something of a traffic jam, Vasantasenā mistakes the coach that is to carry her to her tryst, while the escaping Āryaka leaps into the coach of Cārudatta. (Āryaka is shortly detained, but escapes when one of the constables chooses to defend him against the other and starts a fight.)

In the following act the fugitive meets Cārudatta, who lets him go, himself intent upon finding his mistress. She, meanwhile, was being carried off in a coach that was on its way to pick up her erstwhile pursuer, the Śakāra. This gentleman we find talking with his wit and abusing a Buddhist monk (none other than the barber-masseur who had taken the Buddhist vows earlier). The Śakāra tries to win Vasantasenā, but she refuses him. He then orders his wit and his slave to kill her. They refuse. Feigning calm, he sends them on their way. When they are gone, he begins to beat Vasantasenā, who succumbs. He covers her with leaves and departs. The masseur-turned-monk reappears to hang out his robe that he has been laundering. He finds Vasantasenā, restores her to consciousness, and takes her to his monastery. Since he does this basically out of gratitude, for she had been his benefactress, this act has about it the flavor of satire: the great courtesan being conducted by a lowly friar to a Buddhist cloister.

The satire becomes savage in Act nine, which takes place in a court of justice. The villain accuses Cārudatta of the murder of Vasantasenā (that there is no body does not seem to bother anyone). An interesting parade of witnesses now appears, bearing unwitting evidence that seems to incriminate Cārudatta. First comes Vasantasenā's mother, an old harlot corrupted by brandy and rum. Then one of the constables involved in the fracas centering around Āryaka's escape in Cārudatta's coach testifies to the Pretender's movements: this reflects badly on Cārudatta. To make matters worse, Cārudatta's friend the Fool, on his way to return to Vasantasenā the pearls that she had given to Cārudatta, comes by the court and, in his flustered indignation on hearing the charges, drops the pearls. Further evidence shows that Vasantasenā had spent the night at Cārudatta's house, and that they had had an assignation in the park. All this, plus the powerful presence of the Śakāra, brother-in-law of the king, convinces the judge, who is pictured as a well-intentioned but confused old man, that Cārudatta murdered and robbed Vasantasenā. He sentences Cārudatta to exile (after all, she was only a prostitute). The king, however, understandably concerned with Cārudatta's apparent role in Āryaka's escape, converts the verdict into a death sentence.

The last act sees Cārudatta being led to his death by two outcasts. The Śakāra's servant, who had witnessed the villain's assault on Vasantasenā and had been put in chains, manages to escape and tell his story, but his master discredits him. While the act is melodramatically lengthened to increase the suspense, all kinds of things happen at once: the courtesan and the monk appear in time to stave off the execution, the lovers are reunited, and Āryaka kills the king, succeeds to the throne, and grants Cārudatta a fief. The crowd demands the Śakāra's death—not only did he commit murder, but he is no longer the king's brother-in-law. Cārudatta once more demonstrates his generosity by granting the villain a pardon. All's well that ends well: the lowly monk is appointed by the new king as chief abbot of all the kingdom's monasteries, and Vasantasenā is by royal decree elevated from her caste and thereby made an honest woman, so that she can become Cārudatta's legal wife.

It was certainly not Śūdraka's intention to give a completely realistic picture, nor was it his intention to write a satire on life in Ujjayinī. Nevertheless, he takes great delight in picturing the life of the demimonde. In this he is one of an appreciable number of Sanskrit authors who are fascinated by the way in which sophistication, cleverness, and worldly wisdom establish a realm of conduct outside or indifferent to the dharmic pattern.

Had Cārudatta remained rich, he would never have become so personally involved in all these goings-on. "Poverty," as he says, "is the root of all evil." Had he remained rich, his affair with Vasantasenā would have been decorously conducted, she would have been commensurately recompensed, and that would have been that. In some ways, the hero is a touching figure, finding himself suddenly entangled in a series of events that he can only face as the rich man he psychologically is and with the generosity that his erstwhile fortune has made a habit. Shamefacedly he becomes the recipient of other people's generosity: of Vasantasenā, who freely bestows on him her otherwise expensive love, of his house Brahman, the Fool, who does not desert him even in his misfortune, even of his ex-barber and masseur, who does him good turns albeit unintentionally; and most of all, of his noble wife. For back in that lady's apartments a quiet tragedy goes on, which does not achieve much recognition:

Enter CÁRUDATTA'S WIFE *with* RADANIKĀ

WIFE (*anxiously*): But my gentle husband is really unharmed? And Master Maitreya too?

RADANIKĀ: Yes, ma'am. But the courtesan's jewelry has been stolen.

WIFE *faints.*

RADANIKĀ: Please madam, be calm!

WIFE (*coming to*): Why do you say that my gentle husband is unharmed? It were better if he had been harmed in his life than in his honor! Now all the people of Ujjayinī will say that poverty drove the honorable Cārudatta to a dishonorable deed. Destiny, great God, you play with the fortunes of the poor and they tremble like water drops on lotus petals. This pearl necklace is all I have left, I received it from my mother's family. But even this my husband's great pride will not permit him to accept. Girl, call Master Maitreya!

RADANIKĀ: As it pleases you, madam. (*She approaches* MAITREYA.) Master Maitreya, madam is calling you.

MAITREYA: Where is she?

RADANIKĀ: In here. Go and see her.

MAITREYA (*approaching the wife*): Good day, madam.

WIFE: Good day, sir. Please face me, sir.

MAITREYA: I am facing you now, madam.

WIFE: Accept this gift, sir.

MAITREYA: What is this?

WIFE: I am holding a fast, the Fast of the Pearls. It is prescribed that a suitable gift, commensurate with one's wealth, be donated to a Brahmin, and that he does not keep it to himself. Therefore please accept these pearls for the sake of my fast.

MAITREYA (*accepting*): I thank you. I shall go and give it to my good friend.

WIFE: Master Maitreya, please save me from embarrassment. (*Exit.*)

MAITREYA (*astonished*): Ah, what dignity!

CĀRUDATTA: Maitreya is late. I hope he is not doing something wrong in his confusion. . . . Maitreya! Maitreya!

MAITREYA (*approaching*): Here I am. Take this. (*He holds out the pearl necklace.*)

CĀRUDATTA: What is this?

MAITREYA: The reward of marrying within your station. . . .

CĀRUDATTA: What? My Brahmin wife has taken pity on me! Alas, now I am really poor.[7]

The play moves from boisterous humor to no less ebullient melodrama. It is all a big misunderstanding, sure to be resolved in the end. And nothing is more obvious than the pleasure that the author took in writing the play. He blithely violated stylized prohibitions, as when he permitted on the stage fisticuffs, which were reserved for a farce. But he was also able to create some unforgettable characters: the ineffectual Cārudatta, who was so nice when he was rich, and is so undeservedly poor that good sense demands that his fortunes be returned (as he himself also seems to think, for while he bitterly laments his poverty there are no indications that he intends to do anything about it). He is the rich man's son who excels where the rich inevitably fail—in generosity to a fault. This virtue, which in Indian appreciation can never become a vice, is his sole nature.

Vasantasenā, on the other hand, does not to a Western reader become entirely clear. The Western reader grievously lacks the persuasion of actually seeing her on the stage, and of seeing her with Indian eyes: a free Indian woman, walking and dancing with the cocky self-assurance of the born courtesan, the darling of a sophisticated town, with every gesture excitingly violating all the proper ways for a woman to behave, watched and admired like sin itself. To the fascination of seeing a courtesan on the stage (and the actress was undoubtedly playing herself), there was the added fascination of the courtesan actually in love. The Indian gallant, waited on hand and foot by the women of his house, meets on his escapades women who are out solely to exploit him, pretending the love that, perhaps, he so dearly needs, and throwing him out as soon as he has served their financial purpose. He must have enjoyed the poetic justice of such a woman herself enslaved by the passions she so assiduously and lucratively excites in her men, of seeing her undergoing the same emotions as a proper girl like Śakuntalā.

But it is in the minor characters that Śūdraka excels. The Śakāra is so wicked that he is fun. He has absolutely none of the manly virtues. And he is incredibly ill-educated, mixing up in his conversation all the heroes of mythology. He is the ultimate boor. But he is a boor of wealth and powerful connections. Willing to corrupt a court, able to strangle a woman, unashamed of flaunting his riches and power, a man with not a trace of generosity in him, he is the complete opposite of Cārudatta. Conflict between them, though unsought by the noble merchant, is inevitable; so is the outcome. In the end we find the villain chastened; but are we quite sure that his single-minded brain will not devise a means by which to return to his old power?

The Minister's Seal

Śakuntalā offered little scope for the celebration of friendship. The very paramountcy of the king, champion of the gods themselves, prevents any thought of reliance on friendship. The wisdom of the sage inspires affection, on a universal scale, embracing all living beings and in particular his foster-daughter; it does not embrace the earthy demands of friends. *The Cart*, though its main theme is love, has much room for friendship: the loyal friendship of the Fool for Cārudatta. The Fool is a down-to-earth person, who finds Cārudatta's lamentations exaggerated, disapproves of his affair with Vasantasenā, has great respect for Cārudatta's wife, yet runs all Cārudatta's errands with a loyalty that is appealing. Too, there are the hasty alliances of the down-and-out, the burglar and the gambler and the fugitive Pretender, which form a backdrop of little loyalties against which the affair of the hero and heroine can be played out. And as Cārudatta has his friend in the Fool, so Vasantasenā unknowingly incurs the friendship of the former masseur, whose loyalty, absent-mindedly bought with ten gold pieces, becomes the means of her redemption.

It is in the third play, *The Minister's Seal*, that love completely recedes before friendship. Like *Śakuntalā*, *The Seal* is a *nāṭaka*; unlike *Śakuntalā*, it never leaves the world we live in. Yet its world is utterly unlike that of *The Cart*. *The Seal* moves in the highest realms, which have however a practical awareness of low life and exploit it for such transcending purposes as those of war, peace and status.

Viśākhadatta's play is a very fine example of the Indian playwright's craft. It is single-minded in its plot and ties up neatly all the threads that have been developed. In this the author made the fullest use of his subject matter, which is the implementation of a policy decision. Like a real politician, Viśākhadatta moves his pieces deliberately and calmly against the blundering moves of his audience, who are trying to grasp the rules of the game while it is in progress, finding themselves in the end outwitted and admiring of the master.

Of the author, nothing is known except his name and a brief parentage. It seems certain that he was a contemporary of the flamboyant King Chandra Gupta II, titled Sun of Courage, about whose life Viśākhadatta wrote a play that is unfortunately lost. Probably he was a courtier; his parentage reveals that he was a descendant of local potentates, often people who gravitate naturally to the court of a powerful king.

In his hero Kauṭilya, Viśākhadatta has created a type no less dear to the Indian heart than the sage—the powerful man of affairs. He is minister to the Maurya and represented as the real architect of the great Mauryan Empire. Typically—and here, the sage dominates the man of affairs—he has no ulterior motives or selfish purposes. In a way, he has put himself under the power of his own curse: he was once insulted in full assembly by the old king, and swore an oath to bring him down. His life is spent in the fulfillment of this oath. He has joined forces with Candragupta, the old king's bastard by a slave girl, and has affected an alliance with a king called Parvataka. The allied forces have marched on Pāṭaliputra, the capital of Magadha, and have taken it. The last scion of the old line has for all practical purposes abdicated by retiring to a hermitage.

The minister of the old king was one called Rākṣasa, a man more soldier than diplomat. He pursues a kind of guerilla warfare against the Maurya, and has made several assassination attempts. His partisans, however, have been imprudent, and all the attempts have been smelled out and diverted. One of the attempts was diverted to Parvataka, who held a right to half the kingdom. On that king's death, Rākṣasa's loose loyalty settled upon his successor, his son Malayaketu, who was untried and inexperienced, but who provided a focus for Rākṣasa's need to serve. The play opens with a recounting of the attempts that have been made and the countermeasures taken. It has now become a personal fight between Kauṭilya and Rāksasa, but one which, from his side at least, is unusual: it is his ultimate aim to bring the Maurya and the minister Rākṣasa together, and to have Rākṣasa installed in his place; for, his oath fulfilled, he wishes to retire.

The play thus opens almost as a problem play. Kauṭilya, whose entire statecraft is built on universal suspicion ministered to by a network of spies, has reached the realization of the paradox of international power politics: a king must be able to rely absolutely on the honesty and loyalty of his minister. Every human being is corruptible, everyone has his price, no one can be trusted—but ultimately there must be complete trust in the man who is in charge of the nationwide apparatus of suspicion. What commends Rākṣasa is that he has the faculty of loyalty; even in his present fight his inspiration is his loyalty to his old king:

RĀKṢASA (*with a tear*):

Calamity upon calamity!
The Nandas, who had pacified their foes
With wit and bravery skillfully employed,
Must like the Vṛṣṇis, through their deadly fate,
Still perish in the vastness of their race.
But left awake, my mind ridden with fright,
I stayed to paint the last scenes in, and find
The canvas gone.

Why do I try? Not that the old faith is lost,
Not that I yearn for more sensations, or

Fear for the failing of my breath, or care
To rise to might again. Why do I try
A mind reduced to utter impotence
On subtler schemes but that the king I served
May in his heaven graciously accept
The slaughter of his foes?[8]

In the final analysis Kauṭilya himself does not have this loyalty. He joined the Maurya to fulfill his oath to the world and his promise to himself, that he would exterminate the old dynasty. He is a man entirely by himself, without wife, without children, a practitioner of his own cold brand of the science of statecraft that, in fact, the real Kauṭilya formulated in his textbook, the manual of statecraft, *The Arthaśāstra*. He is the ascetic who is still within the world, whose brilliance cannot prevent him from reaching a pinnacle of power that does not interest him. In terms of *The Bhagavad-gītā*, he is a *karmayogī*, one who does what he has to do, and does it without thought of self or satisfaction. Rākṣasa is a *bhaktiyogī*, one who willingly and happily undertakes the discipline imposed on him by his loyalty. This loyalty that, it seems to Kauṭilya, is Rākṣasa's strength, is also his weakness, through which he can be vanquished.

Like a master spider Kauṭilya in the first act starts weaving the web that will catch his rival. A spy is seen conferring with the minister, reporting on the hostility of a certain Jaina-monk (in reality Kauṭilya's agent), of a scribe, and of a jeweler. The spy has discovered that the jeweler's house harbors the wife and son of the fugitive Rākṣasa (the loyal man is a family man); in fact, when the child tried to dart out of the house a woman's hand had appeared to pull him back in. From the hand had slipped a man's signet ring, too big for a woman's finger, and the spy had recovered it. It bore Rākṣasa's seal.

To build up a system of mistaken loyalties, Kauṭilya has the scribe arrested and, when his execution is imminent, rescued by an agent of his own. This agent, called Siddhārthaka, then flees to Rākṣasa's camp. The Jaina-monk is also feignedly exiled, and joins Rākṣasa. The jeweler is interviewed by Kauṭilya, who admires his loyalty in not betraying Rākṣasa, and jailed. Kauṭilya's pupil (Kauṭilya is a Brahman, and therefore a teacher of his science) reports in consternation the defection of a certain Brahman courtier named Bhāgurāyaṇa and some ranking officers. This is all at Kauṭilya's instigation. In the meantime, Kauṭilya has used Rākṣasa's seal to seal a letter that he had had copied by the scribe who is loyal to Rākṣasa.

The self-confidence of Kauṭilya and the success of his schemes is matched in Act two by Rākṣasa's diffidence and the frustration of his plans. His spy, appearing as a snakecharmer, reports that all the attempts on the Maurya's life have backfired. The new king had had to pass under a triumphal arch before taking possession of the throne, and the arch was to have collapsed on top of him. Instead, the plot was foiled, and the brother of Parvataka had been killed. Parvataka himself had been killed by the touch of a poison girl, a femme fatale, destined by Rākṣasa for the Maurya; and Kauṭilya had engineered the rumor that he himself was responsible, which had caused the flight of Parvataka's son and heir and the subsequent succession of his brother to the allotted half of the realm; the son was in flight, the brother dead, and the Maurya in sole possession of the throne. So too with the other plots: a physician who had prepared a poisoned drink for the Maurya was discovered and forced to drink it himself ("Oh, a great scientist lost," exclaims Rākṣasa); the double agent, the Jaina-monk, had supposedly been exiled, the scribe condemned to death, the jeweler incarcerated.

But while gloom reigns, new hope is imparted by the arrival of Kauṭilya's agent Siddhārthaka, who has helped the scribe escape. As proof of his good faith he returns to Rākṣasa the signet ring he had picked up at the jeweler's house; he asks to join Rākṣasa, who immediately consents. Rākṣasa's spy reports that the Maurya is beginning to resent his overbearing minister, and Rākṣasa sees his chance. But another thread is being woven by Kauṭilya: a merchant offers Rākṣasa some precious jewelry, which he buys, asking Siddhārthaka to see to the price.

In Act three Kauṭilya starts a feint. To feed the rumors of the alienation between himself and the Maurya, he imperiously cancels a festival that the king had deliberately restored after years of war. The king pretends anger, and the minister is insolent and threatening. Finally, he resigns in a fury over the king's ingratitude.

In Act four, Kauṭilya's plans to affect a real alienation between Rākṣasa and his prince are laid by his agent Bhāgurāyaṇa, who insists that he and other defecting officers deal directly with the prince, since they suspect Rākṣasa of playing a game of his own: to disaffect the Maurya from Kauṭilya, so that he can step into Kauṭilya's place. This is of course precisely Kauṭilya's goal. The prince is confused and suspicious that perhaps this is his minister's aim. He is confirmed in his growing distrust by overhearing a conversation between Rākṣasa and a runner, reporting the feigned alienation of Kauṭilya and the Maurya: when Rākṣasa congratulates himself that the Maurya has now come to hand, the prince concludes that his minister refers to a covenant by handshake.

This distrust prevents the prince from deciding on an offensive. And finally, the Jaina-monk, when pressed for an astrologically suitable date for action, stalls and seems to predict a calamity. It is curious that none of the principal characters speak outright lies, preferring double-entendres from which the other may conclude what he wishes: it is the great art of engineering misunderstandings.

These misunderstandings are brought to a head in Act five. The Jaina wants to leave the camp, and Bhāgurāyaṇa is in charge of exit visas. The Jaina says that he is afraid of Rākṣasa who used him in arranging for the poison girl that infected Parvataka, the prince's father, and who wants him out of the way, now that he serves the prince himself. The prince, who had been led to believe that Kauṭilya was responsible for his father's death, is outraged. Bhāgurāyaṇa counsels patience and a cooler head. Just then the agent of Kauṭilya who had rescued the scribe, returned Rākṣasa's seal, and supervised the purchase of the precious jewelry, is apprehended leaving the camp without a visa. He is thrashed and confesses that he is carrying a letter from Rākṣasa to the Maurya; this was the letter that Kauṭilya had had copied by Rākṣasa's loyal friend the scribe and sealed with Rākṣasa's seal. It describes the intended treachery of the prince's main allies. The king questions Rākṣasa about the arrangements for the march on Pāṭaliputra, and it transpires that these main allies are the ones to be stationed about the prince's person. Rākṣasa is perplexed by the letter; it is in the handwriting of the scribe, whose loyalty to him personally was unquestioned, and sealed with his own ring. This evidence practically proves Rākṣasa's duplicity, and Rākṣasa himself is hurt in his most sensitive spot: can the scribe have betrayed his loyalty? Rākṣasa is wearing a piece of jewelry that he had purchased earlier; the prince now recognizes it as one of his father's pieces. The case against Rākṣasa is now complete: the jewelry was Rākṣasa's price for betrayal. The prince then orders his supposedly treacherous allies killed, confusion ensues, and Rākṣasa, whose true faith to the prince has been shredded by the prince himself, sets out, disgraced, on a final errand of loyalty: to rescue the jeweler who was jailed because of his loyalty to Rākṣasa.

In Act six, Rākṣasa has slipped into the Maurya's capital Pāṭaliputra, and has hidden in an abandoned park. There is here a curious and probably not accidental parallelism with *The Little Clay Cart*, where a scene in a park is similarly followed by a scene on the execution grounds. But what in *The Cart* was pure accident and mistake is here carefully engineered design. Rākṣasa has been followed by one of Kauṭilya's agents, who now pretends his own suicide by hanging: Rākṣasa has heard that the jeweler is about to be executed, and he would rather kill himself than see his friend die. Kauṭilya has left only this course, one of final devotion, open to Rākṣasa: he must sacrifice himself for his friend. In Act seven the jeweler is being led to his execution, followed by his wife, who does not wish to survive him. And here Rākṣasa gives himself up to Kauṭilya to save his friend. Loyalty has forced him into the precise situation where Kauṭilya wanted him: at his mercy because of his inability to be disloyal. The master has his condition: he wants Rākṣasa to accept the sword of state and serve the Maurya, while he himself retires. This would resolve all the issues: as minister Rākṣasa could restore his prince (since taken captive after his armies mutinied when the allies were killed) to his ancestral lands, and the jeweler would live. Rākṣasa accepts the condition and pledges his precious loyalty to the Maurya.

This curiously happy ending, when compared with those of Hollywood films, shows up as interestingly Indian. Basically it is the fulfillment of what had been given from the very beginning, although the interference of chance, real or devised, may have obscured the logic of the proceedings. It is the tying up of all the threads that have been spun so that they could be tied up in this way. The classical play is constructed out of its ending: the ending is not an afterthought. The complications are in the final analysis adventitious, and the spectator, having followed the characters through a symphony of moods, relaxes with the serenity that the final resolution of this symphony affords.

The Minister's Seal has no major female characters; its milieu lacks any reference to the emotional dimensions usually associated with the home or female sentimentality. It is both in its mentality and in its representation severely realistic. Intrigue and counter-intrigue take the place of armed conflict, and incidental assassinations of key persons are preferred to massive battles. Even with those who are actually killed, it is hard to pinpoint the guilt precisely: is it Rākṣasa's, who sent the assassins, or Kauṭilya's, who diverted them? There is a pervading atmosphere of conscious deception; but deception is not deceit. Had Rākṣasa been another Kauṭilya, he would have chosen his agents better, pursued the possibilities more open-mindedly, taken his risks more calculatedly. There is no personal enmity between the two. In the execution ground, Rākṣasa asks Kauṭilya not to touch him, as he had been defiled by the touch of the executioners. But in their consideration of others, the two are worlds apart. Kauṭilya is completely self-sufficient, an ascetic of great power who wants no power for himself, unbeholden to anything but the task he has set himself, and pragmatic in the fulfillment of this task. He has no ties and wishes none. That with the Maurya is a tie of expediency, and the whole play is intended for him to be able to renounce even that. One may well imagine him after his retirement, perhaps settling down in a hermitage, a cool recluse, neither as affectionate as Kaṇva (no Śakuntalā seems likely to want his care), nor as irascible as Durvāsas (and no Śakuntalā need fear his curses). A circle of pupils would form around him, while he coolly developed his *Arthaśāstra*, the Science of Material Purpose, holding the world no better than it is, and, in the final analysis, not caring very much for it.

Rākṣasa, on the other hand, is the passionate friend in search of service. He is content that his well-being is interwoven with and contingent on that of others. Such a man will have a wife who wishes to follow him into death; he will have friends whose loyalty is inspired by his own. He is a delicate poet of the beauties of a world made handsomer by his being of it, no less an Indian hero than Kauṭilya himself. If a man like Kauṭilya can defeat him by means of his own virtues, it can only be for the sake of them.

These three plays, which, it is true, belong to the very best of the Indian classical theater, show the latitude that a dramatist was permitted. The *nāṭaka* and *prakaraṇa* belong essentially to the same dramatic genre, even if Indian poetics prefers to distinguish them. Side by side there existed with them a variety of other genres, farces, one-acters, soliloquies, that make the Sanskrit theater one of the richest and most varied in history.

It had its limitations. The prevalence of Sanskrit and the variety of Prākrits that were used demanded of the audience an enormous erudition, and it was at the erudite and the cultured spectator that the play was aimed. In India, the significance of Sanskrit added a peculiar quality to this culture, and the fortunes of the theater were largely linked up with the fortunes of Sanskrit erudition. Not as a matter of course but as a matter of fact was the Sanskrit erudition exemplarily represented by the educated Brahman; and the theater itself, while its first extant fragments from the hand of Aśvaghoṣa are Buddhist in origin, became increasingly his possession.

Hence, greater dignity was given to the *nāṭaka* with its epical and traditional background and its dharmic view of life that is specifically brahmanic. The *prakaraṇa* was entertainment, the *nāṭaka* edification. And once edification was accepted as a proper function of the stage, the subject matter tended to hallow the play. The culmination of this was in the allegorical *nāṭaka*, whose purpose was to dramatize particular philosophical schools. For example, *The Prabodha-candrodaya* or "Moonrise of True Knowledge," written by Kṛṣṇa-miśra in the eleventh century allegorizes the supremacy of the Vedānta, while such sixteenth-century plays as *The Vidagdha-mādhava* of Rūpa Gosvāmin dramatize, not through allegory but through legend, the efficacy of bhakti to Kṛṣṇa.

The erudition demanded of both author and audience contained its own dangers. The author tended to take for granted a particular erudition on the part of his audience, and was content to work within this sometimes narrow scope. Literary inbreeding is characteristic of the theater everywhere: the playwright looks not only at life; he studies other plays. Once the models are set, as they were in classical India by Kālidāsa and Bhavabhūti, their influence is inescapable. Although most certainly the high Sanskrit drama drew to a great extent on popular folk theater, especially in the earlier periods, it became more self-contained as time went on. The mixture of Sanskrit and the less learned Prākrits, which might at one time have been a means of keeping the play popular, in the end worked against any popularizing tendency. Sanskrit remained alive; but knowledge of the Prākrit languages, which had themselves become literary, arbitrarily fixed languages, receded over the centuries. In modern times the play is staged in Sanskrit only, with the Prākrits translated.

Consciously writing within a particular tradition, the playwright was open, and frequently succumbed, to the temptation of trying to outdo an earlier author, in effect becoming imitative and derivative. The easy flow of the Sanskrit of the Gupta period plays, evincing a broad and cosmopolitan Sanskrit culture, gave way to the stilted, elaborate, erudite, and above all self-conscious language of later playwrights. The theories of Indian poetics, which were formed on the basis of the best earlier plays, became part of the erudition within which the later playwright had to work, and which tended to limit him.

Further, while there was nothing to prevent the Indian theater from becoming realistic—as indeed it already is in many scenes in *The Little Clay Cart* and *The Minister's Seal*, its bondage to Sanskrit erudition caused it to become increasingly idealistic; earlier stereotypes, which contained the germs of individual portraiture, were flattened rather than broadened. The very universality of the Sanskrit culture overlaid, in different regions, a variety of subcultures, not always taking account of their peculiarities. But the regional cultures were developing. And as the fortunes of Sanskrit changed and the language became the almost exclusive possession of literati of a specific traditional erudition, the Indian theater slowly declined. (JABvB)

3 Indian Poetics

An overview

Theory follows practice, and it is to be expected that Indian thinkers, with a penchant for analysis and categorization, would be entranced with the problems of poetry and especially the experience of poetry: how can the experience be defined, on what is it based, how is it transmitted, what is its nature? They found the material for their analysis in the drama and in the poetry that was such an integral part of it.

The Sanskrit name for literature is *sāhitya*, a term that appears in many modern languages as well. The word means "joined together," and literature is thus a togetherness of word and meaning. It is on the relationships possible between word (*śabda*) and sense (*artha*) that all utterance is classified. One such relationship, as has been seen (p. 10), is where the sound of the word is the sense (mantra), and where one mispronounces a word at one's peril. Another type of utterance is scientific discourse, or *śāstra*, in which the sense is everything, where the word serves the sense, where the words are replaceable by other words, where synonyms are possible, where tautology is legitimate method. One can say *a plus b squared* in any language, and no thunderbolt falls from the sky. But the type of utterance that interested the poeticians most is that in which neither word nor sense is self-important, where both are indispensable because together they serve the overall structure. This is the joining which is called *sāhitya*.

The Swiss linguist Ferdinand de Saussure once said that the relationship of *signifiant* and *signifié*, the signifier and the signified, the forms and the meaning of words, are distinct and inseparable, like the two sides of a piece of paper; cut one and you cut the other in the same curve. This inseparableness, as Indian thinkers have also pointed out, is not peculiar to poetry. Except in the cases of *mantra* and *śāstra*, it is true of all expression. But in poetic utterance, the relationship becomes usable for a further dimension: a Mobius band, made up of two-sided paper, is an object that has only one surface. The flowing of the two surfaces into one continuum is made possible by one little twist, the obliquity in the use of language: *vakrokti*, the crooked way of saying it, the bend in language or the oblique is the source of the poetic.

There is in all language an obliquity of a sort. There is no natural relationship between a word and its meaning. The three letters of *cat* say nothing of cats, the word has no hint of whiskers and felinity. The connection between word and object is by custom, habit, and arbitrary convention. Before a child is born there is a wide range of possible names; but once a name is securely identified with a person, it becomes the person: mispronouncing it is an insult, forgetting it is a sign of deep hostility. And it is not only that objects are named, that words are at some point in time assigned arbitrary meanings; it is also that some meanings are assigned to words because of association with other words. And it is here that the poeticians begin to ask: what is the meaning of a word? what does context do to that meaning? Some say that all meaning is derived from context: it is the sentence that comes first and gives meaning to the words. They say that literal meanings often do not make sense. In an utterance like *he went out*, the verb can be interpreted literally. But in the utterance *the light went out* a secondary meaning must be assigned the same verb. And sometimes the context completely reverses the primary or literal meaning, as in ironic sentences like "Brutus is an honorable man." All kinds of explicit meanings can be deployed in the strategy of poetry to evoke implicit meanings. Poetics is firmly grounded in the underpinnings of grammatical and semantic theory (see p. 138).

Where then does the meaning of a single word lie? Is it in the individual sounds, or in the totality of the sounds, or is it wholly outside these? One school of thought holds that a word is made up of sounds that follow one another in sequence, and that the meaning of the word is latent until the last phonetic unit is exposed. The last sound detonates the meaning in the hearer's mind, and all that has gone before is at that point redefined, and the sequence makes sense. The sequence is temporal, but the meaning is a-temporal. The referent *cat* is not c first, a next, and t last; the word is one whole, outside the temporal sequence of the sounds that lead to it: time is the path of the fuse, and the explosion annuls it. Yet there is no way of getting to the a-temporal meaning except through the time-sequence.

The situation is similar with a sentence. The words themselves, individually, cannot carry the meaning of the message. The sentence helps us interpret the word. A sentence does not exist without words, but it is beyond words. This is also the significance of the relationship of the poem to its various parts: the whole transcends the parts, incorporates them, and defines them after being created by them. This relationship is called the *rasa*, the "mood" of the poem; it is what is experienced through the poem's parts.

There are the outlines of a theology in this way of looking at things, and as will be seen, poetics and theology do meet and blend at certain points in time. In *The Upaniṣads* the syllable *om* or *Aum*, the word of words that contains all words, is discussed with a logic that has the same design. *Aum* contains the first letter of the Sanskrit alphabet a, the middle letter u, and the last letter m. But the word *Aum*, when sounded rightly, resonates like a struck bronze bell, and the resonance, which is got through the pronunciation of the sequence, is beyond the sequence, and it is the resonance that is its significance. Thus it is too with the man who has passed through all the stages of life, the *āśramas*, and has renounced the world. He no longer has caste, he has none of the vestiges of the past, not even his old name or place in the family. He has no history; and his history is described by a word that means something like "prehistory:" *pūrvāśrama*.

Thus out of precedents in time the unprecedented is created. The same logic is applied to emotional states. In each man's history there are feelings (*bhāva*) of all sorts, and the poeticians single out eight of these: love, mirth, grief, energy, terror, disgust, anger, and wonder. Each of these is, in the poetic context, transmuted into a corresponding mood (*rasa*): grief inspires the mood of compassion, energy becomes a heroic mood, love becomes a loving mood, and so on. In this transmutation the feelings are purged of their original historical and personal meanings, they live and move in the poetic world of which they have become a part, which they make up, participate in, create and are created by. They are impersonal, capable of communication to other men in similar states, and are generalized: they are no longer private and incommunicable. They carry with them all the physical phases of their expression, their allied feelings, their dominants and their consequents in emotional behavior. Each mood has a characteristic set of these, and it is on this fact that the whole analysis of dramatic performance is based, while the dramatic performance in its turn provides the categories for the analysis. The actor, as in a Stanislavsky school, must study the physical stances and expressions that are functions and reflections of the mood, even glandular secretions (tears, etc.) and contractions of the solar plexus: one feels grief because he weeps, joy because his face glows and his eyes dilate. It is a form of physical imagining, as in the story of the village idiot who found the missing donkey by imagining where he would go if he were a donkey. The emotion produces tears and gestures; cannot the gestures reproduce the emotion? And the reader and spectator in his turn goes through the incipient gestures and tensions in himself: the mood creates a condition in which the reader or spectator reconstitutes his own analogous private, incommunicable, and forgotten feelings into this impersonal expression. They are transmuted into the mood (*rasa*). This he enjoys, and thus he can enjoy, paradoxically, even grief. (AKR)

Recent studies of Indian literature have at last begun to emphasize the relevance of Indian poetics to the judgment of Indian literature and to seek in that criticism more perceptive guidelines to the appreciation of an exotic written art than are provided by current or Victorian theories focusing on Western literary traditions.

Western approaches to literature may not only be passively irrelevant to our appreciation of an exotic tradition, but may actually foster and encourage principles of criticism that make unintelligible the literature we wish to study.

It is admittedly difficult to approach an exotic literature from a critical point of view that is itself alien to our own habits and principles of literary judgment. It might even be questioned whether such an approach, even if possible, would yield the immediately relevant and sympathetic understanding of Indian literary works that is one of the important ends of any criticism.

In this survey we will try to characterize the poetic doctrines as they were intended to apply to given genres and types of literature, discussed elsewhere in this book. Such an approach, though it may overemphasize the critical relevance and adequacy of poetic theory at the expense of other possible poetics, does have the advantage of placing the theory in a context of application that is proper to it and is capable of informing the otherwise very abstract cross-cultural or historicistic discussions of Indian poetics.

Little attention can be focused here on the historical evolution of Indian literary criticism—its text history, as it were—for such an enterprise seems inevitably to become mired in technical issues of Indian chronology, philosophic thought, and textual exegesis.

Origins of poetics

The oldest extant works of Indian poetics date from the sixth or seventh centuries A.D., though it is clear that the origins of the subject are much earlier. There are references to categories (for example, simile) that later became the very heart of poetical doctrine in texts of the fourth and fifth centuries B.C.: *The Nirukta* of Yāska and the famous grammar of

Pāṇini. But such writers were interested more in the exegetical powers of the simile than in its poetical overtones. Then too, the doctrine of semantics suggested earlier, which most of the writers on poetics take for granted, was only developed in the period between the fourth century B.C. and the fourth century A.D.

It is difficult to overemphasize that Indian poetics in its origins was a descriptive or applied philosophical study, a śāstra sharing much with related disciplines of grammar, logic, and ritual interpretation, all being aspects of the Indian preoccupation with the spoken word and its powers. Unfortunately, little remains today that clearly belongs to the period of origin. By the time of our older texts, poetics is a recognized and separate discipline: an analysis of literature.

Literature in the sense of belles-lettres was the great innovation of the classical period, from about the first century A.D. This is not to say that there were not hints of the form before that time. Literary composition as other than a vehicle for religious or metaphysical purposes appears toward the end of the first millenium B.C. in portions of *The Rāmāyaṇa* and in the poems and dramas of the Buddhist writer Aśvaghoṣa (though in both cases the "art" is presented in the service of a more noble goal). The innumerable "praises of kings," *praśasti*, some found in inscriptions from the early part of the Christian era, while contributing, as has been seen, to the formation of the epic genre, have poetic qualities. The poetic form emerges full blown in the works of Bhāsa (third century A.D.?) and Kālidāsa (fifth century A.D.?), and in the dramas of Viśākhadatta and Śūdraka—an aspect of the great Hindu "renaissance" of the Gupta era.

Such a thoroughgoing elaboration of new genres of expression does not come about overnight. In effect, the classical literary élan generated a new literary language, based on the normalized liturgical language of Pāṇini. That language in turn became increasingly important in the literature. Despite some notable stylish evolutions the classical Sanskrit language is the language of classical Sanskrit literature. Although Prakrits also are used for literary purposes during this time, they do not appear to have had a decisive effect upon the literary theory. They also became "literary" languages and, metrics aside, utilized the same conventions.

This classical literature presupposes or implies a consciously elaborated poetic. Consistent and utterly sophisticated use of standard literary devices, even in the early work of Aśvaghoṣa, makes this seem certain. Alliteration and simile were clearly worked out into a theory, as was the ever-present pun. Kālidāsa in the ninth chapter of his *Raghuvaṃśa*, "The Dynasty of Raghu," explores systematically a kind of proto-pun called *yamaka*, and alliteration. Aśvaghoṣa even knows what is often thought to be the "late" or "decadent" device of grammatical virtuosity: in certain sections of his *Buddhacarita* are found, for example, nothing but verbs in the aorist, a particularly difficult and rare tense.

Kālidāsa in particular among the early classical writers is remarkable for his sustained use of imagery, recalling in richness and variety the place of importance assigned to the simile (*upamā*) and its variations in the later poetics. His "epic" and lyric poems are often nothing more than chains of beautifully worked out and complex comparisons.

All considerations lead then to the conclusion that down to the fourth century A.D. a form of poetics was in the process of elaboration, conditioning and being conditioned by the increasingly belletristic styles of classical literature. In addition, one of the early writers on poetics, Bhāmaha, mentions several predecessors whose works are not extant.

Two fundamental genres of classical Sanskrit literature, drama and stanzaic poetry (*nāṭya* and *kāvya*), are both attested by Aśvaghoṣa in the first century A.D. These genres continued their separate though related development throughout the early classical period. Because of this, criticism emerged as a discipline with two distinct aspects or traditions, one devoted to the study of the *kāvya*, the *alaṃkāra-śāstra* or "science of the figures," and the other to the study of the drama, the *nāṭya-śāstra*. As has been seen, poetry and drama were interrelated in many ways; and in fact the early critics of the *kāvya* saw their problem as one of differentiating the matter of their concern from the drama, as well as differentiating poetic language itself. (EG)

The poetics of stanzaic poetry: the alaṃkara-śāstra

Keats thought that truth was beauty; had he been able to write in Sanskrit, he would have agreed with Kālidāsa that language is beauty. It was, first and foremost, the rich and balanced elegance of the Sanskrit medium of the *kāvya* that inspired the passion with which the critics of the alaṃkāra tradition described it. Alaṃkāra means "ornament" and is often translated as "figure of speech"; and some writers speak of Dame Poesy doffing and donning these "jewels." In their eyes, figures were only decorative, not essential. But the other view is expressed by the etymology of the word: "that which enables, that which makes adequate." Images are the language of the imagination. All language may be in part imagistic, but when the image becomes, in its complex or sustained use, the chief object of the expression, it is poetry properly speaking. In the simplest case, the image is that understanding of the poetic proposition that, though irrelevant to the poet's topic, strikingly complements it through an emphatic parallelism. The typical image is simile, and this figure is at the basis of all description, as well as being the chief stock of poets:

> "Outspread at the jagged foot of Vindhya Mount thou shalt see Reva-river,
> In channels like ash laid in furrowy streaks on a elephant's frame."[1]

The so-called natural or descriptive poetry of Kālidāsa is often enlivened by an apt but breathtakingly immoderate simile:

> When thou, black-hued as a glossy coil of hair, hast climbed that mountain's peak,
> While its slopes, covered with wild mangoes, gleam with their ripe fruits,
> Surely it will entrance the gaze of divine loving couples aloft,
> Like a breast of Earth, dark-centered, bright the encircling curves.[2]

But the image that accompanies, sets off, or distinguishes the poet's topic need not always be expressed as a simile or comparison. The interest of the alaṃkāra critics in minute differentiation is based on the insight that the content of several poetic phrases may be the same and yet their effects different, because of different techniques. A common variant of the simile is thus *rūpaka,* where the image is identified with the subject; it is often worked out in meticulous parallel detail, as in this image of Kālidāsa's, where the river-woman is approached by the cloud:

> Drawing away from her hips, the banks, her blue water-garment,
> Which seems half-heartedly held by her hand, as reed-branches touch it,
> Bending over her, my friend, it will be hard for thee to depart;
> Who that has known love's savor can leave one whose haunches are bared?[3]

Another extension of simile, *utprekṣā,* is also metaphorical identification, but not of one thing with another. Rather it is the ascription of the mode of behavior of an otherwise unmentioned object to the subject, as in this conceit of Kālidāsa's where the cloud behaves as a weary town resident:

> Thy heart tired of journeys, after dispelling thy weariness on the city's palace roofs
> Fragrant with flowers and marked by the foot-dye of voluptuous women.[4]

There are, in the alaṃkāra-śāstra, tedious lists of the variations of simile—lists made in fact to demonstrate completeness by their tedium—

which conceal rather than explain the acute, sensitive, and above all elaborate tastes of the critics who discussed these figures. The kāvya is most successful as a genre for the way it elaborately interweaves the strands of many semantic lines and stuffs the verse as it were with layers of meaning. The whole is incandescent through compaction and tightly recurrent associations. The medium, as Marshall McLuhan says, is the message. The critics of the alaṃkāra school tried to understand and portray that medium by identifying and isolating the aspects of imagery that are poetry and that, when used coherently and in a sustained fashion, constitute the poem.

The writers on alaṃkāra considered simile the basic figure, theoretically, because it is the most direct way of introducing another level of discourse into the basic assertion. Their emphasis on simile is also practical because so many other figures can be seen as basic simile with the addition of another conceit: in rūpaka the notion of identification is added, and in utprekṣā the ascription of behavior. Such extensions suggest simile, but have their own force. Instead of merely comparing the beloved's face with the moon, the poet can claim that her face excels the moon, or can observe that the moon, because of its blemishes, is less perfect than her face; or he can presume that two such perfect objects must be rivals and jealous of each other:

> Her face wears the sad look of the moon when thy approach
> eclipses its beauty.[5]

After simile, the next important variety of figuration considered is usually hyperbole (*atiśaya*). Here the poet plays on the relation of his subject to its qualities, real or supposed, and the poetic twist derived from the distortion of that relation. As in simile, by speaking falsely a greater truth is told.

The Meghadūta, "The Cloud Messenger," does not present many examples of hyperbole, for Kālidāsa seems in this poem to seek the restrained composure that comes from describing the natural munificence of the Indian landscape (including its women) with exact and parallel, and sometimes understated, imagery. Distortion is of course implicit in all comparison, but the tendency to seek relatively balanced parallels plays it down. In some examples, however, the element of hyperbole appears to dominate the simile form: "Passion for the dear one waxes and becomes a mountain of love."[6] An instance of pure hyperbole, wherein the quality of a thing is distorted without any suggestion of a parallel object, is found in verse 104: "I would that the night's long watches were compressed as a single moment! I would, too, that the day were at all times mild and balmy!" Distortion of duration suggests impatience; distortion of the weather suggests constancy. A quality is replaced by its opposite in verse 49: "Thou too shalt become pure within, black only in outer color."

Grouped together with hyperbole, or perhaps taken as extensions of hyperbole by the alaṃkāra critics, are the many distortions of specific relations such as cause and effect, container and contained, and part and whole. The distortion of the container-contained relationship, here a girl's body and her attributes, is used in the final line of verse 100 of *The Meghadūta* after a series of beautifully balanced images, to bring out the ironical deception of the lover:

> "In the śyāma vine I see thy body; in the eye of the startled doe, thy glance;
> In the moon, the sheen of thy cheek; in the peacock's massive plumes, thy hair;
> In the delicate river-ripples I descry the play of thine eyebrows;
> Nowhere, alas, O gentle one, is thy likeness found in a single place."[7]

Simile and hyperbole constitute the framework of poetry; simile and hyperbole when used for their inherent expressive capacity and not for some extrinsic end of communication *become* poetry (to use a simile). Nevertheless, there are some types of utterance that appear to be poetic and yet lack conceit of any kind. Grouped together as *svabhāvokti* (natural description)—these few "anti-figures" have constituted a theoretically important bone of contention throughout the tradition. Much of Kālidāsa's naturally graceful poetry appears to illustrate just such a possibility:

> "When thy thunder stirs the earth to burgeon with mushroom parasols,
> That music, sweet to the ears of royal swans, will rouse their longing
> For Mānasa Lake; they will form thine escort in the air to Mount Kailāsa,
> Gathering the tips of lotus-stalks to stay them on their flight."[8]

There are some "figures" in this verse (thunder music and the like), but they do not, as in the cases observed above, carry the main weight of the expression, which, by and large, evokes a naturally agreeable landscape, replete with accurate botanical detail.

Another type of alaṃkāra, and the final one discussed here, is *śleṣa* or pun. If any aspect of classical Sanskrit poetry has been singled out for exemplary abuse, it is its tendency to the cultivation of puns. The term "pun" brings to the mind of the English reader the cheapest form of wit by word-association, which does little more than amuse. In fact, the twisted word-play of an Ogden Nash would be condemned by the alaṃkāra critics as puerile. The term *śleṣa* can mean "embrace," and it is defined as "simultaneous expression of two or more meanings." It is possible only when the shape is one and meanings are multiple. Sometimes the linguistic form underlying the two meanings is the same, sometimes different. It is almost a poem in epitome. By putting two meanings into one span, we at once demonstrate the nonliteral character of poetic speech and the limitations of literal speech. English stretches even to involve two words in complementary puns. "Don't labor under a misconception—support abortion reform." In some Sanskrit verses *every* word has two meanings, and the poem is thus two poems, not one. The most extreme instance of this type of ingenuity is the long poem *Rāghava-pāṇḍavīya*: at one reading it tells the story of *The Rāmāyaṇa*, but if the words are divided differently it is the other great epic, *The Mahābhārata*.

Śleṣa, say some alaṃkāra critics, is—when the meanings complement each other—also a "combination" of the other basic figures; it is hyperbolic simile. It is hyperbolic in that the apprehensions take place simultaneously, and thus exaggerate the two meanings taken singly; it is simile in that two meanings are apprehended. The double entendre has its locus in two complete assertions that complement one another and are not mere verbal identities. A good example is from the critic and poet Daṇḍin, lines spoken by a courtier in ironic praise of his royal patron:

> He mounts the eastern mountain, lovely and ruddy orbed;
> The royal moon reaches the hearts of men with its soft rays.[9]

The reference is obviously to the moon. But all of the words, even the verb, are capable of being understood differently. The combined sense of this other reading of the verse, less evident but probably uppermost in the poet's mind, is:

> He has attained prosperity, handsome and beloved by his court;
> The king (still) extracts the people's substance with his light taxes.

The effect of such fusion of senses on a grand scale is intellectually overwhelming; language is turned inside out and made to be, not only itself, but its mirror and its world simultaneously. It is reminiscent of the "hidden" imagery of John Donne or James Joyce; but Sanskrit achieves its end purely through language and rarely resorts to symbolism. The poetry of classical India was both sophisticated and cultivated. It is the literary product of a self-satisfied elite that has seen few equals in those qualities. Not surprisingly, intellectual qualities predominate even in poetry; the śleṣa, properly understood, symbolizes both the direction and the achievement of that literary expression.

The study of poetic figures was the heart of the early poetic schools, and one of the main themes of all subsequent ones. It was not, however, their exclusive concern. There was concern, as has been briefly mentioned, with the phonic substance of poetry. Alliteration, rhyme, and meter were analyzed and categorized as *śabda-alaṃkāra*, *śabda* meaning "word" or "verbal form." The critics properly recognized these figures as important aspects of the acceptability of any poem, although they also recognized that when they constitute the chief interest of the poem, the poem is inadequate. Like those of sense, the figures of sound were thought of as distortions of normal language, as unnatural regularization of the sound features of normal language. Alliteration is the recurrence to an abnormal degree of the same or similar phonemes, as in this verse from Kālidāsa's *Raghuvaṃśa*:

> pautraḥ kuśasyāpi kuśeśayākṣaḥ sasāgarāṃ sāgaradhīracetāḥ
> ekātapatrāṃ bhuvam ekavīraḥ purārgalādīrghabhujo bubhoja.[10]

Rhyme, *yamaka*, is considered similar, in that it also is repetition—of syllables, usually three or more, somewhere within the verse (not only at the verse ends). This can become complex; in the ninth canto of *The Raghuvaṃśa* Kālidāsa employs such yamakas in the same place in each of the first fifty-four verses. Other writers take even more delight in the elaboration of such figures.[11]

Verse itself was the concern of a specialized subdiscipline. Most Sanskrit composition, literary or not, was versified, and thus verse does not appear so closely linked to poetry as it does to the modern West. Nevertheless, certain verse forms were considered poetic par excellence, and these were the ones distinguished for their regularity and complexity: each syllable in the quarter-verse was exactly specified as to length, so that the entire quarter-verse and the verse itself had an utterly predictable syllabic cadence. Moreover, as the poetry became more complex the length of the quarter-verse also grew, from the original eight syllables of the quarter-śloka of *The Rāmāyaṇa*, to eleven, seventeen, twenty-one, and even more. The cadence-patterns obtainable in this way were almost infinitely varied. But certain verse forms continued to be associated with certain styles of poetry; love stanzas, for example, used a particular one, often the Śardūlavikriḍita.

The alaṃkāra critics also discussed topics less obviously related to the capacities of language. Important to them were the concepts of *guṇa* and *doṣa*, "quality" and "defect" of style. To Daṇḍin, "qualities of style" are the properties of the language to produce certain kinds of impressions, both verbal and meaningful, for example "clarity," "vigor," "compactness," and "density of meaning." There are ten of these impressions, and the proper use of all of them evokes the style, the total impact. Daṇḍin recognizes two styles, other writers three, five, or more. Style was probably at first regional variation in literary usage: easterners used more long compounds than southerners. But by Daṇḍin's time, styles had ossified into literary forms, and with time, the definition of style became narrowed more and more. "Stylistic qualities" are reduced to śabda-alaṃkāra, and finally, in the critic Mammaṭa, to types of alliteration.

The doṣa at first appear to be the inverse of "qualities": clumsiness, lack of clarity, unwanted or unfortunate double entendre, and the like. But no one attempted to systematize "non-style," and the "defects" remain an unconnected list of phenomena observed to detract from the aim of the poet.

Alaṃkāra criticism passes over almost without comment the entire range of issues that center around the origin of the individual poem, its context, its appreciation, and its authorship. It does not aim at judgment of individual literary works or at a theory of their origin. But the writers of the school cannot be dismissed as primitive linguistic pedants without considering whether their poetic bears well or ill on the poetry that was its object.

The classical stanzaic verse, the *kāvya*, which found special applications in larger contexts such as drama, epic, and anthological poetry, remained remarkably uniform from the point of view of its techniques of expression. It retained a fundamental unity, the microcosm of the stanza itself. And alaṃkāra criticism was directed toward these units of poetry. That individual stanzas were the basic units of composition is borne out by the fact of their individually finished form and by the manner in which they circulate free of their original, perhaps dramatic, context, to form anthologies. The content, either in the way in which poems are arranged in an anthology, or of the stanza itself, is concomitant rather than essential.

The stanza is a polished and self-complete whole. Larger works were in the main strings of stanzas, as a necklace is a string of pearls. The jeweler spends little time considering the thread on which the pearls are strung; the critic spent little time considering the common subject, in the case of anthologies, or the narrative story, in the cases of drama and epic poem. The value and the achievement lie in the jewels themselves. In these lie the abstraction of much of the critical tradition, for in the stanza it is the complex of formal qualities that determines the effect, and not such larger issues as "inspiration." The problem of the poet was to fill up a verse consisting, for example, of sixty-eight syllables, with language distinguished at each potential level of expression, its sound patterns pleasing to the ear, its words coherent and inoffensive, and its propositions intelligently compact of meaning and charming. The forms dominate the author, and the criticism concentrates on the forms. The vehicle of the poet, the Sanskrit language, itself a highly formulated and "artificial" (cultivated) expression, is inevitably the chief interest both of the poets and of the critics; its poetry, which was seen as a display of the power of that language to please in itself alone (and not in virtue of its "message," however conceived), was in composition more abstract than individual. Although the "problem" of individual variation did receive some attention (the guṇa theory), it did not have the moral force and value that it does for us, and the poeticians expended themselves on understanding (as they conceived it) the *quality* of the poem: its formal power.

It must be said, finally, that the alaṃkāra critics did, in their way, attempt to cope with the "finished" poem, which is more than its component expressive devices. The final "figure," *saṃsṛṣṭi*, or *saṃkara*, "association" of figures, is the coherence of the unique figures in the poem. The figures used must not cancel each other out, but must constitute the unity that is the stanza, now conceived not only metrically but ideally as well.

Certainly, much of the charm of such poetry lies in the expression as content, rather than in the verbal and metrical stuff of the form. The "completeness" of the description is a function of the neat and usually very dense fit between the verse-sentence and the verse form (the "stanza" per se). The "poetry" appears not to be sufficiently accounted for by form alone, for it is more than verbal beauty that we hear. The subject itself is "beautiful."

The figurative schools never went very far in explanation of that apparent paradox; they were by and large content to identify verse as involving an element of the same "charm" that necessarily qualified the more obvious forms, like simile. Later schools will explain the matter in ways that seem more cogent, observing that the beauty of such verse lies not so much in its *form* of assertion as in the latent associations it awakens in the hearer's own experience. The "subject" is beautiful because the rainy season is the season for lovers to pass long uninterrupted days together and, by the same fact, the season for distant lovers to pine all the more. The "thunder," in this view, is more than rumbling in the sky, it is also a sign of perturbation in the lover himself. But before this is taken up in detail, another phase and school of criticism intrudes, that based on the drama. (EG)

Dramatic criticism

As a man lives in this world through his senses, he feels pleasure and pain. He seeks one and avoids the other, and the seeking and avoiding make waves rise and fall in the sea of his consciousness. These movements are called feelings. Some of the waves are large, others small ripples, parts of the larger ones. The larger waves are the eight dominant moods (*rasa*)—love, anger, fear, and the rest; the smaller ones are transitory states, but related to the dominant moods: joy and jealousy, irritation and loss of control, panic and trembling. The moods are excited and heightened by other elements; in the balcony scene in *Romeo and Juliet*, the garden and the moon abet the mood. And the mood in turn leads to actions and responses: tears and sighs and resolutions. All these taken together are defined as *rasa*.

In a play, what the actor acts is not the central mood of love or grief. He acts out the conditions that excite the mood and the responses that follow from it: he shudders or faints or sweats, he weeps and his voice cracks. The Indian theorists spelled this out in great detail, prescribing for each of the *rasas* the correlative consequents, the kinds of dramatic personae, the gestures and scenery and kinds of diction, thus analyzing content into forms.

The feelings of an individual man are based on personal, accidental, incommunicable experience. Only when they are ordered, depersonalized, and rendered communicable by prescriptions do they participate in *rasa*, which is created by them and in turn suffuses them. By this ordering, one's own history is reactivated in an impersonal context. *Rasa* is a depersonalized condition of the self, an imaginative system of relations. Its existence cannot be proved or designed, for "its perception is inseparable from its existence." It is not a "worldly" state, for in the world pity, disgust, and horror are not enjoyed, as they are in poetry:

> Irrational streams of blood are staining earth;
> Empedocles has thrown all things about;
> Hector is dead and there's a light in Troy;
> We that look on but laugh in tragic joy.

And as they are enjoyed in the *rasa* state. The reader experiences the *rasa* not just as himself, but as all men of adequate experience and sensitivity and training appreciate that experience: man is spoken to by man. But if the experience is wholly depersonalized, how does one *rasa* differ from another? Though the taste of all the emotions is dissolved, their essence clings to the *rasa*. The *rasa* is not something apart from them, existing before them. Its generality is not an undifferentiated generality; and the experience of one poem is different from that of another.

But though it is related to personal experience, it is not personal experience. The audience cannot talk to the persons of the drama. *Rasa* comes into being with the work of art and goes out with it. It is outside normal time and space. The Caesar of Shakespeare's play is not the Caesar who crossed the Rubicon; his physiology and biography are irrelevant to the play. Nor is the actor who is playing him Caesar; his biography is also irrelevant. The Caesar of the play is a virtual presence, neither the actor nor the original. It is because of this quality that the spectator sees the play, with all his past animated, but himself being generalized, without resistance or desire, and he sees each thing in its turn: Antony with Cleopatra's eyes, Cleopatra with Antony's, and both with Enobarbus'.

The *rasa* and all its constituents are not in an effect-cause relationship. If they were, as are the pot made by the potter and his wheel, the *rasa* would remain even after the potter is dead and the wheel broken. But when the spectator leaves the playhouse, when the reader lays his book down, the experience is no longer present. Nor is the relationship one of experience and memory. For if it were, the poem or play would be like the lamp that illuminates the pot already made and kept in the dark. *Rasa* comes into being with the experiencing. The critics compare it to the experience of God. It is its own witness, felt in the blood and along the heart through the body laid to sleep, the self in oblivion: a transient twin of the experience of Brahma. *Rasa* is their central concept, but the critics of the drama, like those of *kāvya*, were fond of precision and detail. To be fair to them, their own logic must be followed. (AKR)

The Sanskrit dramas, as we mentioned, have this in common with Sanskrit written literature: they rely at crucial times in the unfolding of the action, on the strophic poetic forms that are the achievement of the *kāvya*. But the drama is a great deal more than its libretto. Not only does the drama involve narrative language (dialogue in prose), which does not conform to the canons of stanzaic criticism, but it is *seen* as well as heard. Its impact lies not entirely, and perhaps not even primarily, in its language, but rather in its visual immediacy. Its poetic or "esthetic" perhaps inevitably centers on the interplay between conceptual and nonconceptual–form, dance, mime, song, characterization (in its simplest form, the idea that *this is Rāma*) in a unity that can only be immediate and therefore affective. In the oldest extant text of dramatic criticism, *The Nāṭyaśāstra*, attributed to Bharata, that affective unity, which is both the goal of the dramatist and the substance of the audience's appreciation, is termed *rasa* (literally, "taste, flavor"), a notion that has remained the most important and influential single concept of Indian criticism to this day.

Like critics of written poetry, the dramatic critic proceeds analytically, considering the elements of dramatic expression. Both consider language, but the point of view is not the same. For the former, it is the whole of his interest, or at least the framework to which other interests must be related; for the latter, it is but an aspect of, and necessarily subordinate to, the chief frame of reference, which, as *rasa*, is an apprehension not conceptual but immediate, an apprehension essentially emotional. Language is considered but one *means* among many others equally symbolic (as dance-gesture, and mime, and characterization). Hence Bharata, though he devotes an important chapter to an abbreviated discussion of the figures and other devices of written poetry (sixteen in most editions) and two other chapters to meter and dialect (fifteen and seventeen in most editions),[12] is chiefly concerned with these issues in the context of the nonverbal means of expression generally: even including such detail as make-up (chap. 21) and construction of the stage (chaps. 2, 3). How these various contexts of symbolism cohere and constitute the drama, itself an obvious mixture of other "purer" genres, is the problem that Bharata seeks to solve with the notion of *rasa* (chaps. 6, 7).

Without *rasa*, says Bharata, no sense emerges from the conglomerate of features that make up the dramatic performance. To the question of how it comes about, he somewhat laconically says, in what was to become one of the most important and controversial phrases of the Indian critical tradition: "*Rasa* originates from the joining of the conditional, the consequent, and the transitory emotions (*bhāva*)."[13] In other words, *rasa* originates from the portrayal of emotion, it has its being in the suggestion of emotion. It is not itself an emotion, though as has been seen it corresponds to an emotion. The subtle transformation of emotion into *rasa* has preoccupied this tradition of criticism.

By the time of Bharata's text, the structural primordinacy of *rasa* was so well established that the only *problem* was to explain its coming into being, its generation out of its occasional elements: the disparate events, scenes, speeches, characters of the play itself.

The question is, *what* does the audience to a drama see and hear? The immediately represented dramatic elements are of four types, three of which are mentioned in Bharata. In the first, *vibhāva*, the conditions of the emotion, figure the background, the scene, the characterizations themselves—those aspects of the drama that are necessary preconditions, but not sufficient causes, of the coherent emotional tone. The first act of *Śakuntalā*, for example, is largely devoted to the delineation of those conditions, which will determine the course of the affair between Śakuntalā and Duḥṣanta. First, the character of the hero, a great hunter yet sensitive to the simple grace of his prey, is established:

> See! there he runs—
> Aye and anon his graceful neck he bends
> To cast a glance at the pursuing car;
> And dreading now the swift-descending shaft
> Contracts into itself his slender frame:
> About his path, in scattered fragments strewn,
> The half-chewed grass falls from his panting mouth;
> See! in his airy bounds he seems to fly,
> And leaves no trace upon th' elastic turf.[14]

And in acceding to the hermit's plea to respect the sacred grove, Duḥṣanta shows his nobility:

> Well does this act befit a prince like thee,
> Right worthy is it of thine ancestry.

His character, established immediately in the play, remains constant throughout it; only, as will be recalled, through external intervention is he made to "forget" Śakuntalā. The drama does not concern his character, though he suffers; the suffering is a complication that assumes his steadfastness as a precondition, as a *vibhāva*.

Similarly, Śakuntalā is introduced as having the virtues of naïve faithfulness, which remain with her throughout. Her character is at first played off against the forest setting: "Father Kaṇva . . . assigns to you who are yourself as delicate as the fresh-blown jasmine, the task of filling with water the trenches that encircle [the shrubs'] roots." The king responds:

> The sage who would this form of artless grace
> Inure to penance—thoughtlessly attempts
> To cleave in twain the hard acacia's stem
> With the soft edge of a blue lotus leaf.

The static impression that much of Sanskrit drama gives is from the structural point of view a function of the care paid to such delineation of situation and condition. But although dynamic qualities are thus absent, this care renders the elements of the action more purely forceful and emphatic. Only because of such preparation can the scene of the meeting of Śakuntalā and the king become a paradigm of lovers' sport:

> Although she mingles not her words with mine,
> Yet doth her listening ear drink in my speech;
> Although her eye shrinks from my ardent gaze,
> No form but mine attracts its timid glances.

The conditions of character and setting, then, are constant; other kinds of conditions vary to heighten the peculiar effect of a given scene. The scene of the meeting of Śakuntalā and the king is built up by the pretext of the bee (drawn to Śakuntalā, she has been identified with the forest flowers), which calls forth the king in his already established role as protector, and the information given to the king about Śakuntalā's past, which permits him to aspire toward her; such factors determine and promote the major sentiment and mold it to circumstance. They are carefully selected, not for their "real" or "dramatic" effect, but for the way in which they nurture the fledgling sentiment. Irrelevancy, contradiction, all the qualities of the actual human situation that do not serve this purpose are rejected.

The conditions of an emotion, including character, are constant and are thus in a sense the subject matter of the drama. Movement is in the actions and reactions of the characters and in the conditional background. These actions and reactions are the "consequent" factors of the play, the vocabulary of the mood. Most important in the expression of these consequents is the language of the characters itself. Even straightforward descriptive speeches constitute the reactions of characters to their circumstantial milieus; they convey not only context, *vibhāva*, but the sense or perception of that context. The peace and tranquillity of the penitential grove is evoked by the king's elegant stanzas:

> The gentle roe-deer, taught to trust in man,
> Unstartled to hear our voices. . . .
> Laved are the roots of trees by deep canals,
> Whose glassy waters tremble in the breeze;
> The sprouting verdure of upward curling smoke
> From burnt oblations; and on the new-mown lawns
> Around our car graze leisurely the fawns.

The language is subordinate to the establishment of the *rasa*.

Throughout the play, language is the premier mirror of emotion, particularly for the reader who, unlike the theatergoer, is deprived of visual excitants and expressants. But even to the reader, the visual quality of the play is not entirely lacking. Speeches of the characters often evoke vividly the physical surroundings. Sometimes there are stage directions: "Śakuntalā gazes bashfully at the king." And sometimes the physical reactions of the characters themselves are portentously stated: the king's arm throbs as he enters the hermitage, and the reader knows that this is a stylized portent of rendezvous. When the play is on the stage, such consequences as stuttering in anger, sighing in delight, and so on are even more explicit; the craft of the actor and the skill of the poet must combine to make clear the emotional tone in which both of them, and the audience, are absorbed. Success cancels individual awareness on the part of the spectators, actors, and poet; it is the empathetic fusion of all elements into the mood that is *rasa*.

The consequents (*anubhāva*) are tokens of an emotion. The emotion itself, of course, is never real; it can only be suggested. Paradoxically, any irruption of real emotion, which is by its nature grounded in individual awareness, would terminate the process of suggestion and therefore terminate the drama as well. It is at this point that the poetic theories of India and those of Greece most clearly differ; for Aristotle appears to wish to put the emotions of pity and fear into his audience, to "cleanse." A real emotional transformation, a real experience, was intended. In Sanskrit drama emotion is tamed, cultivated, and sentimentalized. The notion of suggestion is thus crucial; it is not only the means of communication, it is the very being of the play.

In this surrogate world, the dominant emotion does not "live" per se; it lives only in terms of cleverly maintained and sustained contrasts with other emotions. Oedipus does not stand before the audience with eyes plucked out; it is rather the constant interplay of various transitory emotional states with or against the dominant emotional tone that both establishes that tone and maintains it as fresh and vivid. These transitory emotions, called *vyabhicāri-bhāva*, constitute the third category of expressive factors. As emotion, they too are only suggested, but as they are more immediate and constitutive of the action, they are often the direct locus of the expressive factors. The king's amazement at Śakuntalā's charm: "The lotus with the Śaivala entwined / Is not a whit less brilliant. . . . This lovely maiden in her dress of bark / Seems all the lovelier"; the girl's embarrassment at the king's unexpected appearance; his fear that he may not be able to sue for Śakuntalā; her pretense of anger at her companion's rather too direct allusion to her nubility—all these transitory states serve as the context of awareness of the developing *rasa*. The *rasa* cannot be long maintained in pure isolation: saying the word "love" does not convey the profundity or complexity of that emotion. It exists in suggestion and by contrast, provided by conditions and expressive consequents themselves organized into transient nuclei that give their content to the *rasa*.

The Nāṭya-śāstra describes thirty-three such transitory emotions,[15] which are suggestive in different contexts of different dominant moods. These dominant moods, which all factors combine to suggest and express, are called *sthāyi-bhāva*. It is the sthāyi-bhāva that the audience perceives, and in this empathetic perception is the *rasa* of the play. It is in cultivating and maintaining this dominant emotional tone that the crucial question of organization or plot arises. The dominant emotion is of course lost irretrievably if for a moment the sequence of events fails, is incoherent or confused, or if it does not reflect the *sthāyi-bhāva* itself at all times. Aristotle says that the plot (*muthos*) is or ought to be the chief end of the poet and that it is the soul of the play; is this true of the Indian drama?

In the first place, the Indian drama cannot be considered an "imitation of actions," a mimesis. Its "objective" correlate has already been revalued and subordinated to the status of an already emotionally determined "factor." The organization of factors to sustain the dominant emotion proceeds on principles that bear little relation to a calculus of events. The action does not have to be subjected to canons of probability nor to the tyranny of the three unities, nor is it discussed in terms of knot and dénouement. Not only is the action of the Sanskrit drama not real, it is not even a function of the characters themselves, who remain constant and uninvolved. As has been seen, whatever dramatic imbroglio occurs is not because of defect of character, but from the arbitrary superimposition of chance, as the curse of Durvāsas; it is the proper business of the drama to dispel this, resolving the characters again into their original, constant state. It is for this reason that plays with plots as different as those of *Śakuntalā*, *The Little Clay Cart*, and *The Minister's Seal* can be formally identified.

The way in which Indian dramaturgists speak of plot strikes the Westerner as psychological rather than structural. They speak of five progressive elements of plot that reflect the underlying desire or motivation that is to be realized in the play: "The undertaking (ārambha) is a movement that carries the soul toward an object ardently desired."[16] "The effort (prayatna) is a febrile élan toward the object that is not offered immediately to the desire."[17] "The possibility of success (prāptyāśā) is the state where success appears possible . . . ."[18] But at this point obstacles still remain. Obstacles are adventitious and external. "The certainty of success (niyatāpti) results from the absence of obstacles."[19] And finally, "success (phalaprāpti) is the attaining of the desired object in all its plenitude."[20] The reader can apply this analysis for himself to the plot, for example, of *Śakuntalā*.

The organization of the play, then, is not of the action at all. It is an organization of the elements of the nascent emotional tone, recast as the "will" or "volition" of the characters. Stream of consciousness is substituted for Aristotle's objective references. Yet the plot remains in a sense the essence of the play: it is the conscious organization of all the factors of drama that together suggest the dominant emotion, which is what the play is all about.

The dominant emotion of a play does not exclude from that play other emotions, which in other plays might themselves be dominant. In fact, the greatest achievement of the dramatic poet consists in his use of other, potentially dominant emotions as subordinate motifs in his statement of the primary emotion. When this occurs, the subordinated dominant functions as a transitory emotion, with subtle differences. In *Śakuntalā* the dominant is love. But the fifth and sixth acts are devoted to expressing the *rasa* pity, first of the shunned Śakuntalā, then of the king despondent at what he has done. Mere transitory emotions could not be maintained at the level of intensity that the *rasa* pity is in these two acts. At the highest level, then, the poet must employ other *rasas* to state a contrast with his chosen dominant. In plays of love, another *rasa* is usually the sentiment of separation—pity or pathos—that provides the contrast. But the comic is also used, for relief, both in love stories and in those whose theme is heroism. Transitory emotions express the *rasa*; but other *rasas*, by qualifying it, bring it to life and mediate its intensity.

The dominant emotion is dominant not only structurally, but inherently: only a few states of emotional awareness are so basic, so universal, so fundamental in human experience as to serve as the organizing principle of a sustained dramatic production. These, as has been noted, are sexual passion, humor, sorrow, anger, perseverance, fear, disillusion, and amazement, to which a ninth, calm, is sometimes added in late texts. For each of these there is a corresponding *rasa*, which is the apprehension of the emotion suggested in the play, an apprehension that is abstracted from all the conditions of the play and of life itself, and is general and common to all men who are receptive. It is perhaps akin to the emotion itself through the chain that links psychological reality to the *rasa* through personal experience and memory. Abhinavagupta, whose explanations of Bharata most modern critics follow, speaks of latent impressions, of personal history buried in the past. The *rasa* is the awakening of these impressions. The play reveals an aspect of the mind usually hidden and only implicit; this is its function and uniquely pleasurable quality; it can do this only through representation, through events that are themselves unreal, already understood as paradigmatic and not individually meaningful. (EG)

The dhvani school of criticism

The figurative and dramatic modes of criticism and theories of art were the chief loci of literary studies during the classical period. Toward the end of that period, in the ninth century or perhaps somewhat earlier, a new way of thinking about literature appeared. The school, called *dhvani*, "tone" or "suggestion," was better suited to explain, and therefore perhaps rose in response to, the then nascent forms of medieval literature, the devotional and dramatic song. For as early as the seventh century in South India, but gradually spreading over the whole subcontinent, there took place a resacralization of literature, corresponding to an increasing emotionalism, personalism, and devotionalism in religion—*bhakti*.

The Śaivite saint Sambandar (seventh century) speaks thus of the name of Śiva:

> Who utters it with tears of love, receives both life and guidance;
> It is the very essence of the four Vedas, the name of the Lord:
> Glory to Śiva.[21]

And somewhat later, Māṇikka Vāsagar (late seventh century) describes his Lord in terms of mystic sweetness:

> Shall I call you honey on the branch,
> Or nectar from the sounding sea?
> I know not what to say, O our Hara!
> Our precious balm, our King! . . .
> I know one thing: I miss you;
> And what I have, I disdain.[22]

At first popular and vernacular, this type of poem only slowly, and then never completely, won its way into the classical literary tradition represented by Sanskrit. Still, one poem above all others gained favor as the perfect expression of the new devotionalism, the exquisite *Gīta-govinda* of the twelfth-century Bengali Jayadeva, written in a Sanskrit of wholly new artistic dimensions.

Poetic theories are best understood when they are seen as attempting to deal with the actual poetic genres of classical India. Poetics is not limited, except by the poetry with which it deals. A theory of "stanzaic" criticism can be spoken of because, to a remarkable degree, the poetry of classical Sanskrit is formally and conceptually uniform. That the poetic seems insensitive to other issues, such as distinguishing what are clearly subgenres like epic and lyric in poetry, is more the fault of the poets than the critics. Similarly, the theory of drama was very much a creature of the peculiar symbiosis of the literary and kinesthetic styles that made up the drama. In drama, the arts coexist, and drama must be understood as their affective coherence. The theory of dramatic criticism, in contrast to the purely literary theory of the figurationists, more resembles a modern "esthetic": it aimed at explicating an expression not primarily linguistic.

It was perhaps inevitable that the newer forms of devotional expression should call for a poetic based more on the dramatic mode than on the stanzaic. The love of God subordinates linguistic to other values, and makes of language a handmaiden to the inner strivings of the soul. But more than that, the very terms of dramatic criticism, the structuralism of emotions, the transcendence of the *rasas*, of which the chief and model was love, the entire emphasis on tone and suggestion—all these aspects of dramatic criticism seem to apply cogently to the poetry of devotion.

This does not mean that the *dhvani* theory applies only to the poetry of devotion. Indeed, *The Dhvanyāloka* (ninth century), the chief text of the *dhvani* school and the high water-mark of Indian literary criticism, is full of examples drawn from earlier works, secular and often downright sexy in tone. Nor does it mean that religious poetry was unknown to or ignored by earlier critics. Indeed, it would be hard to pick a poem from classical times whose theme at least was not religious; *The Meghadūta* is an exception. But the earlier religious poetry, for example the hymns to the Sun God, *The Sūryaśataka* by Mayūra (seventh century), are most remarkable for their egregiously classical form. The *bhakti* poetry is a new form, direct, often naïve, simple in idea but complex as song, and deeply felt. The *dhvani* theory remains today the Indian poetic par excellence not only because it cleverly redeployed older theories, but because it represents a general point of view; it can claim convincingly that it reconciles and explains the older genres of drama and stanzaic poetry.

The *dhvani* theory, a theory of "suggestion" or "tone," is in fact a modification of the *rasa* theory, again applied to an entirely literary genre. Both aspects of this syncresis are important: the *dhvani* is the translation of *rasa* into the purely expressionistic terms of written poetry; at the same time, the *dhvani* is *rasa*, for *rasa* (in the drama) is the thing to be suggested.

The *dhvani* theory, as expounded by Ānandavardhana in *The Dhvanyāloka*, has its theoretical focus in and derives its context of discussion from an ancient model proposed by the grammarians and philosophers of language. The theory was that a word has three powers: to denote (*abhidhā*), to indicate or betoken (*lakṣaṇā*), and to intend (*tātparya*). The *dhvani* is an extension and development of the third function, but cannot be understood apart from the other two. The word "Ganges" denotes the river. But in the phrase "a village on the Ganges" the same word must have other than a purely denotative value; if the village were literally on the Ganges, it would sink. "Ganges," then, betokens the shore of the river. The literal sense must be logically incompatible with its specific use to be understood as "betokening." Further, the word "Ganges" has many associations that are not necessarily incompatible with its primary meaning: sanctity, ritual purification, disposal of the dead, pilgrimage, origin on the brow of Śiva or the footsteps of Viṣṇu; and some or all of these meanings are associated in the mind of the reader with the village on its banks. This then is the third function of the word.

The *dhvani* writers situate true poetry in this third power or function: poetry is that form of language that has as its major aim the conveyance of another sense through suggestive association. Here and elsewhere aspects of the "new" *dhvani* theory harken back to traditional critical viewpoints, and this is a slight but important alteration of the *alaṃkāra* view. *Vakrokti* becomes *dhvani*; nonliteral usage becomes supraliteral usage. The newness is that *dhvani*, once established as a separate and general power of language,[23] is developed and given content by constant re-reference to the other powers of language. A series of tripartite distinctions emerges that can be illustrated from *The Gīta-govinda*.

A poem in which *dhvani* predominates will derive its content sometimes from the world of fact, sometimes from the world of figurative usage (fact as refracted through the betokening power of language), sometimes from the essentially connotative realm. The last is and can only be affective, an emotion. The *rasa is* the *dhvani* with itself as content.

The Gīta-govinda is a series of poems on the theme of the love between Rādhā and Kṛṣṇa, and in it the *śṛṅgāra-rasa*, the *rasa* of love, is of course predominant. The poems tell of love in earthy, sensual terms; it is a love, however, that is to be understood as a paradigm of the divine. The first type of *dhvani*, in fact rare in the poem, can be seen in a stanza from the fifth chapter; the "fact" suggested is that of the beloved on her way to a tryst:

Depart, my friend, now to that grove, impenetrable in this dark,
and put upon yourself your cloak of black;
Discard the anklets on your feet, betraying—noisy, timid foes—
that dance with clatter in the sport of love!

He dwells, the garland wearer, in the forest by the Jamna, in the
gentle breezes there. . . .[24]

The suggestion is in the circumstances of the tryst: the black coat to make her invisible, the lack of ornaments to escape detection.

The second type of *dhvani*, whose content is figurative usage (the *alaṃkāra*), is found in profusion in the poem; the complex of metaphorical identifications in the following stanza suggests not only the "painfully" amorous context, but also the further simile that Kṛṣṇa will succumb ultimately to the wiles of Rādhā, as Śiva had previously to Pārvatī. Kṛṣṇa speaks:

Not the king of serpents this lotus necklace upon my bosom,
Not the gleam of poison upon my neck this chain of blue lotus,
Not ash this unguent of sandal dust upon me;
Mistake me not for Śiva, O love god, assail not me! . . .

On Rādhā, embodying his victory, Love, who conquers all things,
Placed his bow, her sprout-like eyebrows; his arrows, her
fluttering glances;
His bow-string, the tips of the curves of her ears—the weapons
of love.
So your arrow of eye-play placed on your bow of an eye-brow
wounds me. . . .[25]

By the reference to Śiva, whom the love god with his bow and flower-arrows attempted to entice as he sat in meditation, the poet's figures interrelate subtly, weaving through and behind the basic simile.

The third type of *dhvani* is crucial to the whole theory. Its content is itself. But it is also an intensification of the poetry of the natural description, of the *alaṃkāra* school. Nothing suggests the *rasa* of love more eloquently than the endlessly beautiful variations on the themes of voluptuous intoxication and despair that are the glory of *The Gīta-govinda.*

Sandal and garment of yellow and lotus garlands upon his body
of blue,
In his dance the jewels of his ears in movement dangling over his
smiling cheeks.
Hari here disports himself with charming women given to love.[26]

The visual and audial qualities of the lines recapitulate with their vividness and sonorousness those factors of the *rasa* that were in fact in the drama seen and heard; here they are evoked linguistically. To this voluptuous awareness the musical cadence and extraordinary alliteration of the Sanskrit contribute. The part of the verse given, without its refrain, consists of two long compound words; its moric meter, largely restricted to short syllables, conveys a lilting breathlessness:

candana-carcita-nīla-kalevara-pīta-vasana-vana-mālī
keli-calan-maṇi-kuṇḍala-maṇḍita-gaṇḍa-yuga-smita-śālī

Or again:

I who follow you devoted—how can you deceive me, so tortured
by love's fever as I am?
O Kṛṣṇa, like the look of you, your body that appears so black,
that heart of yours a blackness shall assume![27]

The rich and sensuous imagery approaches the sharpness of touch itself.

If you speak but a little the moonlike gleam of your teeth will
destroy the darkness frightful, so very terrible, come over me;
Your moon of a face that glitters upon my eye, the moon-bird's
eye, now makes me long for the sweet of your lips.
O loved one! O beautiful! give up that baseless pride against me!
My heart is burned by the fire of longing; give me that drink so
sweet of your lotus face![28]

The imagery itself becomes fact; sense merges with emotion.

O make him enjoy me, my friend, that haughty destroyer of Keshi,
that Kṛṣṇa so fickle!
To whose act of desire accomplished the anklets upon my feet
bejeweled
Vibrated sounding, who gave his kisses seizing the hair of the head,
And to whom in his passionate love my girdle sounded in
eloquence sweet.[29]

This type of *dhvani*, which in itself is the *rasa*, demonstrates a linguistic function that has the power of nonlinguistic modes of expression. In the drama, dance, music, and rhythmic movement played a role alongside language in the evocation of the dominant mood. In *The Gīta-govinda*, language becomes a surrogate of the entire object world, and in its empathetic and imagistic fervor encompasses also the entire subjective world of thought, feeling, and desire. In form, too, *The Gīta-govinda*, like medieval devotional poetry generally, illustrates new techniques to express the *rasa*. New metrical forms, adapted from popular poetry, emphasize the rhythmic and musical lilt of the lines rather than their balanced syllabic sequence.[30] And the constant use of end rhyme and refrain in the individual songs introduces new principles of organization, no longer based on the stanza but on the song itself. Such repetitions, as well as the brilliant alliteration of sounds and words, again suggest that structures of thought are secondary to the poetic goals; the *rasa* has in fact become the poet's goal, and the poem is now organized "dramatically," in terms that affirm the *rasa*.

In a way these formal innovations and the preeminence of the *rasa*/*dhvani* represent an impoverishment of poetry; *dhvani*, though still possessed of several aspects, is in essence conditioned by the range of major human emotions and in practice by one of them alone: love. The pervasive theme of the devotional religious tradition was also love of God, and despair at his absence. It is no accident that *The Gīta-govinda*, the most perfect *rasa/dhvani* poem, came to be the most influential single example for the religious poetry of the medieval period.

The *dhvani* theorists, of course, allow for poetry in which the *dhvani* does not predominate, but their treatment of it is brief. Just as the *dhvani* was distinguished with the aid of the old tripartite division of word-signification, so are distinguished the kinds of poetry wherein the element of *dhvani* is subordinated to some other principle. There are two versions of this classification.

(a). In all the types illustrated above, *dhvani* was both the aim of the poem and its function, both end and means. Differences among poems concerned, in effect, subject matter. A type of poetry is possible wherein *dhvani* still constitutes the end, but whose means and content ("meaning") must be supplied by another power of the word. *The Dhvanyāloka* discusses only one case, in which the *dhvani* is based on "betokening" (*lakṣaṇā*): irony and its derivatives, when the statement means not what it says, but its contrary or opposite. Suggestion is intended, thus the *dhvani* is real; but it is brought about by negating the literal sense. Brutus is not really an honorable man. And the young lonesome girl says to the traveler: "Sometimes my mother-in-law sleeps there, sometimes I; look what time it is! Traveler, blinded by the night, don't fall into our bed!" From this "prohibition" the traveler is supposed to derive an invitation to come back when it is safe.[31]

(b). The second type is poetry wherein another expressive function is not only present, but is itself the end. This would be poetry in name only, for the element of suggestion, of *dhvani*, is here adventitious or nonexistent. If the poet intends chiefly some striking expression or figure, a *dhvani* may accompany or complement it. And finally, there is a type in which *dhvani* is absent; this cannot properly be called poetry at all. Turns of phrase alone constitute the charm of the *citrakāvya*, pictorial poetry. Other instances are puns, conundrums, poetry that must be seen to be understood, and the like: simple denotation is again dominant.

The influence of the *dhvani* reinterpretation of the *rasa* in literary terms has been profound. Because of it, one can speak of literature in the same vein as music and dance. Most modern Indian criticism is based squarely on the *rasa/dhvani* theory, and cultivates a belief in the universality and subjective motivation of art. At the same time it has a disdain for the older theories of drama and particularly *alaṃkāra*. There are two main threads in the later history of poetics, which come down to the present day almost intact. The first is eclectic: writers reacted to the array of theories before them by trying to arrange them into a coherent whole, irrespective of origin or relevance. In this tradition, as a concept that already spanned two major schools, *rasa* remained the chief element of poetry, though more and more thought was devoted to the definition of those figures that were thought best to express a *rasa*. Some writers, accepting the *dhvani* theory, put emphasis on the interesting question of the logical interrelation of the various modes of figurative expression. But on the whole, the whole eclectic movement was a part of the classic tradition, in which classical values were maintained by isolating, insofar as possible, the older and more "genuine" works.

The second aspect of post-*dhvani* poetics was involved with the reigning, increasingly popular, and vernacular-oriented salvation cults based on *bhakti*. The close fit between the *rasa/dhvani* poetic and the theological universe of these devotional cults has been mentioned in passing. In later centuries, the theologian increasingly borrowed from the poetician until, in the sixteenth century, in the hands of the Bengali Rūpa-gosvāmin, the entire *rasa* poetic had become a theology, dominated by the various forms of divine love. *Bhakti* itself becomes the chief *rasa*, a sure sign of release from the cares of the mundane, self-contradictory real world. The *rasa* of love is no longer the image of salvation; it is salvation.

The topic of poetics thus becomes nonliterary again and merges with traditionalistic or devotional frames of reference. This in itself has its fascination. In the blending of poetic and theology can be seen what might have been the Platonic poetic, had not Plato been so keen a moralist and interested only in literature as edification. Art and religion have generally in the West been considered antithetical modes of expression. Periods of great religious fervor are associated with the most stringent censorship. Litterateurs take refuge either in an Aristotelian mode of criticism, which attempts to establish the foundations of appreciation in categories proper to the work of art, or in something akin to Longinus' ideal of beauty, an esthetic transcendent peculiar to art—art for art's sake. In the West, the Platonic doctrine of ultimate interrelation of all modes of expression, insofar as they are true, has not been applied effectively to art and to the "truest" of all social forms, religion. T. S. Eliot attempts to "esthetify" religion as he listens to the ritual mass as an art form; but this approach makes trivial the popular impact of religion itself. The other possibility has been taken up and explored by the Indian psychoreligious schools, wherein the fundamental identity of mankind's feeling, trusting soul is seen *as* the religious experience, not as its model or antithesis. The sexual imagery, so easily censored by the theological puritan, becomes when reinterpreted on the level of integral man the most poignant mode of expressing the solitude and fulfillment of the thirsting soul. Religion is not Art, say these Indian thinkers, but Art is Religion. All forms fall before the need for union. (EG)

4 The Lyric Poem: *Various Contexts and Approaches*

The Sanskrit lyric: a genre analysis

Poetry is as old as Indian civilization itself. Embedded in the oldest Indian literature are passages of lyric beauty. *The Ṛgveda* contains over twenty hymns to the dawn, and even one to "night," perhaps the loveliest of all:

> The goddess Night comes forth, vast with stars;
>   she wears all beauties.
> Constant Night invests all space above, below;
>   her glory banishes the dark.
> Divine Night follows behind her sister Day;
>   may darkness flee away!
> At your coming we go home like birds in trees to nest;
>   remain with us today!
> All creatures now lie down to rest—men, hoofed beasts, and
>   birds . . . the great swift-moving hawks.
> Tremulous Night! keep us safe from wolves and thieves;
>   may we pass the night in peace.
> The black, bright darkness, all-adorning, shrouds me;
>   O Dawn, like a debt drive it away!
> I have prayed to you as kine, O Daughter of the Day;
>   accept these words like an oblation to a conqueror.[1]

The worship of the gods was in the early Vedic period often expressed in song, and a connection of the lyric mode with religious observance is one of the constants of subsequent Indian literary history. In *The Atharvaveda* are addresses to gods in lyric form that sometimes have overtones of sympathetic magic. And even the early Buddhist literature, which overall is known for its puritanical and intellectual bias, contains two collections of songs describing in vivid colors the difficulties and pleasures of renunciation:

I was born high, to wealth and fortune given,
Perfect in hue and beauty; Majjha's own daughter.

Sought for by princes, by guildsmen desired;
Came an envoy to my father, requesting my hand:

"Upon the scales, as much as she weighs,
Eightfold I'll give you in jewels and gold!"

But I had found Buddha, all-wise, best of men.
I gave honor to his feet and sat in a lonely place.

Compassionate Gautama taught me the *dhamma*.
Seated on that seat I touched the third fruit.

So, cutting my hair, I wander, homeless;
This is the seventh night since my thirst is quenched.[2]

Likewise, both Indian epics are interspersed with "lyrics"; for example, among others, in *The Rāmāyaṇa*, the passage describing Sītā's poignant decision to accompany Rāma to the forest and exile.

But despite such occasional outbursts, during the first fifteen centuries of Indian history the lyrical mode is clearly not considered a genre. As poetic and cultural expression, the lyric becomes important only when its form—its structure of conventions, aims, and achievements—is established. The overwhelming predominance of religious, ritual, and philosophical preoccupations provided little scope for distinctive styles whose focus was primarily literary until the end of first millennium B.C. Similarly, the historical origins of the lyric are of little importance for understanding the consciously realized and conventional genre of the classical period. The lyric as a form must be described in its own terms.

The first extant examples of the three types into which lyric poetry was grouped throughout the classical period are from the first centuries A.D. The three types are, first, narrative *kāvya* or *mahākāvya*, an example of which is *The Saundarananda* of the Buddhist Sanskrit writer Aśvaghoṣa (first century A.D.); second, as has been seen, the strophic poetry of the drama, exemplified in the partially recovered dramas of that same writer; and third, the thematic anthology, an example of which is the Prakrit collection called *Sattasaī*, attributed to Hāla (perhaps second century A.D.). Historically, these three contexts of the Indian classical lyric remain quite distinct, so much so that it is usual to treat them as separate subgenres; yet the variety of contexts has had remarkably little effect on the style, structure, and aims of the poetry itself. There is a uniformity of tone and inspiration across the three contexts, at least until the beginnings of the medieval period, when the devotional lyric returns to more popular song models for renewed inspiration.

As has been seen, the classical Indian lyric strives for a unity of expression and imagery that is coextensive with metrical unity: the stanza. The stanza, however, may be, and usually is, an extremely complex form; the unity it imposes is capable of considerable variation. That variation can best be understood in terms of the tension created by two formal extremes. To reiterate, the first is the tendency of Sanskrit vocabulary to rotundity of expression, richness of connotation, suggestive overtone, expansive synonymy, and double entendre: a potency of meaning-stuff unimaginable in the utilitarian vocabulary of Western languages. On the other hand, restraining this tendency to echo upon echo after echo, are the precise, formal limitations of a rigid syllabic metric and the syntax of the language, tending to compaction of thought, both in terms of an expressive variety of inflections and a penchant for compounding words to the point of eliminating most inflection.

So classical Indian poetry is "microcosmic" unit poetry, the unit consisting of the stanza. And poetic compositions longer than the stanza are in effect merely sequences of stanzas, the "subject," if any, serving as a pretext for elaborate repetitive inventions on a given theme. The stanza, therefore, tends not only toward a grammatical and formal independence, but, as the focus of composition, becomes in itself the poetic world. The imagination of the poet achieves a finished form in each stanza, which becomes *par contre*, the affirmation of an image—complete, often rotund, perfectly balanced, its beauty deriving much from the éclat of structured repose. This complex idea, partly formal, partly contextual, is expressed, as we have seen, in the Indian poetics in the doctrine of *alaṃkāra*, "ornamentation" or "figuration," a true theory of formal imagery in its major types and varieties.

Anthology verses

The tendency to individualize the stanza at the expense of the more extended "work" is best seen in the anthologies. The great bulk of the lyrical poetry of classical India is preserved for us in this form. Since each stanza was in theory capable of standing by itself as an expressionistic whole, many poems, though sometimes parts of larger works, came to be included in one or another anthology. The lovely description, already noted, of a deer fleeing before the hunter's chariot in the first act of Kālidāsa's *Śakuntalā* is likewise included in many anthologies such as *The Subhāṣitaratnakoṣa*:

> Lovely the bent neck—
> Her glance fixed on the chariot following;
> Hind quarters outpacing forelegs from fear of the falling arrows,

The track strewn with half-chewed bits of grass fallen
From the panting mouth.
Look! She leaps so that she seems less earthbound than airborne.[3]

The oldest anthology, *The Sattasaī* of Hāla (second century A.D.), is in Prākrit.[4] Most critics presume that the Sanskrit "lyric" represents in part a genuine poetic élan suited to the sophisticated tastes of classical court life; but it is also in part a Sanskritization of more popular, more vernacular, less stylized poetry. The anthology of Hāla appears to confirm this interpretation. Its scenes show a life more humble, more variegated, more realistic than in most classical Sanskrit poetry.

Friend! Such are lovers—devious as the veins of a young crab!
Don't cry; do not avert your gentle moonlike face. (1.10)

The Sattasaī focuses primarily on the village rather than on the court, and on petty intrigues, jealousies, amours:

Tonight I must go through the thick black darkness to my beloved;
Does not Mother put the house in order with her eyes
closed? (3.49)

It is a precious picture of a life that we know must have been lived, but which was not often thought worthy to report. The scenes are direct and vivid—moments captured in their own eternity:

One day more allow me to weep, dear friends;
Tomorrow he is gone; if I am not dead I will cry no more. (6.2)

The slim moon arrayed on the red sunset of the sky!
Like a love-scratch on the bride's breast, half-seen beneath the
crimson silk. (6.69)

Has she not slain me, the wanton, with the sharpened arrows of
her playful glance
Slung out from the bow of her blossomlike brow? (6.4)

Lyric as love poetry

Although in the anthology of Hāla, the lyric or stanzaic form is made to express a wide variety of "naturalistic" moods, the style becomes in subsequent centuries more and more closely associated with the central theme of emotional life itself—with *śṛṅgāra*, love. The most perfect expression of the classical lyric style is found in the anthology of one hundred verses attributed to Amaru (late seventh century A.D.), *The Amaruśataka*, which is justly famous for its vignettes d'amour; but the love it treats is always the light love of flirtation, youth, and easy conquest; though there are jealousies and complications, partings are always temporary.

> An angry embrace with arms as gentle as vines—soft snares,
> She draws him to her chamber at evening, friends shyly watching.
> "Will you leave so soon . . .?" her hesitant voice proclaims his crime;
> The lover, scolded with playful regrets, smiles. (9)

> "Will not those parted soon return? Grieve not
> On that account for me! You are so pale!" My sad speech done,
> She gazed at me with eyes of languid shame, crying pale tears, and
> With a wild laugh, seemed bent upon an eager death. (10)

> She wards him off with frightened hands from the wound of her lower lip,
> "Stop, leave me alone, you wretch!" Her lashes dance to the angry words,
> Her eyes half-closed in passionate sighs; he steals a kiss from his haughty love
> And gains an immortality of sorts; why did the foolish Gods exhausted churn the ancient ocean? (36)

> The parrot listened quite intently to their prattle in the depths of night,
> And next day began to speak it back with all the in-laws there! Ashamed,
> The young wife plucked a blood-red ruby from her earring, and
> Pretending it a pomegranate seed, thrust it into his beak, to silence him. (16)

This specialization of the lyric form to love poetry is at once the most "secular" application and the most sustained lyric development of the classical poetic form. The anthologies' tendency to group poems around certain themes is preserved; but in the love poetry of Amaru, for example, the net result of this concentration on the manifold aspects of a single theme is to give the collection the character of a highly individualized work of art.

In this "secular" context the poetry of Bhartṛhari (early seventh century) must also be mentioned. Three "centuries"[5] (collections of one hundred poems) are attributed to him, one of which is on the theme of love. But the tone of it is not quite the same as that of Amaru. Instead of the delights of dalliance echoed in amorous fantasy, Bhartṛhari sees a somber, transient, intense but inevitably momentary passion. His angle is not that of the roué, but that of the deeply sensitive man who knows that his moment of delight is a mere glimmering in the abyss of time—he is revealed as a man too honest to disdain, but wise enough to regret, his own passionate nature. Bhartṛhari is one of the rare "individuals" to emerge from the classical literature, a man seen at the moment of conflict itself.

But, for Bhartṛhari, poetry is "secular" on the level of appearance only; deeply religious motives, as they are understood in India, guide its expression. These motives are more clear—indeed, paramount—in his other "centuries," which are devoted to topics of the moral life and the urge for salvation.

> Above, the lowering cloud, beside, the peacocks dance;
> The earth is white with petals: Where, wanderer, rest your
> glance? (18)

> Remembered, she is anguish; seen, intoxication;
> Her touch is madness—and yet I call her "treasure." (100)

There is an apocryphal story that Bhartṛhari was so torn between the delights of sense and the needs of the soul that he entered a monastery seven times, each time to return. Certainly the three sets of poems assigned to him by tradition bear out this indecision: not that of a weak man, but of one suspended between irreconcilables. The solution, for Bhartṛhari, comes only with old age and death.

The religious lyric

The "secular" developments of the stanzaic lyric, for all their brilliance, are yet of a fleeting and almost unperceived character. Though the love poetry of Amaru was permitted by the development of an urbane and sophisticated civilization around the courts of the Gupta kings, the basic tone of that poetry, the emotional aspiration toward the beloved object, was itself difficult to distinguish from the spirit of devotional adoration that had from the earliest period been a theme of Indian religious life and was to become in the post-Gupta period the basic concept of Indian religion itself: *bhakti*. The earlier lyricism, Vedic, epic, and Buddhist, was strongly colored by religious devotion. Nor is it surprising that deeply religious minds seek an expression of their longing and their satisfaction, their love for the source of all beneficence, in terms analogous to those of secular lyricism. The emotional conviction is the same in both cases; only the contexts differ. So in the classical period, the stanzaic mode finds an application in service to beloved deities—beloved, and, of course, feared. And at this time and in this way the stanzaic mode achieved its most evident "literary" form: highly elaborate, employing many of the technical virtuosities of the Sanskrit language—long compounds, difficult words, elegant alliterations, interior rhymes, even puns. At first glance, such formal sophistication in religious lyrics (in the classical period called *stotra*—"praise") might be understood as a sign of less serious devotion, less intense feeling. This is of course possible. But perhaps a truer picture emerges if one considers the elaborateness of the poetry in the light of an offering to the God: for both deity and devotee, a perfect, finished offering alone suffices. Westerners might tend to question the "honesty" of the classical Sanskrit poet in considering the appropriateness of his poems; but the gushing soul has never been, in stylized India, a sign of quality. And the religious poets were the first to recognize the appropriateness of the more extreme, perfect, finished stylistic adaptations to this most important of contexts.

The religious poetry of classical and medieval India is vast. The oldest collections are among the best, but a definite historical transition in style is perceptible.

Two poets from the high classical age, Bāṇa (seventh century A.D.) and Mayūra (seventh century A.D.), have left collections of "praises," the former to the goddess Caṇḍī, the latter to the sun god Sūrya. In these the character of the anthology is preserved; there is a thematic unity, and no dramatic or narrative enchainment. Mayūra is also author of some highly esteemed erotic poetry (*Mayūrāṣṭaka*), but it is in his "century" of songs to the sun god (*Sūryaśataka*) that this aspect of the lyric genre achieves its most finished product:

> Deep in the blooms of the lotus, upon salient sharp-thorned peaks
> Alike falling; uniform at birth of day and at the evening hour of
> rest—
> May the sun's effulgent rays protect you!
> Like travelers arrived in chorus on the courtyards of three worlds,
> They bestow torrid merit, born of thirsty journey's toil. (3)

In the generations following these poets, religious devotionalism became increasingly emotional. With this change, religious poetry in Sanskrit lost something of its studied elegance. It assumed, on the one hand, the guise of a cruder iconographic realism, but on the other became again a true song of divine love. The poem *Gīta-govinda* of Jayadeva will forever be the archetypal religious lyric of the Sanskrit language. Late classical Sanskrit poetry like the *Gīta-govinda* (twelfth century A.D.) undoubtedly drew upon the resources of more popular, even oral poetry; in this unique poem, however, the Sanskrit language seems to gather strength from its contact with new forms and recaptures in sheer verbal beauty much of the naïve innocence of ages long past. In this canto, Kṛṣṇa repents his dalliance with rivals of his beloved Rādhā:

Kaṃsa's foe, forsaking the damsels of Braj, took
To his heart Rādhā, chain of wandering memory's prison.

Heart pierced by the wound of the arrow of love, searching for
Rādhā,
Unhappy Mādhava mourned in a bower by Yamunā's bank.

She would not stay by me, the artful women near;
I held her not, constrained by guilt and fear.

Cursing my fame, my name disdained, angry she left.

What will she say, what will she do, so long alone?
What good to me now wealth and friends, my life or home?

Cursing my fame, my name disdained, angry she left.

I remember her face, brow frowning with weight of wrath,
A crimson lotus cloudy under bees' black path.

Cursing my fame, my name disdained, angry she left.

I court her in vain in my violent heart,
I pursue her in forests and mourn her apart.

Cursing my fame, my name disdained, angry she left.

Rādhā! I know your jealous heart is grieved;
My love will persevere, though you had cause to leave!

Cursing my fame, my name disdained, angry she left.

I see her! Back and forth alone she paces,
But welcomes me no more with fond embraces.

Cursing my fame, my name disdained, angry she left.

Be kind this once, and from your side I'll never turn;
Bestow a tender glance on me whom passion burns!

Cursing my fame, my name disdained, angry she left.

This song is sung and offered to Hari
By suppliant Jayadev, moon of Kindubilva's sea. (7.1 ff.)[6]

It has been seen that in language too Jayadeva's poem is extraordinary. Abandoning complex grammatical formalism and metrical styles, he adopts, for the first time in Sanskrit verse, the easy moric meter of Hāla, emphasizing the music of his song. At the same time, he reformulates the classical "discipline" of poetry by placing stringent restrictions on the pattern of heavy syllables: they occur rarely, or only at the beginning or moric units. The songs of Jayadeva have unparalleled lightness and verve, played off against a regularity of beat and an alliterative style unapproached by any other Sanskrit writer: the love of God sings in every syllable; it is a paean of love, uniting, insofar as it is possible to do so, the separate genres of secular and religious lyric. Not only is it a poem of adoration of Kṛṣṇa, but it is a poem to Kṛṣṇa himself as divine lover. The poet speaks as both himself and Rādhā, and this has much significance for developments to come. Much has been made of the apparent deviation of this poem from the classical norms; it has been called un-Sanskrit, popular, a calque on vernacular poetry. It is possible also to think of it as a poem so perfect it could not be equaled. Like the classical period, the middle ages demanded a serious formulation in Sanskrit; Jayadeva is *the* medieval Sanskrit poet.

The tradition of religious lyricism continues to the present, most usually in the regional languages, as will shortly be seen. In some senses, *The Gīta-govinda* is transitional. In many ways it provides a model for later religious poetry. And in it, the old anthology form is somewhat altered. Rather than each stanza being a scenario in itself, the poem is constructed as a number of monologues, each of which, though unitary, fits into and continues a larger story—that of the seduction of Rādhā. The narrative element, so late in influencing the religious/erotic lyric, on the other hand, had been an important aspect of another variety of stanzaic lyric from the very beginning, the "epic" or *Mahākāvya*.

Mahākāvya: the narrative lyric

The older epic or narrative poetry, as demonstrated in *The Mahābhārata* and *The Rāmāyaṇa*, though sometimes showing considerable poetic inspiration, was basically an oral, panegyric literature that happened to be written down at a certain point in time. Stylistically it varies from the crude to the sublime, but its intellectual mode suggests more popular, conventional inspiration. This vast and important literature had too its classical formulation: certain of the epic narratives were "poeticized" in highly sophisticated stanzaic form. But although narrative, the stanzaic integrity of the poetry is stringently maintained. The "stories" serve as pretext and liaison, but they are of no more inherent significance than is the "frame" of the anthology. With rare exceptions, the poetic individuality of the stanzas is not subordinated to the requirements of sequential narrative. The result is that the *kāvya* we call "epic" seems by and large devoid of dramatic interest. It is a mistake to look upon these epic poems as stories; despite their epic theme, they are from this point of view for the most part sequences of digressions—on the moonrise, the beloved, the spring, the great hermitage of the Himālaya. In Kālidāsa's *Kumārasaṃbhava*, "The Birth of the War God," the conflagration of the god of love by the flaming eye of a Śiva who is enraged at the distraction of his meditations requires one stanza, but the lament of the love god's wife takes an entire chapter. Such disproportion is characteristic of all *mahākāvya*: the story is unimportant. *The Śiśupālavadha*, "The Killing of Śiśupāla," of the poet Māgha, for instance, treats in twenty chapters (about 1,800 highly ornate stanzas) the dramatically very minor episode of *The Mahābhārata* involving the challenge and combat of Kṛṣṇa and the arrogant Śiśupāla. But individual stanzas are not without merit, and there are moments of strange realism, as in the description of an army camp:

> An ass, frightened by an elephant, violently reared back, provoking
> laughter in the watching crowd,
> And a courtesan, surprised at the sudden movement of the
> saddle, fell, her garment slipping from her ample hips. (5.7)

Kālidāsa, by everyone's admission, has excelled in this genre of *kāvya* as in all others he tried (he wrote no prose). His two narrative *kāvyas*—*The Kumārasaṃbhava*, a picaresque story of the seduction of Śiva by Pārvatī, and *The Raghuvaṃśa*, "The Dynasty of Raghu," a "history" of the family of which Rāma was the most famous representative—are masterpieces of the genre. In style they show the classical stanzaic poem at its best and most varied. The set patterns of thematic description that appear to stereotype the narrative stanzaic poetry are in fact a sign of the great latitude that the rigid form of the poetry can encompass, in contrast to the restricted thematic material—love and devotion, for example—of the classical anthology. An example is Kālidāsa's description of the Palk Straits, in *The Raghuvaṃśa*:

> Vaidehī, see the vast, foam-covered waters, still split by the
> bridge, even to the far southern mountain,
> Like the starry brightness of an autumn sky rent by the Milky Way.

> The sea seems churned by towering clouds, like some primeval
> mountain come to drink the waters from stormy whirlpools.

The further shore forms the sea's horizon, now a disc of iron,
Its sands dark with forests of palm and tamāla like a row of spots
on the rim of some enormous wheel.

The shore wind refreshes your face, lashes arching, with odorous
ketaka pollen,
Impatient to adorn you, as though it knew my thirst to kiss those
full red lips.

Now the speed of our car attains the sea's sandy shore, where
heaps of pearls are strewn among
Broken oyster shells, and rows of betel trees are bent with heavy
fruit.

Exquisite Sītā, cast your glance back, whose glances are those of
a doe;
The earth with its forests now rushes away from the distant sea!

My car moves at times on the path of the gods, at times with the
clouds or the birds;
Wherever the cast of my mind inclines, there it goes![7]

Traditional critics agree that the *mahākāvya* shows the classical stanza at its best and appears to satisfy most completely the esthetic requirements of that very strict form. But for that reason, it is the most difficult of all Indian poetic styles to convey in translation, and renderings in Western languages can be only bare shadows of the original. It is here that the expressive capacities of Sanskrit—its love of suggestion, double entendre, its compaction and density—are most compellingly put to the test. These *mahākāvya* poems do not have the universal appeal of the erotic anthologies, nor have they "subject matter" in the true sense of that term; they are exercises in the delights of language, its limitations and transcendency. They must appear forever dim and mysterious to those outside the Indian tradition. And even within it, many poets, unable to meet the discipline of this pure form, cannot preserve the calm integrity and wholeness of Kālidāsa's two works, but are drawn into realms of formal experimentation: use of difficult and archaic terminology and of obscure punning that overburdens sense, and strange syllabic arrangements that stray far from poetic requirements, to say nothing of "lyric" inspiration.

The opulent imagery of the final stanza of *The Śiśupālavadha* may convey in some measure the frustration this poetry offers to translators:

Proceeding from the form of the headless (Śiśupāla),
His glory, praised by assemblages of poets,

Was made visible to the amazed eyes of human Indras [kings]
As it entered the body of Indra's younger brother, Kṛṣṇa–
A glory anointed by beauty, accompanied by a shower of flowers
and the drums of divine thunderclaps,
Dispersing with its effulgence the rays of the author of days.

An exception

As has been seen, there are many contrasts of usage and context that to some extent fashion and modify the original idea of the integral stanza in classical lyric poetry. The lyric becomes anthology, erotica, "epic"; in its stylistic elaboration, it often appears to lose all meaningful relation to its "lyric" or "song" sources. There is, however, one poem that does not fit into any of the lyric categories so far noticed. It is such a chef d'oeuvre that it must be considered a genre by itself: *The Meghadūta*, "The Cloud-Messenger," of Kālidāsa. This is a short poem of somewhat over a hundred stanzas, all in one very elegant meter. It is a love song of an exiled spirit sung to a cloud, in the hope that the cloud in drifting across the plains of India will convey his plaint to his beloved. The poem is an address to the cloud or the beloved, and at the same time a narrative of love and a description of the pastoral and urban beauties of India.

The Meghadūta is less a "new" genre than a clever blend of the existing lyric genres: thematic anthology, erotic poem, epic narrative, stylized description. There are even a few lines of address to a god.[8] And with this blending, Kālidāsa approaches what the West might consider the lyric par excellence: an extended outpouring of elegant sentiment. Yet such a form was so difficult or peculiar in the Indian setting that it provoked no further development. The poem to all intents and purposes stands alone, its uniqueness clouded only by a large number of banal imitations.

The problems of comparative literature across time and culture are epitomized in such anomalies as these; on the one hand we see, in India, the development of an increasingly arid *mahākāvya* form, and on the other a failure to take up and explore the challenges of a real lyric tradition, stillborn in *The Meghadūta*. Most historians have offered sociological explanations of this literary fact: in the postclassical period, after the twelfth century, Brahmanism was becoming increasingly parochial and true intellectualism was on the decline. In other words, the capacity of the educated to write sensitive poetry was lacking. This explanation strikes a very *ad hominem* note: it effectively projects the tastes of the present day on cultural forms that have totally different modalities. It is possible that in some degree the withdrawal of Sanskrit from secular pursuits, its growing liturgical bias, could have prevented the expression of "lyric" enthusiasm; yet it is dangerous to argue individual cases from a generalized development that lasted nearly a thousand years. Until well into the medieval period the Sanskritic community maintained many "secular" interests; the lack of interest in the generic possibilities of *The Meghadūta* form has certainly less to do with the supposed pedantry (or lack of it) of the typical educated Indian than with the difficult problem it posed for the canons of poetic style. It was too original to encompass within the creative possibilities of classical formalism. These verses are unique in classical poetry, in imagery and in language:

> You will find her voice subdued, my wife and second life
> While I'm away—a single dove, longing for its mate.
> Her heart does yearn as these heavy, lonesome days go by;
> She has become, it seems, a wild lotus struck with frost.
>
> O my belov'd; her eyes are swelled with tearful sobbing,
> Her full red lips are pale from the ardor of her sighs.
> A hand is placed against her faded cheek; her disheveled face
> Wears the mad look of a moon seen pale and hazy through the
> racing clouds.
>
> When you find her, she may be withdrawn into holy worship, or
> About to paint, distracted, my haggard and impassioned form.
> She sometimes asks, too, her caged, sweet-throated myna bird
> Does it remember with delight her lord—for the bird was mine.
>
> Or, on her lap, the careless garment soiled, she lays a vīṇā,
> Wishing to sing the song whose words I wrote, and sing my name.
> She strums strings wet with tears, yet somehow now forgets
> Cadence and chord she once played over and again.
>
> The months still left, beginning with the day of our divorce,
> She counts and puts a flower on the ground for each of them;
> Perhaps she tastes, in memory, the perturbation of my embrace. . . .
> Such are the moods, when love is far away, of women lost in
> love. (*Meghadūta* 2.20–24)

Yet, from a certain point of view, the spirit of *The Meghadūta* does appear again in the lyrical brilliance of *The Gīta-govinda*. There is likely no connection between the two; still *The Meghadūta* may be taken as the oldest "modern" poem, for Jayadeva has had an enormous influence on poetic development in the regional languages of India. (EG)

The religious lyric in Bengali: an analysis of imagery

This influence of Jayadeva was, for example, powerful on both the form and the theme of the Vaiṣṇava religious lyrics of Bengal. Much of Jayadeva's imagery, meter, and highly elaborate verbal figures appear again in the lyric poems of Vidyāpati, who lived in Mithila, between present-day Bengal and Bihar, in the fifteenth century. But it was Jayadeva's treatment of the theme of the love of Rādhā and Kṛṣṇa that captured the Bengali literary and religious imagination. His masterpiece came to be read and sung, and later lyrics on its theme came to be written, both as literature and as expression of devotional religion.

A religious interpretation of an erotic theme is in no way peculiar to the Vaiṣṇavas of Bengal (it operates also in Kannada poetry), nor even to India. The Persian poet writes of his Beloved, whose long tresses are black as night, whose lips are rubies, whose body is graceful as the cypress in the nightingaled garden, whose eyes are pools to drown in. And Saint John of the Cross hears his soul, the Bride, sing:

> There in my festive breast
> walled for his pleasure-garden, his alone,
> the lover remained at rest
> and I gave all I own,
> gave all, in air from the cedars softly blown.[9]

And the great troubadour Bernard de Ventadour sings, somewhat more bluntly:

> If only she were bold enough
> to lead me, one night, there, . . .
> and naked take me in her arms . . .[10]

Neither Ḥāfiẓ nor Saint John, and quite possibly not even Ventadour, is speaking of a real woman, a real love or lust. Saint John encloses in his gladdened breast, as though in a scented grove of Lebanon, the divine object of his desire. So it is with Ḥāfiẓ, whose Beloved's eyes are fountains of all life. So too perhaps with Bernard, whose desire for the naked and unashamed body of his beloved stops short of actual union, for Christian satisfaction of religious yearning does not allow the thought of union with the Christ or God.

In most literary situations, unfortunately, anthropological dissections cannot be made, nor scenes observed. When context is not known, and text must stand alone, it is not always clear whether the poet is writing of God, or a real woman, or both. Tertullian notwithstanding, it is not unlikely that The Song of Songs (The Song of Solomon) is a love poem, a love poem of extraordinary beauty, to be sure, but secular, and that it was through a series of historical accidents that it found its way into the Christian canon. Once there, of course, it had to be accounted for, so it became an allegory of the love of the soul for God, or of that between Christ and the Church. It is equally possible that *The Gīta-govinda* of Jayadeva, like The Song of Songs, was intended as a series of lyrics on a divine but nevertheless fully sensual love, and that, because its principals are the divine Kṛṣṇa and Rādhā and because of the natural allegory, came later to be accepted as canonical literature and reinterpreted.

Indian thought seems inclined to look at things as three-dimensional. It slowly circumambulates facts and ideas, carefully and delightedly observing how the shapes and shadows change, how the movement of a fraction this way or that yields a totally and entrancingly new form. One's role in society, if he moves a trifle to the left, becomes duty; duty becomes, perhaps, the attainment of wealth; wealth becomes pleasure; pleasure becomes esthetic enjoyment; esthetic enjoyment becomes religion, and religion changes, just a bit further on, back into esthetic delight.

Viewed in this way, the religious and esthetic experience are but different aspects of the same: if *rasa* is the ultimate esthetic enjoyment that is detached from the self, it is almost by definition also religious. The manifestations of the two are the same. The yogin sits in meditation, contemplating and repeating his *mantra*, his sacred formula, oblivious to all that goes on around him in the bustling world. He is much like the man enraptured by a painting; "swallowed up by beauty," he no longer hears the talking of others in the museum and is in fact no longer conscious of time or place. Again, the true nature of God, of Kṛṣṇa, is *ānanda*, bliss, the ultimate pleasure. Man, being man, seeks pleasure. Therefore, whether he knows it or not, he seeks Kṛṣṇa. Kṛṣṇa is the ultimate in esthetic satisfaction. He plays the most entrancing possible music on his flute, and his body, gracefully bent as he plays, absorbs the mind in pure delight. His color, burning like a blue jewel, cannot be caught by earthly pigment. And the drama of his love-play with Rādhā is the ultimate drama, the play of pure passion, a projection of the condition of the human heart itself, in its eternal union and eternal separation. It is a drama of human love, but on a divine, abstract plane, beyond the reach of petty personal involvement: and the experience of it is *rasa*. His devotees are so absorbed by it that they are transformed into Gopīs, perhaps even into Rādhā herself, in perpetual and actual love with Kṛṣṇa. The poet, as he sings, has been transformed:

Love, I take on splendor in your splendor,
grace and gentleness are mine because of your beauty.
I remember
how I embraced your feet, holding them
tight to my breast.

Others have many, I have
only you,
dearer to me than life.
You are the kohl on my eyes, the ornaments
on my body,
you, dark moon.[11]

As has been seen, esthetic theory assumes several kinds of *rasas*. Like the Sanskrit erotic anthologies, the religious poetry of the Bengali sect of Kṛṣṇa-devotees known as Vaiṣṇava stresses only one: *Sṛṅgāra* or love. The reason for this is twofold. First, in the stories of Rādhā and Kṛṣṇa, the devotional tradition of Indian religion has cast up a symbol of the proper relationship of man to God; for the Gopīs, the cowherds' wives, even in their restrictive society, were prepared to give up husbands, family, honor, everything, for the sake of Kṛṣṇa. Whether the scene is religious or secular, this is true love. Second is the observable fact that in human love, relationships have two essential phases, union and separation. It is the nice observation of the Vaiṣṇavas among other schools that these are in fact two sides of the same coin: separation is latent in union, and union in separation; it is much like Dylan Thomas's feeling that a man's death begins at the moment of his conception. This is the Indian view of things in the round: what seems to be "becoming" is really "being." But one cannot circumambulate indefinitely. At any given point in time one must take a posture. The usual Vaiṣṇava posture is to view proper love as love in separation, and to stress in their poetry, the pain felt in separation, *viraha*. They also observe that separation is certain and especially painful if no final union is possible, i.e., if the woman is married to another.

Therefore, stressing the *viraha* theme, the Vaiṣṇavas have a ready-made symbol for the essential doctrinal position of any devotional religion: there is an absolute separation between human and divine (for if God and man were the same, one is in the awkward position of being devoted to oneself). The soul, symbolized as the cowherd woman, sings in separation:

Let the earth of my body be mixed with the earth
my beloved walks on.

Let the fire of my body be the brightness
in the mirror that reflects his face.
Let the water of my body join the waters
of the lotus pool he bathes in.
Let the breath of my body be air
lapping his tired limbs.
Let me be sky, and moving through me
that cloud-dark Śyāma, my beloved.[12]

As was noted in regard to the Sanskrit anthology verses, secular love poetry can offer a variety of themes. But while in religious love poetry, too, the love relationship can be viewed from all the subtle angles that a complicated love affair presents, there must be, underlying it all, a doctrinal position. The Vaiṣṇavas then have no alternative to a poetry of separation. Even in the joy of the moment of union, which these poets are by no means averse to describing, it is the transitory that is emphasized:

When they had made love
she lay in his arms in the grove.
Suddenly she called his name
and wept—as if she burned in the fire of
separation.
    The gold was in the corner of her sari,
    but she looked afar for it!
—Where has he gone? Where has my love gone?
O why has he left me alone?
And she writhed on the ground in despair,
only her pain kept her from fainting.
Kṛṣṇa was astounded, and could not speak.[13]

While, as will be seen, the love lyrics in Tamil have a whole interior landscape in which to wander, the Bengali Vaiṣṇavas have access to only one part of it. They are fenced in, on the one side by their doctrines, and on the other by the ancient Sanskrit literary tradition upon which they drew.

Though convention sometimes imposes a certain sameness upon the more pedestrian poetry within it, it also has advantages for the poet. Though skill with language and image is required, a poet can evoke with relative ease a mood or chain of associations in those readers who are familiar with the same conventional system. Thus the Tamil anthology poet, merely by setting his scene on a mountain peak, suggests the union of lovers. There is no need to be more specific, and his freedom to move around within the suggestion is thereby increased.

Within the Sanskritic convention, the same is true of the Bengali Vaiṣṇava poets. Here are three examples, not in chronological order. The first is by the modern Bengali poet Buddhadeva Bose. It is the first part of a poem called in the poet's own translation, "A Parting."

After the first thousand nights we had to part.
Rain fell on the river, the water rose in flood.
Between the bamboos, like a hidden hope,
One or two fireflies fitfully gleamed.
The sky was closed in cloud, but not quite,
For the wound throbbed sometimes, as lightning flicked
And a long low moaning perished in the pain
Of trying to utter the inexpressible.
Urgent, uncertain, ruthless, full of violence,
The water foamed and spread and disappeared
Into the final silence of the fates
When I left my love in the hand of God.[14]

The imagery is clear enough. Darkness is lostness, or death, or pain. Fireflies, stated symbols of hope, flicker and die away. But on another level, the imagery is conventional. Compare this verse, by no means atypical, by the Sanskrit poet Yogeśvara:

After the rain a gentle breeze springs up
while the sky is overlaid with clouds;
one sees the horizon suddenly in a flash of lightning;
moon and stars and planets are asleep;
a heady scent is borne from *kadambas* wet with rain
and the sound of frogs spreads out in utter darkness.
How can the lonely lover spend these nights?[15]

The meaning of the verse is not literally that the storm makes it impossible for the wanderer to go abroad. The verse is not only descriptive; it too is conventional. The wanderer is less likely to be felled by the rains than by his own grief: for the season is that of reunion with the beloved and he is still abroad. The convention is perhaps best shown by the citation of a Bengali Vaiṣṇava verse, signed with the nom de plume "Vidyāpati."

O my friend, my sorrow is unending.
It is the rainy season, my house is empty,
the sky is filled with seething clouds,
the earth sodden with rain,

and my love far away.
Cruel Kāma pierces me with his arrows:
the lightning flashes, the peacocks dance,
frogs and waterbirds, drunk with delight,
call incessantly—and my heart is bursting.
Darkness on earth,
the sky intermittently lit with a sullen glare . . .
Vidyāpati says,
How will you pass this night without your lord?[16]

The convention underlying all three verses is that the rainy season is the time when lovers should be together: the air is cool, the breeze sweet-scented. To be parted in this time is doubly painful.

There is one other convention involved. The second line of Bose's verse, "Rain fell on the river, the water rose in flood," is identical with a line from a popular Bengali nursery rhyme, *bṛṣṭi poṛe ṭāpur ṭupur, nodi elo bān*. Within this more narrow convention, this would suggest the hope of childhood, and with it change, decay, and the despair latent in hope.

Later developments

There is a saying in Bengal, possibly a mot of the late scholar Haraprasād Śāstri, that *kānu bine gān nāi*, "without Kṛṣṇa there is no song." The story of the love of Rādhā and Kṛṣṇa has been so close to the surface of the consciousness of many Bengalis, be they Vaiṣṇava or Śākta, Hindu or Muslim, that many a love affair in literature finds itself under the shadow of this prototype. Except for the obviously Muslim name of the poet, the following lyric could easily have been written by one of the early, purely Vaiṣṇava devotees:

I die, burning in *viraha*;
where has he gone—Hari, dear to my heart?
I do not see his bending body on the banks of the Kalindi,
or beneath the kadamba tree;
no more, in Vṛndāvana, does his flute call
his beloved Rādhā.
I lie in sleep, and see him in my dreams.
Awakening, I can only weep.
Vṛndāvana is empty; he who holds the flute
comes there no more.

Kāmār Āli, wretched, says:
the image of your beloved is in your mind.

Hari, dear to your heart,
Will come and fill your eyes.[17]

But apart from devotional songs written by non-Vaiṣṇavas, the Rādhā-Kṛṣṇa theme has often been used as a point of departure for poetic reflections on purely earthly love affairs. Orthodox Vaiṣṇavas, of course, have their objections to such a use of the sacred theme. They have little sympathy from any point of view with such as the so-called *kabiwallas*, who flourished from the mid-eighteenth century to the end of the nineteenth. The usual view is that of S. K. De: "This spiritual inadequacy of the songs of the Kabiwallas necessarily involved a lowering of the literary ideal."[18] The kabiwallas were poets who extemporized upon a theme for the amusement, and sometimes the titillation, of their audience. For wealthy people in Calcutta, and in the houses of families outside the city, it was fashionable to hire two, or sometimes two groups, of these poets to entertain guests on festive occasions. The most colorful aspect of this custom was the *kabi-laṛāi* or verse-battle, which has had a long and respectable history in India from the time of the poets in the court of King Chandra Gupta II; the two kabiwallas or sets of kabiwallas would exchange verses on a theme, a reward being given on the audience's judgment as to the better verses of the two. For a long time, it was the custom for the poets to decide the theme among themselves, before the contest began. And not infrequently the theme was an exchange between Rādhā and Kṛṣṇa, or between one of the other Gopīs and Rādhā. And since this theme was a familiar one, both audience and poets knew roughly what to expect. Later on, however, the exchanges grew more freewheeling, and yielded such as this, between Ṭhākur Siṁha and, somewhat surprisingly, a Portuguese named Antony:

Ṭhākur Siṁha: Antony, I want to know this single thing: why do you wear such dress? Why don't you any longer wear a shirt?

Antony: I am quite happy in Bengal, wearing a Bengali's dress; when your sister came into my bed I put aside my hat and shirt.[19]

With increasing value being placed on surprise and shock, treatment of the Rādhā-Kṛṣṇa theme often became a little gross, and sometimes scurrilous.

In the late eighteenth century, the stream of Vaiṣṇava creativity had become a mere trickle. But although the primary motives, psychological and metaphysical, of the Vaiṣṇava tradition had all but disappeared from the scene, the poetic forms and conceits remained. The kabiwallas took the theme and to some extent the conventions of Vaiṣṇava religious poetry and made of it a poetry of secular love. Some of the results, needless to say, were appalling. They were no more than shallow mimicry of poets who, while not always themselves literarily brilliant, had at least the saving grace of substantial religious fervor. The lyric, secular love poetry in the Sanskrit erotic anthologies, becoming religious with Bhartṛhari, reaching a zenith of devotional fervor in the songs of the Bengali Vaiṣṇavas, had come full circle.

Although in the hands of some kabiwallas the Rādhā-Kṛṣṇa theme was a mockery, in the hands of others it took on a strange and interesting new life. When the old Vaiṣṇavas spoke of Rādhā, they meant both Rādhā the woman participating in a love affair and Rādhā the symbol of the human soul. The kabiwallas did not concern themselves overly with symbolism. In their eyes, Rādhā's love was not a state of grace; like that of any young person, Rādhā's love brought with it pain and lust and general confusion.

When I was a girl, I was happy.
I did not desire happiness.
I knew no lover, nor did I know the joys of love;
the lotus of my heart was closed.
But now the hundred-petaled lotus, closed and warm,
has been opened
by the touch of time.[20]

Or again, very much in the spirit of Hāla's Prakrit verse:

My heart aches, my friend,
that what I had to say to him remains unsaid,
for modesty.[21]

"Spiritually inadequate" though these songs may be, they have a warmth and directness too often lacking in those closer to the classical conventions:

He is mine! I am young, and spring has come,
and he is in another land.
But when, at last, he comes laughing to me,
and when I see him laugh, and swim in my tears,
how can I refuse him?
My heart longs to hold him to my breast,
though my modesty says no.[22]

As devotional religion gained predominance, in medieval times, the religious and erotic blended imperceptibly with one another. Circumambulating this poetry of love, the Vaiṣṇavas saw it one way, the kabiwallas another. The duality is inherent; in Rabindranath Tagore's English *Gitanjali*, the book that moved Yeats and Pound to such high praise in 1912, it seems to be Rādhā who speaks, just as she spoke in the sixteenth century:

> Clouds heap upon clouds, and it darkens. Ah, love, why dost thou
>   let me wait outside at the door all alone?
> In the busy moments of the noontide work I am with the crowd,
>   but on this dark lonely day it is only for thee that I hope.
> If thou showest me not thy face, if thou leavest me wholly aside,
>   I know not how I am to pass these long, rainy hours.
> I keep on gazing at the far gleam of the sky, and my heart
>   wanders with the restless wind.[23] (ECD)

The Kannada vacanas of Mahādēviyakka: love as metaphor

> Look at
> love's marvellous
> ways:
>
> if you shoot an arrow
> plant it
> till no feather shows;
>
> if you hug
> a body, bones
> must crunch and crumble;
>
> weld,
> the welding must vanish.
>
> Love is then
> our lord's love.[24]

In its love-imagery, in its strength, and in its sudden final transposition of "profane" to "sacred," this *vacana* by Mahādēviyakka,[25] a woman-saint of twelfth-century Karṇāṭak, is representative. *Vacanas* are the "sayings" or prose-poems of medieval saints belonging to the Vīraśaiva sect of South India. Each of these saints had a central cluster of metaphors that articulated his experience of God. As in the writings of Saint Theresa, or Mīrā Bāī, or indeed the Vaiṣṇava poets of Bengal, in the *vacanas* of Mahādēviyakka the central metaphor is that of love; the poet is the beloved, and the Lord the lover.

In most religious literature, there are two types of love-relationship between God and man, depending upon who takes the initiative. God may be represented as pursuing man (or woman, in some mythologies) with His love: grace is the Hound of Heaven. This is the case in Greek mythology, as shown by the story of Leda and the Swan, in Christianity, as the Immaculate Conception demonstrates, and in the classics as well as tribal lore in India, where often the Lord comes down to earth as the lover and husband of some beautiful woman. The Sōliga tribesmen on the Biligiri hills of South India call Viṣṇu their brother-in-law, for He married one of their sisters.

The second type of relationship is that which has already been noticed: the human soul, represented as feminine, yearns for and, if doctrine allows, attains the Lord. The poetry of their relationship describes all phases of such love, in separation and in union. Here is another of Mahādēviyakka's *vacanas*:

I have Māyā for mother-in-law;
 the world for father-in-law;
 three brothers-in-law, like tigers;

 and the husband's thoughts
 are full of laughing women:
  no god, this man.

And I cannot cross the sister-in-law.

But I will
give this wench the slip
and go cuckold my husband with Hara, my Lord.

 My mind is my maid:
 by her kindness, I join
 my Lord,
  my utterly beautiful Lord
  from the mountain-peaks
  my lord white as jasmine,
and I will make Him
my good husband.[26]

There is behind this poem a whole framework of love conventions: the heroine, for example, steals out of a houseful of people to meet her lover, as did the Gopīs in the Kṛṣṇa story. There are also the allegoric equations of various members of the household with various abstractions. Some of these are explicit: *Māyā*, or illusion, is the mother-in-law, the world the father-in-law. And some of them are assumed (and pointed out in commentaries on the poem): the three brothers-in-law are the three *guṇas*, the three ultimate components that, in philosophical literature, make up material nature. The husband is *karma*, the ego's many past acts and lives. The sister-in-law is apparently *vāsanā*, the binding memory or smell of the past, that goes with *karma*. Furthermore, all relationships mentioned are those of marriage—the house is full of in-laws, legal social relationships—there is not one related to the poet by blood. This is the net that binds her, knotted by convention, not by birth. And this is the net that is torn to shreds by the adulterous experience of God.

The Vaiṣṇavas of Bengal point out that the Gopīs were the wives of others when they fell in love with Kṛṣṇa. Here too, the true relationship of the soul with God is necessarily an illegitimate one, from the point of view of law and social order. It is a violation of expected loyalties, a breaking-down of the predictable and secure. The Lord is the illicit lover, and the world of *karma* and normal relationships must be violated and trespassed, if one is to know God.

Many such motifs are common in Mahādēviyakka's work. One of them is the contrast between human and divine as lovers. "No god, this man" is a notion often found. Legend has it that Mahādēvi, like Mīrā Bāī in Rajasthan, was actually married to a local king and left him in search of her true love, Śiva.

I love the Handsome One:
he has no death
decay nor form
no place or side
no end nor birthmarks.
I love him O mother. Listen.

I love the Beautiful One
with no bond nor fear
no clan no land
no landmarks
for his beauty.

So my lord, white as jasmine, is my husband.

Take these husbands who die,
decay, and feed them
to your kitchen fires![27]

This poem also points up an insistent paradox in Mahādēvi's poetry. Her Lord is impersonal, not made up of material nature; he has no attributes, no death, no form, no particularity. All the imagery is of physical love, but the object of that love is without body, parts, or passions.

O swarm of bees
O mango tree
O moonlight
O koilbird
I beg of you all
one
favour:

    If you should see my lord anywhere
    my lord white as jasmine

call out
and show him to me.[28]

The heart in misery
has turned
upside down.

    The blowing gentle breeze
    is on fire.
    O friend moonlight burns
    like the sun.

Like a tax-collector in a town
I go restlessly here and there.

    Dear girl go tell Him
    bring Him to His senses.
    Bring Him back.

My lord white as jasmine
is angry
that we are two.[29]

The first part of the above poem is pure *śṛṁgāra*, in the classical mode. But the second part returns to Mahādēvi's preoccupation: oneness in a world of dualities.

If He says
He has to go away
to fight battles at the front
    I understand and can be quiet.

But how can I bear it, girl,
when He is here in my hands
right here in my heart
    and will not take me?

O mind, O memory of all pasts, my help in love, my girl,
if you will not help me get to Him
how can I ever bear it?[30]

In the opening lines, which are marvelously concrete, the Lord is spoken of as a warrior who might have to go away; but soon it is seen that he is not in fact away, but here. In the third section everything is rendered abstract by the way the poet calls her mind, the memory of her pasts, her helpmeet in love. This assimilation of the abstract to the concrete and the rarification of the concrete to the abstract is characteristic. Even when Mahādēvi actually describes the beauty of her Lord, as the Vaiṣṇava poets describe Kṛṣṇa, her poem ends on an abstract note:

Locks of shining red hair
a crown of diamonds
small beautiful teeth
and eyes in a laughing face
that light up fourteen worlds—
    I saw His glory,
and seeing, I quell today
the famine in my eyes.

I saw the haughty Master
for whom men, all men,
are but women, wives.

I saw the Great One
who plays at love
with Śakti,
original to the world,

I saw His stance
and began to live.[31]

The image of Śiva in the first part of this poem is unlike the usual description in the *vacanas*, and is suspiciously like Kṛṣṇa in his crown of diamonds; but it quickly moves to the idea of the Master to whom men are wives, thus metaphorizing the imagery of physical love, and ending with a description of Him as the Lord, the husband of the Original Śakti herself.

Probably it is the nature of religious poetry to oscillate as Mahādēviyakka does between the personal and the impersonal, to use human and concrete forms to express the ultimate yet intimate nature of the religious experience. The *bhakti* schools, which have deities conceived of as having name, form, and attributes like the Rāma of Kabīr in Hindi and the Kṛṣṇa of the Bengali Vaiṣṇavas, often inconsistently identify their Kṛṣṇa or Rāma with an impersonal godhead; and schools that hold their deity absolute and formless have ways of making the concrete details of poetic imagery tend toward the dissolution of such details. When these poets really succeed, as Mahādēviyakka does, in making their utterances articulate the oscillation from "home to heaven" and back, the movement that seems to be essential to the devotional experience, they are not just saints, they are also poets. In them, the "profane" is a form of the "sacred," and the distinctions between "sacred" and "profane" vanish. As Mahādēvi says of the body:

If one could
draw the fangs of a snake
and charm the snake to play,
it's great to have snakes.

If one can single out
the body's ways
it's great to have bodies.
The body's wrong
is like mother turning vampire.

Don't say they have bodies
who have Your love,
O lord
white as jasmine.[32] (AKR)

The interior landscape: classical Tamil poetry

In the Kannada *vacanas*, the atmosphere is quite different from that which pervades the devotional lyrics of the Vaiṣṇavas of Bengal, and although resemblances can be detected in the landscape, we are quite clearly in another country.[33] Resemblances may be due in part to psychological limitations on metaphors, that can be used to express the religious experience. Differences may be due to those of doctrine, and perhaps to some extent to those of variety in poetic convention.

The theme of the simultaneous unity and diversity of Indian literature has been running throughout this book. In the case of *The Rāmāyaṇa* it was seen that versions of the story occur with some variations and sometimes widely differing interpretations in different parts of the subcontinent. But despite these differences, *The Rāmāyaṇa* represents a pan-Indian set of moral and literary values.

The situation is quite different for lyric poetry. For in this case the Sanskrit tradition offers a set of values and conventions valid only for those languages and literatures of the north that claim Sanskrit as a natural literary ancestor. Bengali religious poetry owes a great deal to the forms and conventions of the puranic repertoire, the anthology verses, the erotic lyric, and also the poetics of Sanskrit. It will be seen that Urdu, though linguistically related to Sanskrit, owes much less; Urdu accepted only the small loan that Sanskrit literature extended to all of North India by the mere fact of its presence; far greater is Urdu's debt to Persian. And the debt of the classical Dravidian language, Tamil, to Sanskrit, is practically nil in the early centuries of the first millennium A.D. Tamil secular lyric poetry belongs within its own, non-Sanskrit, set of conventions. Some of these are common property to all of India, and peculiar to India in the world. But others belong to the Tamil tradition alone, and here diversity is at its greatest.

One of the eight collections of the oldest Tamil poetry is an anthology called *Kuṟuntokai* (ca. A.D. 100), short love poems between four and nine lines long, comprising 400 verses by 205 poets; of these, ten are anonymous and several are only identified by a phrase in the poem. For instance:

> What could my mother be
> to yours? What kin is my father
> to yours anyway? And How
> did you and I meet ever?
>   But in love our hearts are as red
> earth and pouring rain:
>   mingled
> beyond parting. (*Kuṟuntokai* 40)[34]

The poet is known by the phrase *cempulappeyanīrār*, "the man of the red earth and pouring rain."

The poems are simple in their setting. To appreciate fully their conciseness and density, a little knowledge of the poetic behind them is needed. The poems create their own world, they introduce and establish their own conventions of symbolism. But the poetic adds to the poem itself. It adds nuances, confirms impressions, and works as a kind of reference-glossary to the symbols of the poems. And it will be of interest to note the differences between the Tamil system, as presented in *The Tolkāppiyam*, the authoritative treatise on the grammar and rhetoric of classical Tamil, and the Sanskrit system.

All poetic themes in Tamil are divided into those of *akam*, the inner world, and *puṟam*, the outer world. *Puṟam* poems have to do with the community or the kingdom; the central relationship they present is that of the poet to the king, the most poetic experience they express is that of war. In these poems, names of kings and places are mentioned: the poem is placed in a real society, a real history. *Akam* poems, on the other hand (*Kuṟuntokai* is an *akam* anthology), have the inner world for their subject. Here the central relationship is that of man and woman; the most poetic experience is love, in separation and in union, in fidelity and infidelity. No names are named; stylized individuals, not historical ones, are the dramatis personae. Landscapes are more important than places that can be named.

The love themes of the *akam* poems are of seven types:

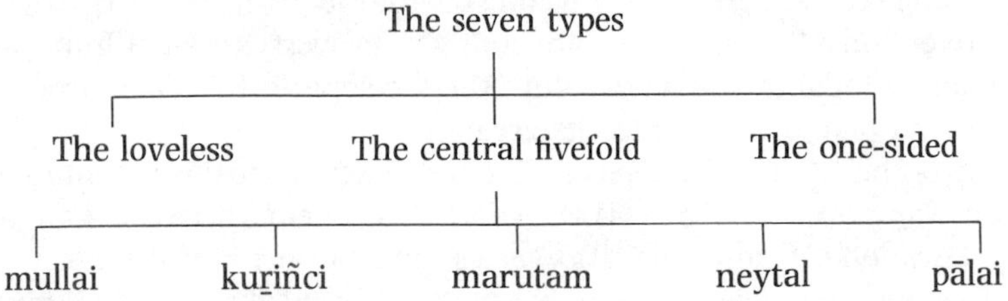

One type of man-woman relationship is the loveless one: a man and a woman get together for desire, duty, or convenience. Such a relationship is considered abnormal, undignified, and fit only for servants. The one-sided type is mismatched or unrequited love. Neither of these is the proper subject for *akam* poetry.

The fullest poetic potential appears when man and woman are well-matched in several ways: beauty, wealth, virtue, rank, and so on. Such a couple alone is capable of the full cycle of love, and that cycle is represented by five landscapes.

Every landscape is a mood, said Amiel. And the five landscapes of the Tamil country are the settings for the five moods or phases of love; these are not unlike, in a different art, the Books of Hours in the Middle Ages. Each landscape has its characteristic flower or tree by which it is named or evoked, its best time of day or time of year. Thus, when the forest landscape is evoked, with its wild jasmine *mullai*, and evening time, and the season of rain, it is the time and place for the waiting and reunion of lovers; the mere mention of these, or any other of the birds or trees or men of the forest, will suggest the time of waiting. The poet thus has freedom in his imagery; the design is given but the details are his to choose.

The landscapes, their regions, names, compatible seasons and times, and moods, may be roughly summarized thus:

The flower	*The region*	*Compatible seasons and times*	*The mood*
mullai	forest	the rainy season; evening	patient waiting, domesticity
kuṟiñci	mountain	the cold season; night	lovers' union
marutam	fields, city fringes	summer; dawn and early morning	conflict; infidelity
neytal	seashore	summer; sunset	anxiety, separation
pālai (an evergreen tree)	wasteland (or fields and forests parched by summer)	summer; midday	elopement; separation from parents

In addition to these landscapes and themes, there are many subthemes and elaborations, each of them as in Sanskrit classified and described in detail by the rhetoricians. For example, according to a rhetorical text, here is a symptom of love: "Mild exudation on the forehead of the heroine, due to fear or some reserve in her mind as she is being stared [at] by the hero." There are smiles, and attempts to conceal them, and many skillful ways in which the heroine hides the different amorous propensities aroused in her. There are exactly eight preliminaries to the approach by the lover. Some are in this poem:

> The hero praised me often.
> And watched like a big game hunter
> fagging out the stalked animal;
> he bowed abruptly
> and touched me, and my heart went faint.
> And like an elephant in heat
> evading the cruel hook of the master,
> bowed again, again,
> and touched me.
> I thought he was a fool. (from *Kalittokai* 55)

And there are six different acts of the love-stricken lady, and thirty-six places where she can speak out (e.g., when the hero leaves), and the physical symptoms of morbid love:

> It would help, dear friend,
> if we could get someone
> to go to him
> with some of those rain flowers

of the sponge gourd
that grows so lush
with leaves among the tall wet grasses
on our farm
and tell him: Look,
the girl's fair brow
has yellowed like these
with love. (*Kuṟuntokai* 98)[35]

The rhetoricians, establishing these classes, also recognize what they call *tiṇaimayakkam* or "overlap of classes." The rule, they say, is to keep the main poetic mood, the human elements; all else may be fused, ignored, or rearranged toward that end.

Finally, a distinction is made between two kinds of proprieties, the proprieties of the mode of drama (or literature) and the proprieties of the mode of the world. All the proprieties so far mentioned are part of the dramatic mode. When a poet wishes to make a poem he deploys both. He embodies the things that belong to the real world in the time, place, and settings of the dramatic mode. In this view of the relationship of reality to poetry, the Tamil rhetoricians seem to be anticipating Marianne Moore:

til the poets among us can be
'literalists of
the imagination'—above
insolence and triviality and can present
for inspection, imaginary gardens with real toads in them,
shall we have it. ("Poetry")[36]

In this way, everything is done to define the input of the poem beforehand, to depersonalize the poetry, till poetry becomes like language. As in natural language, the words are given, the syntax is given. But every sentence uttered is new, because the possibilities of combination are infinite. So in these poems, the speakers, the moods, the landscapes, the contents of each landscape, even the audience within the poem, are given. We only overhear what the hero or heroine or their friends say to one another; every poem is a dramatic monologue.

The following poems will be examined from these points of view. The basic question is: given all these conventions, how does an individual poem manage to be different from other poems? In the first one, the poet uses the various parts of the scene to speak about the actors:

Bigger than earth, certainly,
higher than the sky,

more unfathomable than the waters
is this love for this man

of the mountain slopes
where bees make rich honey
from the flowers of the *kuṟiñci*
that has such black stalks. (*Kuṟuntokai* 3)[37]

The *kuṟiñci* is a mountain flower, and mountain slopes are places of tryst, according to convention. Bees drawing the richness of honey on mountain slopes are clearly enacting the lover's action: where he is is what he is. Large abstractions open the poem: "Certainly larger than earth, higher than skies . . ."; but it ends with the concrete and minute: the black stalks of the *kuṟiñci* flower. The abstract love and knowledge of the virgin who is speaking become the acute, focused concreteness of experience. And with this the obvious identification of the flower with the virgin girl is no longer conventional.

O girl
with those long cascades of hair
and face bright as a lotus
and brow like the moon,

did you see passing by
a deer
with an arrow in its body?

The initial elaborate and loving description of the woman soon identifies the stricken deer as the speaker himself. Even the deer might be an excuse, a metaphor. The factual question "Did you see a deer?" becomes a statement about the speaker: the hunted deer itself becomes the hunter.

The *vēṅkai* tree plays a crucial role in this poem:

O lord, I fear the way's danger
when you come in the dark through the thick of the forest
with only the smell of the *vēṅkai* blossoms
for a clue. (*Kuṟuntokai* 358)

The *vēṅkai* tree has another name, *kaṇi*, which means "foreteller"; its blossoming foretells a wedding. Its blossoming also coincides with the ripening of the millet harvest, after which no one needs to watch the fields any more. The ambiguity of the poem lies in the danger of the forest and the closeness to love's consummation, presented by the smell of *vēṅkai* flowers in the double darkness of the forest in the night.

This poem too has the *vēṅkai* tree, signifying expectancy:

O bright jeweled maid
I heard the bells
of my man's chariot horses
and went out
only to find that it was the birds
on the *vēṅkai* tree. (*Aintiṇai* 60)

In all these poems there is an interesting correlation between the speaker and the type and range of imagery used. For instance, the heroine's images are confined to what she knows of her own landscape; when her girl friend speaks the imagery ranges more widely, for she is of a lower class and her experience is wider; for the hero, as he is a hero, there are no limits to experience and therefore no limits to imagery. The following poem is by the heroine:

O long white moonlight,
you do him no good at all
as he comes stealing
through the night in the forest

where the black-stemmed *vēṅkai*
drops its flowers
on the round stones
and makes them look
like tiger cubs
in the half-light! (*Kuṟuntokai* 47)[38]

The *vēṅkai* again suggests the approaching union. But the *vēṅkai* itself looks in the moonlight like stripes on a tiger's skin, and the stones like tiger cubs. The night is ambiguous again, filled with *vēṅkai* flowers but menacing: the very moon that lights the lover's way produces the illusions. Both the *vēṅkai* and the tiger cubs are signals, the one of expectancy, the other of anxiety—for where there are cubs there are lurking tigresses. But yet the imagery is confined. Compare it with this poem, spoken by the foster-mother or nurse:

Man-eaters, male crocodiles with crooked legs,
cut off the traffic on these waterways.
        But you,
in your love, will come to her swimming
through the shoals of fish in the black salt marshes.
        And she,

she will suffer in her simpleness.
        And I,
what can I do but shudder in my heart
like a woman watching her poisoned twins? (*Kuṟuntokai* 324)[39]

And here is a hero's poem:

Let us mount our chariot of ivory
white as the foaming hill-stream
its bright wheels sunk three-fourths in the earth
like a young moon,
let us go and by evening return
to my love. (*Kuṟuntokai* 235)

So the imagery, by its narrowness or width, marks out the characters and the classes to which they belong.

The landscape does other things as well. It is not only a metaphor to bring out likenesses, but is a device to include other worlds. The heroine speaks to her friend about her lover, who is gone:

Will he remember, friend?
Where the curve of the parrot's beak
holds a bright-lit neem
like the sharp glory
of a goldsmith's nail
threading a coin of gold
for a new jewel,

He went across the black soil
and the cactus desert.

Will he remember? (*Kuṟuntokai* 67)[40]

The goldsmith's nail is brought in not simply as a metaphor, but to parallel man's festivities to the festive springtime of nature—the parrot's beak holding the bright-lit neem. But the lover has gone across the desert. The movement of the poem is from the colors of the parrot and the goldsmith's jewel to the bleakness of the black soil and the cactus desert.

"A landscape is a mood." While the landscape is very much external in its detail, it is very much internal as evocative design: it is an interior landscape. A change of scene may mark a change of heart. Here is a mother looking for her daughter, who has eloped with her lover across the desert:

O women
I have only one daughter
and she is gone with the man of the keen spear
over the mountains and down the valleys
she's gone,
across the wild impassible desert.

O women
you ask me to hold my heart
and like it.
My inmost flesh is set on fire
when my sweet pearl, my girl, learned to walk;
I burn when I suddenly see the blue nocci flowers. (from *Naṟṟiṇai*)

The growing-up of the girl is traced in terms of landscapes: she grew up among blue nocci flowers, she has moved among the mountains—places of tryst and the mountain-lover, down the valleys—places of lovers' quarrels and estrangement and waiting, and now through the desert, which is the setting for elopement and parting from parents.

This mother is more ready to accept the situation:

Let no sun burn
may trees shade the little ways to the hill
may the paths be covered with sand
may cool rain
cool the desert roads
    for that simple girl
    her face the color of the new mango leaf
    who left us
    for a man
        with the long bright spear! (*Kuṟuntokai* 378)[41]

From the little ways to the desert road: it is a virgin's progress from innocence to experience. The other images are also functional: the cool rain is propitious to love; and the poem is filled with sunlight, beginning with the sun, ending with the bright-faced lover, as if the lover *is* the sun.

The following poem by a waiting heroine also enacts the movements of her heart from the constriction and timidity of her yard to the daring of the long dark sloping mountain ways:

Once: if an owl hooted on the hill,
if a male ape leaped and loped

out there on the jackfruit bough in our yard
my poor heart would melt for fear. But now
in the difficult dark of night
nothing can stay its wandering
on the long sloping mountain-ways
of his coming. (*Kuruntokai* 153)[42]

Such designs are not accidental, for they appear in poem after poem:

You know he comes from
where the fresh-water sharks in the pools
catch with their mouths
the mangoes as they fall, ripe
from the trees on the edge of the field.

At our place
he talked big.

Now, back in his own,
when others raise their hands
and feet,
he will raise his too:

like a doll
in a mirror
he will shadow
every last wish
of his son's dear mother. (*Kuruntokai* 8)[43]

Here the movement is from the outdoors (the mango and the streaming fish) to the indoors (the dressing room and mirror), tracing the man's movement from his mistress's house to his wife's, from his bravado to the henpecked shadowing of his wife's nods.

In these poems whole lists of abstract virtues are outweighed by one experience:

I had, as you'd wish,
courtesy,
friendship
honour
usefulness
culture
and a considerate way
with others,

I had them all
before I set eyes
on the cold rich eyes
of this woman. (from *Naṟṟiṇai* 160)[44]

Another:

O crab with crooked legs
I ask you please
do not efface the wheel-tracks
of my lord's chariot,
he is the lord of the seashore;
please
let me look at the trace
of his wheel's designs. (*Aintiṇai*)

The seashore spells separation. But there is an irony in the notion that crooked-legged little crabs can efface the wheel-track of the seashore's lord. Here is another poem on this theme:

My mother asked me
why I wept.
I told her
the waves have washed away my doll
and my house of sand.

The lover has taken away not only her hopes, but her girlhood.

The dilemma of the lyric poet is that he wants to be both Daddy Longlegs and Floppy Fly, as T. S. Eliot has put it. But

One never more can go to court
Because his legs have grown too short;
The other cannot sing a song,
Because his legs have grown too long.[45]

The lyric poet knows or feels it is impossible to write a "long poem" yet is dissatisfied with the small compass of the short lyric. He wants to say many things while saying one thing. He wants to set up not a single resonance but a whole system of resonances while striking a couple of notes. He wants to find an astronomy in specks and flashes. Sanskrit poets set the conventional theme for the Vaiṣṇavas of Bengal and the poet-saints of Kannada, against which these could register their observations on the life of the soul by speaking of the body. The Tamil poets found a different formal world of symbolism in five landscapes and their various contents, which allowed them to speak one thing and say far more than one. (AKR)

Ghazal and taghazzul: the lyric, personal and social

Background

It is from one point of view surprising that there was much interaction between the Muslim literary traditions of Persian and Urdu and those of the Hindus. From another point of view, it is surprising that there was not more. When Islam came to India in strength, it came as a fully developed culture, with loyalties and legalities well defined. The great Muslim empires, centered in Delhi, employed Hindus in the government, but the establishment was such that areas of authority were carefully delineated, and there was little overlap. And on the lower strata of society, though Hindus and Muslims lived side by side in the villages, the orbits of their daily activity were largely separate. On the other hand, there was an aspect of Islam that was receptive to religious syncretism. The Great Mughal, the Emperor Akbar, attempted to found a new syncretistic religion, the Din-i-ilahi, which took tenets from Hinduism and Christianity as well as Islam; Abu'l Fazl, Akbar's great minister, and such as Prince Dara Shikoh were scholars of both Hindu and Muslim philosophical and religious texts. And the teachings of certain orders of Islamic Sufis, notably Chishtiya, were most congenial to the emotional, devotional love-centered worship and doctrine of many Hindu *bhaktī* cults. One small result of this has been noted: Muslims writing lyrics in Bengali on the Rādhā-Kṛṣṇa theme.

From about the fourteenth century through the seventeenth century, a wave of *bhaktī* or ecstatic devotionalism swept across northern India, down the Gangetic plain into Bengal. The movement which had begun many centuries earlier in the south, with the writings of the Tamil Alvars (ninth and tenth centuries), caught on in Maharashtra in the late thirteenth century; the text *Jnānesvarī*, an interpretation of *The Bhagavadgītā*, was written by Jnanadeva or Jnanesvara in 1290. Other famous poet-saints of Maharashtra followed: Nama-deva, Ekanatha, and Tukaram; but by the fifteenth century the *bhaktī* movement had spread also to northern India, and Ramananda, the great *bhakta* and guru of the even more famous Kabir, was preaching against idolatry and that devotion alone is the source of release. And, preceded by the two great *bhaktī* poets Candidasa and Vidyapati (both early fifteenth century), the great reformer Caitanya was born in Bengal (1486).

The primary characteristics of the *bhaktī* movement were four: devotion to the deity as an exclusive means of the attainment of the ultimate goal (the deity was usually Kṛṣṇa, though especially in North India Rama is popular), a somewhat more liberal attitude toward caste and frequently a receptive attitude toward Islam, the use of regional languages instead of Sanskrit for religious expression, and anti-Brahmanism.

Devotional religion was not at this time new to India; it had been stated in *The Bhagavadgītā* and given fuller and more poetic expression in the ninth- and tenth-century *Bhagavata-purāna*. The iconoclastic attitude of the *bhaktī* movement toward caste was also nothing new. The Buddhist and Tantric traditions had from time immemorial offered religious systems in which caste played no part at all. But in the *bhaktī* movement the attitude took a new and vigorous form. The *bhaktī* poet Kabir, for example, has a Muslim name (an appellation of God in the Qur'ān). Legend has it that he was the illegitimate son of a Brahman widow, who was cast off by her and picked up and raised by a Muslim of a weaver caste, who was childless. Kabir was educated as a Muslim by his foster parents, but read Hindu texts also. Kabir's reaction to matters of distinction in caste and religion was strong, but not atypical. One song attributed to him says:

> A Brahman wears a sacred thread that he himself has made. If you are a Brahman, born of a Brahman mother, why haven't you come into the world in some special way? If you are a Turk, born of a Turk, why weren't you circumcised in the womb of your mother? If you milk a black cow and a white cow, can you distinguish between the milk that they give?[46]

There is in modern Bengal a group of mendicant singers and devotees who, dressing themselves in cast-off garments of both Hindus and Muslims, wander the countryside singing their songs of devotion. Some of these songs are modern, and use the imagery of the lights and tram-cars of Calcutta in expressing their contempt for the glitter of external life. Others are very old, handed down from guru to disciple over many generations. These Bauls, as they are called (the word means "madmen"), sing in no uncertain terms of their hatred of caste and all other divisive institutions:

> Go to visit Jagannatha—see there how caste is kept. A Candala brings a Brahman's food, and the Brahman eats. Kabir was a Jola—but Jagannatha, the lord of *dharma*, does not want caste, for he is lord of *bhaktas*. In such measure as one lives by caste, in such measure is he evil. . . . If he does not root this out, he will never gain the feet of Hari. Do not sing the praises of caste, saying "Do

> not touch him." . . . Lalan says, if I could take this caste in my hands, I would hurl it into the fire.[47]

It is certainly true that some of the leaders of the *bhaktī* movement did not understand or care about the social consequences of their position on caste. Some of them acted "on ritual, not individual" grounds: when the scene was religious, they acted in one way; when the scene was not religious, they acted in accordance with their training in the Brahmanical tradition. In *Maharashtra* the great poet and devotee Tukaram (ca. 1700) approved of the traditional ordering of society, and wrote:

> I tell you, O saints, that the different castes have been born of some Being according to their merits and demerits.[48]

And Chaitanya (ca. 1486–1538), the great *bhakta* of Bengal, approves positively the attitude of one of his disciples who refuses to eat with high-caste people because of his low status. Yet Chaitanya can say that the *bhaktī* of Kṛṣṇa is for all people, that a Shudra is not one who is born in a lowly Shudra family, but is one of any caste who has closed his ears to the preaching of the *bhaktī* of Kṛṣṇa.

The third characteristic of the movement was its attitude toward orthodox religion. To the *bhaktas*, the traditional paths of ritual and knowledge, and even that of Yogic discipline, if followed without devotion, are not only meaningless, but downright evil and dangerous. Kabir says:

> O brother, when I was forgetful, my true *gurū* showed me the way. Then I left off rites and ceremonies, I bathed no more in holy waters; then I learned that it was I alone who was mad, and the whole world beside me sane, that I had disturbed these wise people. From that time forth I knew no more how to roll in the dust in obeisance. I do not ring the temple bell, I do not set the idol on its throne, I do not worship the image with flowers. It is not austerities which mortify the flesh which are pleasing to the Lord. . . .[49]

Again, the Bauls are even more outspoken about the matter:

> The Vedic cloud casts fearful darkness, and the day's jewel cannot rise. . . .[50]

> As much as you read the Vedas and the Vedanta, so much will your delusion grow. . . .[51]

> Some say that praying to Hari instead of to Kali is an error.

Others say that praying to Kali instead of to Hari is an error. I have thought much on these things, and have gone mad. . . .
I used to make a great show, bathing three times a day in the Ganges, reciting many *mantras*, performing Yogic exercises, and all I got was out of breath. I fasted day after day, and all I got was a pain in the belly. . . .[52]

It is significant that this revolt was directed not only against Hindu orthodoxy, but against Muslim orthodoxy as well. A Baul sings:

> The path to God is blocked by the temple and the mosque, and though I hear your call, O Lord, I cannot find the way. Against me stand both *gurū* and *murshid* [*murṣid*] . . . on the gate are many locks: Puranas, Qur'an, *tasbī*, *mālā*—such outward show makes Madana weep in sorrow.[53]

And Kabir again:

> I have seen those who observe the practices of ceremony, and those who are very pious, who bathe every morning. . . . I have seen many elders, *pīrs*, and Muslim holy men who recite the Qur'an and . . . worship metal and stones. They have become mad with pride of having made the pilgrimage . . . they have lost their reason, singing words, and know nothing of the soul. . . .[54]

These poets, then, looked for the good in all religions. Their enthusiasm stemmed from the conviction, not unfamiliar to the West, that there was no need of a ritual intermediary between God and man. As time went on, of course, the movement took on some of the very qualities against which it was reacting. In the generation or two following men like Chaitanya and Kabir, the enthusiasm died away, and sectarian organization took the place of the strong bond of emotion that had held the *bhaktas* together. The story is that after the death of Kabir, there was controversy among his followers as to whether the body should be burned, according to Hindu custom, or buried, according to the custom of the Muslims. In the midst of this argument, the body disappeared, and in its place was left a pile of flowers. These were equally divided between the two groups, to be disposed of according to belief.

What runs beneath, however, is the feeling that a man is first a man, regardless of his nominal religious affiliation. There is the story of Haridasa, who was a follower of Chaitanya, but who had been born in a Muslim family of high station. Because of his supposed defection, Haridasa was brought before a Muslim judge. They questioned him, and ordered him to recite the Qur'ān. Haridasa replied:

> Now hear me, lord. There is one God, of all people. Only his name is different, between Hindus and Muslims. This one God is the highest meaning of both Puranas and Qur'an. There is but one pure, eternal, unchangeable truth, which fulfills the meaning of our lives by dwelling in our hearts. . . . The one Lord speaks, in each man's heart, of names and qualities, and that man writes. The writings may differ, but the Lord is the same. If a man is born a Hindu, perhaps even a Brahman, if God within says that he is a Muslim, so he is. . . . Should he be punished for that? If I have sinned, punish me.[55]

He was whipped through twenty-two marketplaces.

It is hardly that at this, or any other, period, all men looked upon each other with respect and love. But at least one attitude is summed up by Abu'l Fazl, minister to Akbar, who wrote in the *Ain-i-akbari* (*ā'īn-e akbarī*):

> It was for me then indispensable, to place in full evidence the Hindu system of philosophy, the degree of interior discipline, the gradations of rites and customs of this race, in order that hostility to them could be eliminated, that the temporal sword be able to abstain from drawing blood, and that the thorn of strife and hatred be caused to bloom into a garden of peace.

It is then into two contexts that Muslim poetry in India must be fitted. Islam and its literary tradition took a particular form in India. Islamic literature was colored by its Indian environment, just as some Hindu *bhaktī* poetry was colored by its juxtaposition to Islam. But at the same time, the repertoire of some Islamic poetry is that of Persia, not the Sanskrit tradition of India. The Urdu ghazal (*ġazal*) is a foreign gem in an indigenous setting.

Ghazal and taghazzul

In 1956 when the question of reorganizing the states on linguistic grounds was being hotly debated in the Indian Parliament, C. D. Deshmukh, a member of Nehru's cabinet but also a supporter of the United Maharashtra movement, concluded a long and angry speech against his own party with some Urdu verses by a Pakistani poet. Immediately Nehru got up and after suitably defending his party's position, ended with the remark: "My distinguished friend quoted a Pakistani poet to embellish his argument; I can only answer in the words of the famous poet from my home town, Allahabad,

A mere sigh, and we get a bad name;
He commits murder, and no one comments."

This very well known and quite typical *ghazal* couplet of Akbar Allahabadi (d. 1921) expressed the late prime minister's feelings more poignantly than any other remark could have, as was evident from the thunderous applause that followed. In quoting a couplet from an Urdu *ghazal*, Nehru expressed not merely his personal inclination but displayed a habit common among the millions of admirers of Urdu poetry who come from all parts of the subcontinent and from all strata of society. Of all the gifts that the comingling of the two great cultures, Hindu and Persian-Muslim, brought forth in India, perhaps the greatest is the Urdu language and literature; and the most precious part of that literature is the Urdu *ghazal*.

In formal terms a *ghazal* is a collection of couplets, each couplet containing a separate thought and being often semantically disconnected from the other couplets in the collection. What the various couplets of one *ghazal* have in common are two formal devices, meter and rhyme. The meters are many, and are almost all of Arabic origin, only a few having been developed by the Persians. The rhyme scheme in a *ghazal* is always as follows:

aa ba ca da ea fa ga, etc.

The rhyme may consist of only one element, a final rhyming syllable called *qāfiyah*, or two, a *qāfiyah* followed by a *radīf*, i.e., a word or phrase repeated without any change whatsoever. The first couplet of the *ghazal* in which both the lines rhyme is called the *maṭla‘*. The following is a *maṭla‘* by Ghalib (d. 1869).

har qadam dūrī-e manzil hai numāyāN mujh-sē
mērī raftār-sē bhāgē hai biyābāN mujh-sē

Each step shows how remote the destination is.
The wilderness runs away from me at my speed.

In it *numāyāN* and *biyābāN* are the two *qāfiyah*, and *mujh-sē* is the *radīf*. The last couplet, in which the poet usually mentions his real or literary name, is called the *maqta'*. There is no restriction as to the number of couplets a *ghazal* may have, but there should be at least five. Originally, there was a continuity between couplets of the *ghazal*; this came to be neglected and was soon discarded completely. Each couplet is now considered complete in itself, highly condensed and effective in thought, and resembling the other couplets only formally.

Ghazal is a word of Arabic origin and is variously translated as "to talk with women" or "to talk of women." As a separate form of verse the *ghazal* did not exist in the pre-Islamic poetry of Arabia. In the Arabic odes, however, there used to be an initial section, called *nasīb*, in which the poets talked of their beloveds' charms and reminisced about the days when they were young and their loves successful. After the brief amatory prelude the poet would continue with whatever happened to be the main theme of the ode—eulogizing himself, or his tribe, or some worthy person; or perhaps satirizing with equal power his enemy. For Arab poets were more often than not recorders of tribal events that they would immortalize in their verses.[56]

These amatory preludes, which in the beginning were only one part of the ode, slowly gained prominence and, by the first century of the Muslim era (seventh–eighth century A.D.), were popularly treated as separate poems. The so-called *Udri* poets of Hijaz were pioneers in this respect. Their love poems were usually recited in literary meetings by the poets themselves or by special readers called *rāwī*. Often they were set to music. Thus from the very beginning the element of musicality was important. These two practices are still followed in the world of the Urdu *ghazal*. In areas where Urdu is spoken and understood, whether in small towns or in large cities, symposia of poets, called *mushaira* (*muṣā'irah*), are regularly held. These *mushairas* usually last five or six hours and are attended by literally thousands of people. And about 90 percent of the poetry read at them belongs to the genre of the *ghazal*.

With the transfer of power to the Abbasids and the migration of Arab tribes, Arabic traditions reached Persia. The Persians were not without a poetic tradition of their own, though present knowledge about it is not very extensive. It seems they were aware of the necessity of rhyme in poetry; also, for them poetry was closely related to music. Beside more lyrical themes their poetry included religious and ethical ideas. This was in contrast to the Arabic tradition, where pre-Islamic poets never wrote on religious matters and Muslim poets hesitated to rival the Qur'ān. The Persians took over the existing Arabic verse forms and invested them with further refinement and a new vigor. Apart from inventing a new form of poetry, *mathnawī* (*masnawī*), for narrative purposes, they paid most attention to the *ghazal* and expanded and enriched its traditionally limited scope. The Persian poets used the *ghazal* to express a wide range of human emotions—religious, mystic, ethical, as well as philosophical and totally secular. The *ghazal* especially suited the needs of the developing cult of Sufism. The Sufis, the mystics of Islam, were not all necessarily poets, but some of them were, especially one of the greatest among them,

Maulana Jalaluddin Rumi (d. 1273), who, beside producing a prodigious amount of marvelous poetry, also established music and singing of verses as an integral part of Sufi practices. The Sufis found the *ghazal*'s lyric tone and love imagery most appropriate, even essential, to the satisfactory depiction of their love for the divine beloved.

With the advent and settlement of Persian-speaking Muslims, the *ghazal* reached India. In Persia it had already reached the pinnacle of achievement, and it was the most popular form of poetry not only there but also in Turkey and Arabia. Urdu speakers, who looked toward Arabic and Persian for their literary traditions, adopted the *ghazal* as their own, and since that time, about the sixteenth century, it has been the most popular form of verse in Urdu as well. More recently, it has been taken up by poets of other languages, especially of Punjabi, Sindhi, Pashto, and Bengali in Pakistan, and of Punjabi, Sindhi, Gujarati, and Hindi in India.

It should be noted that the *ghazal* is not the only form of verse used in Urdu. For narrative and descriptive purposes there is the *mathnawī*; for elegies and panegyrics there are the *qasīdah* and the *musaddas*; for ethical and moral aphorisms there is the *rubāʿī*. It is that which is beyond these more prosaic and didactic purposes that is expressed in the melodies and concise couplets of the *ghazal*.

Urdu critics and poets, in their discussions of *ghazal* poetry, have developed a concept of *taghazzul* (*taḡazzul*), *ghazal*-ness or *ghazal*-like quality. A couplet—not the *ghazal*, for that is only an arbitrary collection of couplets, but a couplet itself—is significant only to the degree of *taghazzul* that it may contain. *Taghazzul* is not, however, just one element; it refers to many diverse features, which combine in a couplet.

Ghazal poetry is essentially introspective. A *ghazal* poet seeks the source of his poetry deep within himself. His view of the world and this universe is purely subjective. Looking within himself he finds everything —his heart is the mirror in which the entire universe is reflected. The external world exists for him only to the extent to which it relates to human emotions. For a *ghazal* poet his imagination (*taxayyul*) is the greatest reality. A story is told of Mir (d. 1810), the foremost *ghazal* poet of Urdu, that once he was given by the Nawab a room to live in that opened onto a garden. One day a visitor noticed that the window on the garden had never been opened. He pointed that out to Mir, adding that the Nawab expressly wanted him, a poet, to enjoy the beauty of the garden. Mir replied: "I am always busy tending the plants and blooms of my imagination. How can I find time to look at these ordinary flowers!"

Like Mir, a *ghazal* poet considers nature only in that aspect in which it provides a backdrop for human existence. Nature is never assigned a separate or independent existence. The external world is always in some way relative to the interior world. The cypress is tall, but is it taller than the beloved? The rose is red, but why? Is it because it has been put to shame by the beloved's beauty?

Cypress trees beside the brook, poppies, roses, and jasmine—
Everywhere, you see in bloom, a garden of colorful thoughts.
(Mir)

The bud has learnt to bloom, but only a little,
From the drowsy eyes of the beloved.
(Mir)

Mistakenly hoping they can catch a glimpse of you,
the flowers rush to bloom, one after another.
(Ghalib)

As we said earlier, it is the imagination of a *ghazal* poet that gives significance to his experience. His imagination helps him discover all the dimensions of the experience; it also helps him maintain his uniquely introspective point of view. For a *ghazal* poet the external phenomenon and his response to it are not divisible; his imagination unites them. Reality, thus, is what he creates for himself from within himself by means of his imagination. This attitude of the *ghazal* poet is called *durūn-bīnī* in Urdu, and its origin can be traced back to the introspective aspect of mystic love that asks the seeker to plunge deep into his own heart and discover there the presence of the divine beloved. The result is that the *ghazal* poet considers himself unique, considers himself and his beloved as the center of the universe or, to put it more precisely, considers his love as the center around which the universe rotates.

There is no eternal theme in the world, Majruh.
But the theme I touch, becomes eternal.
(Majruh; b. 1919)

We never saw even the outside of the ka'bah or the temple.
Without stirring we saw, within the heart, the two worlds.
(Mir Hasan; d. 1786)

The most important theme in the Urdu *ghazal* is the theme of love, especially that of the love of flesh and blood. This love, however, is not what Mir once called *cūmā-cāṭī*, or love play. Love (*'iṣq*) is an ennobling process as well as a vital process that sustains this universe. To the *ghazal* poet, as to Dante, the universe is based on love, on "relationships which exist between all its elements and between it and its creator." These relationships are not causal in essence, but sympathetic. God created mankind and everything out of His love. And the creation partaking of this love has its own unique and vital role:

> The goblet of colorful sights rotates at your will.
> It is my amazed eye that sets mirrors around it.
> (Ghalib)

It must be borne in mind that this attitude, though being very similar to that of a mystic, does not imply that the poet-lover is a practicing mystic in other respects.

Here is what some of the *ghazal* poets have to say about love.

> My nature found the pleasure of life through love—
> A remedy for its pain, and a pain without remedy.
> (Ghalib)

> An increase in love increases light in the world.
> It is the only lamp in this dark place.
> (Zauq; d. 1854)

> There are many more worlds beyond the stars.
> There are still more tests of love to come.
> (Iqbal; d. 1938)

It is love that draws the moth to the flame, the nightingale to the rose, the river to the ocean, the breeze to the garden, the poet to his beloved, and the creation to its creator. For some this love appears in a simple garb.

> Perhaps this is what is called love—
> This fire that seems to burn my heart.
> (Shefta; d. 1869)

And for others, like the Persian poet Urfi (d. 1591), the pain of love ennobles and enriches the mundane experience.

> In my heart mundane sorrows of life turned
> into sorrows of love. Though the wine was raw,
> the cask brought it to maturity.

The path of love is not easy. It is full of hardships, and there is no one to lead the way. The mystic may find a master (*murṣid*) to guide him on the path of divine love, but in the blazing desert where the poet-lover finds himself, there is no guide except his own heart (*qalb, dil*). Those who preceded him in this desert were true lovers, but they were not as true as he is; and this assertion of the uniqueness of his love is made again and again, in many ways. The popular romances of antiquity, the loves of Majnun and Laila, or Shirin and Farhad, of Yusuf and Zulaikha, the metaphors of the flame and the moth, the rose and the nightingale, the wave and the ocean, all these are recalled in various forms but only to prove that the poet's love is far superior in its intensity and purity to them. There is even a code of love that only the genuine lover knows.

My sense of propriety sustained me in my love.
All my life I found gains in defeats.
(Mir)

The dust of Mir settled away from her.
Without love one does not learn such manners.
(Mir)

Life was spent following the rules of love.
We never expressed our heart's desire.
(Hasrat; d. 1951)

In this love the poet is not unaware of his own personality, and quite often carries a sense of pride in his love, even to the extent of feeling that his love is independent of the beloved. His own feelings of love, his passion, his yearning, his faithfulness, are of the utmost significance to him. Like the troubadours, he would even prefer a constant separation to a union that might kill his passion and yearning. His high individualism and his introspection make the *ghazal* poet consider himself the source of all phenomena, of all the relationships that sustain this universe, and thus in a sense independent of all relationships. At that stage he is not far from the point at which the mystic cries out, "I am the Truth."

What is love? What is beauty? Who knows the answer?
But without the cup wine cannot appear, and
without the wine, the cup remains worthless.
(Jigar; d. 1960)

Who cares for the tavern, who cares for the Saqi, let our
selflessness increase a little and it will create of itself cups,
goblets, and wine.
(Jigar)

If you ask me the truth, love is in no way inferior to beauty.
If beauty is what the lovers desire, it is love that gives them life.
(Hasrat)

The elements of innocence and chastity in love have been of utmost importance from the very beginning. The "Udri" poets of Arabic of the first century of Hijrah also insisted on this element of chastity. Though they talked of their love for real people, they never mentioned any sexual act as the goal of their love. Again, like good troubadours, they cherished the chastity of their beloveds, who were usually married to someone else, who always refused to meet the poets and kept a distance between them. In the Urdu *ghazal* the poet-lover is very rarely successful in the usual sense of the word. But, unlike the "Udri" poets, he does not go to the extent of renouncing all desire for a union. He suffers pangs of separation and, like all lovers, desires union, yet he is also aware of the propriety and dignity demanded of him by his love. The goal of his quest is perhaps not so important to him as the joys and sorrows of the quest itself, for essentially there can never be an end to his quest—a union with the beloved does not mean the end of this desire.

> If you think desire ends with union,
> look at the wave, see how restless it is
> even in the bosom of the ocean.
>
> (Ghalib)

Another characteristic of the Urdu *ghazal* is the use of masculine forms of adjectives and verbs. Unlike the Bengali Vaiṣṇavas, for whom, metaphorically, Kṛṣṇa is the sole male of the universe, the *ghazal* poets use a masculine vocabulary even when they are using feminine imagery. Even the women poets use masculine gender for themselves and for the beloved, to maintain the tradition. This may at first strike the Westerner as quite unnatural, but there are several reasons for it. It is not that the poet is a homosexual, as some critics of Urdu *ghazal* hastily conclude, but because he has been brought up under certain traditions. The ethics of Islam demand that names and specifics should be avoided to preserve the purity of the object of love, to which we should also add the requirements of a clandestine love, which was all that was possible in Persian and Indian Muslim societies, and which is still very much the case. This is not to deny the existence of male homosexual love in those days. No doubt it existed. After all, the *sāqī* of those times was not a voluptuous maiden, as we now see in the illustrations to the Rubaiyat of Khayyam, but a young slave. There is some linguistic influence evident also. In Urdu, if one wants to avoid the particular, and wants to generate universality, one uses a masculine form of the verb. Further, Urdu makes a gender distinction; Persian, from which almost all the similes and metaphors have been borrowed, does not have grammatical gender. But the most important factor, perhaps, was that this tradition enabled the poet to maintain that very popular dual reference (sacred-profane) aspect of the *ghazal* poetry, i.e., the love described in the *ghazal* could be interpreted to be not the love for a maiden but the love for God, or the love for the guide (*murṣid*) on the path of Sufi love.

On the other hand, to be fair to the morally inclined critics of the Urdu *ghazal*, it must be mentioned that in every age there have been poets who were not so reticent in describing their loves. There were also poets whose homosexual imagery is quite impossible to interpret as mystic love. But those poets and *ghazals* never gained any permanent popularity, and among them only those who retained some semblance of metaphor in their language were considered superior.

From the very beginning, mystic love was a most popular subject in *ghazal* poetry, or rather, *ghazal* poetry came to be a favorite of the mystics. The metaphorical and symbolic language of the *ghazal* was especially suitable for describing the secrets and mysteries of mysticism. Like the love of the *ghazal* poet, the love of the Sufi is subtle, impressionistic, and emotional; it dislikes detail and the logical explicitness of rational discourse. On the other hand the mystic themes of non-conformism, simple piety, humanism, universalism, self-cognition, as well as selflessness, all found favor with the poet-lovers, most of whom were in no sense practicing mystics. The Sufi and the poet-lover of the *ghazal* found understanding and sympathetic friends in one another.

Iqbal in his lectures on "The Reconstruction of Religious Thought in Islam" offers what he considers to be the four main characteristics of mystic experience:

1. First is the immediacy of the experience: "We know God just as we know other objects. God is not a mathematical entity or a system of concepts mutually related to one another and having no reference to experience."

2. The second feature is the unanalyzable wholeness of the experience: "The ordinary rational consciousness, in view of our practical need of adaptation to our environment, takes Reality piecemeal, selecting successively isolated sets of stimuli for response. The mystic state brings us into contact with the total passage of Reality in which all the diverse stimuli merge into one another and form a single unanalyzable unity in which the ordinary distinction of subject and object does not exist."

3. The third feature is that "to the mystic, the mystic state is a moment of intimate association with a unique Other Self, transcending, encompassing, and momentarily suppressing the private personality of the subject of experience."

4. It is an incommunicable experience in the sense that "it is essentially a matter of inarticulate feelings, untouched by discursive intellect."

While its contents cannot be transmitted, it can be interpreted to others in the form of propositions.[57]

As one looks at the *ghazals* of the mystic poets of both Persian and Urdu one is struck by the urgency and immediacy of their experience, projected through the use of a very concrete imagery and not through shallow abstractions. The high subjectivity, the personal and emotional tone, the mad joy of self-abandonment, the intensity of the felt anguish, all these find expression. The gnostic nature of their love, its intimacy and secrecy, its passionate ecstasy, found expression in a picturesque and often quite erotic symbolism, just as in the religious lyrics of Bengali and Kannada. Just as the coquetry of the beloved and its fatal effects can be expressed only by utilizing the symbols of dagger and whip, so with the experience of the mystic lover:

> Though try we may to talk of divine and mystic visions—
> Yet, if not cloaked in "Cup" and "Wine," they make no sense.
> (Ghalib)

And it takes a sensitive heart to receive the message:

> O you, who are not aware of the significance of our constant intoxication, know that we have seen the beloved's face reflected in this cup.
> (Hafiz of Shiraz; d. 1390)

This erotic-mystic symbolism was utilized and expanded by the Persian Sufi poets, often to a fault, so that many later treatises were prepared by their followers to explain and interpret practically everything mentioned in their *ghazals*. Some of these "keys" to Sufi poetry are highly curious in their elaborateness:

> The Ghazals or odes [of the Sufi poets] are, to those who possess the key to their symbolic imagery, the fervent outpourings of hearts ecstasied, or, as they express it, intoxicated with spiritual love. For every word has its mystical signification . . . The "Fair One," for whom in these ghazals Man the "Lover" sighs, is the Deity; as is also the "Loved One" whom he entreats to throw off the veil that conceals His perfect beauty from view. The "Ruby Lip" signifies the unspoken but heard and understood, words of God; "nestling in the Fair One's tresses" denotes comprehension of the hidden attributes of the Divinity; the "Embrace" is the revelation to man of the divine mysteries; "Separation" or "Absence" from the "Loved One" is the non-attainment of oneness with the Deity. "Wine" is the Divine Love; the "Cup-bearer" the

> spiritual instructor, the "giver of the goblet of celestial aspiration"; the "Libertine" the Saint who has become careless of human conventionalities; the "Tavern" a place where one mortifies sensuality, and relinquishes his name and wordly fame. The "Zephyr" is the breathing of the Divine Spirit; the "Taper," the heavenly light kindling the "Torch" which is the heart of the lover, Man: and so through every detail.[58]

Even if we disregard, and quite justifiably so, such farfetched interpretations, the fact remains that the subtlety and ambiguity of the language of the *ghazal* and the refined concept of love of the *ghazal* poets made it possible for both kings and visionaries to patronize this form of poetry. Besides, it would be altogether wrong to suggest that the mystic interpretation of these symbols decreased their essential universality. The images and metaphors are still highly in vogue, and the contemporary *ghazal* poet depends upon them for achieving maximum communication. Just as Ghalib (d. 1869) deemed it necessary to cloak "divine and mystic visions" in "cup" and "wine," so does Faiz Ahmad Faiz (b. 1911), a contemporary poet with liberal, socialist affiliations, feel a need for those old symbols to express his modern idea.

> Come, Faiz, and speak of Farhad and Parwez,
> For those who are knowledgeable shall see the truth.

The contemporary poet tries to evoke a reality of experience in his reader's heart—for the appeal is still to the heart and not to the intellect—when he invokes the names of these two characters from an old Persian romance. The story as it is generally known in India is as follows. There was a certain king of Persia named Khusrau Parwez whose favorite wife, Shirin, was unsurpassed in beauty. Farhad, a common sculptor, fell in love with her, and the intensity of his passion made its mark on Shirin's heart, too. Learning of these affairs, Khusrau promised Farhad to award Shirin to him if he would, single-handed, dig a canal from a distant mountain to his palace. It would have discouraged any ordinary person, but Farhad, intoxicated with love, took up the task and began to carve through the heart of the mountain. When he was nearly finished, Khusrau, in order to avoid making good his promise, sent him false news of Shirin's death. On hearing the news, Farhad killed himself with his pick. Later, Shirin also committed suicide. The earlier *ghazal* poets used this story extensively to express the intensity and fidelity of their love. They identified themselves with Farhad, and their rivals with Khusrau. They often also compared their own love with the love of Farhad, and found the latter inferior.

> He couldn't kill himself without using a pick-axe.
> Farhad was a slave to customs and traditions.
> (Ghalib)

Later, for example in Iqbal's poetry, Farhad represents a sincere and courageous man whose blood warms the heart of the universe.

> Of the truth of Life seek the clue from the man who broke the rocks.
> An endless toil, a flashing pick, a rocky trail is Life.
> (Iqbal)

There is another very interesting example from Iqbal (d. 1938), though this time the references are very topical.

> So what if the toiling hands of Labor hold the power, for yet the guiles of Khusrau thrive in the guise of Farhad.
> (Iqbal)

Here "the toiling hands of Labor" and "Farhad" stand for the National Coalition government of England, whose formation in 1931 had aroused the expectations of the Nationalist leaders in India. "Khusrau," of course, represents the Conservative party, archenemy of the Nationalist movement.

In the contemporary Urdu *ghazal*, especially in Progressive circles, the struggle between Farhad and Khusrau represents the class conflict between labor and capital. And now the poet compares himself with Farhad, not because he too is willing to make a deal with Khusrau, but because he feels inspired, as was Farhad, by an untiring devotion to his cause. He feels that though, like Farhad, he may fail to gain a final victory, his individual effort will not be completely lost.

A left-wing poet, Majruh, writing in 1951 about the Korean war, curiously symbolized President Truman by Khusrau and Communist China by Farhad.

> Lo, trembles and falls in dust the crown of Khusrau's glory. Lo, onward strides Farhad, crushing the rocks to dust.
> (Majruh)

Thus, even though they have no programmatic poetry and shun logical discourse, *ghazal* poets do respond to their age.[59] Using the same symbolic and metaphorical language, they make reference to the changes in their milieu and respond to those changes and events. The fact of the matter is that in such verses the more common lyrical meaning is not ruled out—for it sustains the universality of their observations; but it is possible to understand at the same time a more particular derivation. Perhaps an example will help at this point, and will also add to an understanding of the concept of *taghazzul.* The story from the literary chronical of Mir Hasan of Delhi is that when Raja Ramnarayana Manzur, a close friend of Sirajuddaulah, Nawab of Bengal, heard of the murder of his friend after the battle of Plassey, in 1757, the raja expressed his grief in a spontaneous couplet:

> O fair gazelles, you know the truth, tell us of Majnun's death.
> Tell us how fares with the desert now that the madman is dead.

The identification of the young prince who died a tragic death with the hero of an old Arabic romance, the identification of the ardor of the one with the passion of the other, the mention of the desert and the gazelles, the fair-eyed ones, all these elements make this couplet a most beautiful and poignant one. Explicitness would have ruined its effect. If one compares that couplet of Manzur with this couplet of Mir, he can easily see which is better:

> Those kings whose feet's dust was like collyrium of jewels,
> I have seen those very kings being made blind.

This couplet has a strong moral tone of a universal type. Its historical reference is also easy to recognize. In 1788, the Mughal king, Shah Alam, was imprisoned and blinded by a rebel noble, Ghulam Qadir. The decline of the Mughals and the plunder of Delhi were witnessed by Mir. Yet this couplet lacks greatly in that manylayeredness that was the chief quality of that of Manzur. The second couplet is more explicit, and though it arouses sympathy, it does not express the extent of the poet's involvement with his experience and, consequently, it fails to reach the deeper emotions and to make the listener live that experience with him. Except for its moral tone it is not much different from the couplets of some of the modern Progressive writers. It lacks *taghazzul.* For, after all, the *ghazal* poet is not so much concerned with the presentation of a fact as with depicting his own involvement with that fact. In other words, it is not the depiction of an external phenomenon but that of his own deep personal attitude or response to a phenomenon that is significant for him. His goal is not to delineate in sharp contrasting colors, but to present a totality of facts and emotions in a muted style, in metaphorical language, in the most condensed expression, with the utmost of musical effect, with the aim of reaching the heart rather than satisfying the intellectual curiosity. And the more successful he is in achieving these goals in his verses, the more *taghazzul* he achieves. It is this multifaceted quality of *taghazzul* that is the secret of the *ghazal*'s popularity and makes it possible for a raja to express his sorrow at a friend's death, a Communist poet to attract and keep the attention of his workingmen audience, and a prime minister to refute the arguments of the Opposition. (CMN)

5 The Story Literature

Introduction

When the lovelorn spirit of Kālidāsa's *Meghadūta* directs the monsoon cloud to his home town in the Himālayas, he insists that the cloud make a detour and visit Ujjayinī, the splendid capital of the Gupta dynasty. It is the city of the Avanti country, he continues, "where the village elders are experts in recounting the Tale of Udayana." This is an apt comment on what the Indian folktale is: it is told by the old people of the countryside, and it is known as well by the sophisticates of Ujjayinī.

The story is universal in India, and has persisted over many centuries. It has also been one of the greatest gifts of India to the world outside. The stories with which the early Buddhist preachers, perhaps the Buddha himself, embellished their sermons and morality tales are still being recounted everywhere on the subcontinent, and many of them have become part of the folklore of the world.

A story cannot be dated. The only datings must be random ones, marking the point in time at which for various reasons a story emerges from the leisurely narrators of illiterate villages into the literary language of the moment and region. While this chapter confines itself to the literary or semiliterary tale, it should not be forgotten that this is merely the visible top of an immense submerged mountain.

Yet fate, together with the delight that India has shown in the telling of tales, has seen to it that there exists a massive record of the kind of stories that have been told from the beginning of this era. Reflections of an existing oral literature can be seen in the Brāhmaṇa texts (1000–500 B.C.), but it is only from the beginnings of the Buddhist period that finished stories are available. It is esthetically pleasing and thoroughly appropriate that these first stories have been transmitted in a Buddhist context, for the Buddha had instructed his followers to speak to the people in their own tongue. His monks did not only that, but the stories they used for instruction were also those of the people. (JABvB)

Gnomic stories

Buddhist tales are now known as the *Jātakas* or "Birth stories." This name, however, does not refer to the contents of the stories, but to their function. As "birth stories," they tell of the Buddha in his innumerable previous lives. In fact, now part of the Pāli canon of the Buddhists, they function as a running commentary of life, its perils, rewards, follies, virtues, and general unpredictability. A typical story might begin: "Once when Brahmadatta was king of Benares, the future Buddha was born as a tree spirit." From this tree, the future Buddha then watches how a clever crane inveigles the fishes of a drying pond into letting it carry them to another pond that he had first shown to an emissary, an old, one-eyed, and generally dispensable fish. Trusting the crane, the fish are carried off and eaten. Finally one crab remains. The gluttonous crane suggests it carry the crab to the same pond. But being wilier than the fish, the crab insists on holding the crane by the neck with its claws, and, on discovering the pile of bones under the tree where the future Buddha is watching it all, the crab strangles the crane. The moral is that the crane was clever but not clever enough. Elsewhere the future Buddha may himself play a role in the story, when in one of his former lives he happened to be a monkey, or the disciple of a brahmin, and so on. In structure the stories are not religious, but in the anthology they function as religiously inspired admonitions about the ways of the world and how not to be taken in by them.

It was suggested that the *Jātaka* stories are the earliest ones; but it is not to be concluded that stories were not recorded earlier. *The Mahābhārata* contains a great many of them, and *The Rāmāyaṇa* is itself really a romance. But there is a distinction between the predominantly supernatural tales of the great epic, with its legends of sages, its myths and sagas, and the less pretentious and more popular stories of the *Jātakas*. It is significant also that the *Jātaka* stories appear in Pāli rather than in Sanskrit. A story in Sanskrit is removed from its popular context; it leaves the folk tradition and becomes a part of the great tradition. Because the Sanskrit language became the vehicle of a highly sophisticated and artificial culture, a story in that language no longer has much relation to the way in which it was originally told.

Another collection, wholly devoted to *nīti*, "conduct in life," is a collection of fables harking back to the older *Jātakas*, and is called *The Pañcatantra*, "The Five Chapters." The frame narrative is that a king is upset by the problems of educating his sons. A venerable Brahman volunteers to teach them in fables the "five chapters" of successful royal conduct. The individual chapters also have frame narratives, within which other stories are fitted. The first chapter deals with the Alienation of Friends, admonishing the reader to prevent false advisers from creating enmity between fast friends. The second deals with the reverse: How to contract an alliance. The third treats the all-important matters of war and peace. The last two, rather poorer in fables, are miscellaneous: On Losing What One Has, and On Rashness.

The Pañcantantra has had an incredible history; it has been said, perhaps without exaggeration, that no book except the Bible has been so widely spread. Two hundred different versions are known in some sixty-odd languages. All the Western versions derive from one early translation by a Persian doctor into Middle-Persian (ca. 550), now lost but preserved in a Syriac version (570) and in an Arabic one (750), called *Kalīla and Dimna* (corruptions of Karakaṭa and Damanaka, two important jackals in the chapter on Alienation). The *Kalīla and Dimna* became the basis for the Western European versions. Through a Greek translation it came into the Slavic languages, through a Hebrew version translated into Latin by John of Capua (1270) into German and Italian, through the Italian version of Doni (1520) into Elizabethan English in Sir Henry North's rendering, *The Morall Philosophy of Doni* (1570). Ever since they have in one way or the other been part of Western folklore. The following story will sound familiar to most Westerners:

> Once in a certain country a sage was about to rinse his mouth after his bath in the Ganges, when a young mouse dropped from the mouth of a falcon and fell into his hand. Perceiving it he placed it in a leaf of a banyan tree, and bathed once more and rinsed his mouth and performed the rites of expiation and the like and set out for home. And remembering the mouse he thought: "It was a cruel thing that I did in abandoning the little mouse that has lost its father and mother. This was sinful of me; because I am now her guardian." So thinking, he returned, by the power of his penance changed the mouse into a maiden, and took her home and gave her to his wife, who was childless, saying: "My dear, here is a daughter for you; take her and bring her up carefully." From that time on she brought her up and cherished her fondly. Now when in the course of time she had reached the age of twelve, the sage began to think about her marriage: "It is wrong to let her time [of puberty] pass by; for this would be a sin of my part. And it is said: 'But if a maiden beholds her flux in her father's house, unmarried, that maiden is unmarriageable; her parents are considered to be śūdras.' Therefore I will give her to a powerful husband worthy of

herself. And it is said: 'Only between two persons who are well-matched in means and in blood should there be marriage or friendship, but not between the high and the low.' " With this thought, he summoned the venerable Thousand-rayed Sun, and said: "You are powerful; marry this my daughter!" But that venerable god, the World-protector, who sees all things immediately, replied to him: "Reverend sir, the clouds are more powerful than I; they cover me so that I become invisible." The sage said: "That is true!" and summoning a cloud he said: "Take my daughter!" But he said: "The wind is stronger even than I. It blows me hither and thither in all directions." Then he summoned the wind also and said: "Take my daughter!" Thus addressed the wind said: "Reverend sir, the mountains are more powerful than I, since I cannot move them so much as a finger's breadth." Then he summoned a mountain and said: "Take my daughter!" He replied: "We are indeed 'immovable,' but the mice are stronger than we; they make us full of countless holes on all sides." At these words the sage summoned a mouse and said: "Take my daughter!" Thereupon he said: "This is out of the question. How can she enter into my hole?" At which he said: "Very true!" and by the power of his penance turned the girl into a mouse again and gave her to the mouse. Moral: one cannot change one's birth.

Apart from incidental and external detail, there is nothing peculiarly Indian about this story and many others. And the ease with which Indian stories could get into some of the most famous collections in the world, the Arabian Nights, the Fables of La Fontaine, the stories of Grimm, the fairy tales of Andersen, proves the immortal appeal of the stories that are Indian only insofar as they originated there.

Nevertheless, many of the most famous collections of stories, originally written in languages other than Sanskrit, exist now only in Sanskrit versions. The original versions have been lost, for the two reasons suggested earlier. In the first place, the extreme perishability of manuscripts gives them a very short life; thus the preservation of texts depended on the willingness of individual people, from generation to generation, to copy them. This willingness was dictated by individual interests. In the second place, in the course of time learned men's erudition narrowed, ancient languages other than Sanskrit were no longer studied, and the texts of those languages lost. An impression of the lost originals is all that can be got, through their Sanskrit versions. (JABvB)

Pure narrative: The Great Story

All the gnomic literature was written partially in verse and partially in prose. The usual pattern is that the narrative sections are in prose, with the moral stated in verse, perhaps thus reflecting the popular origin of the form (most Indians, like Molière's Frenchman, speak prose). The purely narrative literature, literary versions of folk tales, also traces for us the development of prose used for literary purposes. The most famous example of pure narrative is *The Bṛhat-kathā*, "The Great Story"; its oldest forms are in verse, but later versions are in prose. By the eighth century, however, in *The Daśakumāra-carita*, or *Tales of the Ten Princes*, by Daṇḍin, the penchant for literary refinement had again taken over, and Daṇḍin's stories, while prose, are *kāvya* in all but metrical form.

The Great Story, which is attributed to the otherwise unknown author Guṇāḍhya, was written in the form of Prākrit called Paiśācī and survives in two partly parallel Sanskrit translations, *The Ocean of Story*, or "Ocean to the Rivers of the Great Story," by the twelfth-century Kashmiri Somadeva and the *Summary in Verse of the Great Story* by Budhasvāmin. Its original probably dated from the first centuries A.D. It provides some strong contrasts with the *Jātakas*, but also some similarities. Though far from exclusive, the animal tale or fable is typical of the *Jātaka*. It has a rural aura about it; after all, that is where the animals live, where their behavior is observed and likened to the conduct of various human characters. *The Great Story*, however, is wholly urban. It recounts the romantic adventures of Udayana and his wives and of his son Naravāhanadatta and his amorous conquests. Its scenes are those of the real and powerful cities of Ujjayinī, Vidiśā, and Kauśāmbī. This is the romance that Kālidāsa's village elders were so expert in telling, and it shines with splendor, riches, and intrigue.

After the Greek sailor Hippalus had discovered the secret of sailing directly from the Red Sea to the ports of western India by using the trade winds, commerce with the Roman Empire had increased tremendously. India provided the luxury goods for the wealthy citizens of Rome, Antioch, Alexandria, and Edessa—the fine textiles, the emeralds, beryls, rubies, and sapphires, and above all the spices. The silk route from China forked through Afghanistan into northern India and when wars were raging on the frontiers of the Roman Empire, the silk was routed through Ujjayinī and Bharukacha and from there shipped to Egypt. The cities waxed rich and both in northern and southern India a city culture flourished. It was a culture subsidized by the merchants who "filled the hell-hole of royal cupidity" so that the king could surround himself with the luxuries of culture. The stories of *The Great Story* do justice to the merchants. To the romance of love is added the romance of adventurous travel, of shipwreck and miraculous recovery, of fortunes made and lost and recouped on a scale beyond the wildest dreams of the *Jātakas*.

The Great Story, or the cycle of folktales on which it was based, not only continued to inspire the development of the literary tale, it also inspired the theater. While the heroic drama went for its heroes and sagas to the great epic, the fantasies, in which the author invented his own subject matter, were often based on the story literature. Several of the plays ascribed to Bhāsa, among others *The Dream of Vāsavadattā*, owe their material to the Udayana cycle.

But this cycle was more of a spiral than a closed circle. In a culture where the story is so popular, it is not surprising to find that the characters in the stories themselves are given to the telling of tales. At the least provocation a person recalls a tale, so that stories, and sometimes stories within stories, become embedded in the narrative itself. This is the technique that the Western reader knows from *The Arabian Nights*, one which, considering the influence that the Indian story has had on the Middle East, probably originated in India.

In style the stories of *The Great Story* type are sophisticated yet not overly elaborate. The authors are aware that a story is being told that has to cater to the diminishing attention-span of the listener. But once these stories were accepted into Sanskrit they were embellished into a highly literary form in which the point is less to tell a good story than it is to write an elaborate prose, with all the structured devices, save meter, that have been noticed in Sanskrit verse. It is no longer a matter of an hour's entertainment, but of a lifetime of polishing over dozens of pages whose elaborate armies of similes dissolve in the simple statement that a girl appeared at the court of a king.

The function then of some stories was to provide the artist with a simple framework for a work of laborious art; the function of others, an older function, was to teach the listener a good lesson. Some of these edifying stories have been the most popular, for as has been noted, wisdom is, and always has been, loved in India. Such stories must have a point. In the early collection of the *Jātakas* the point is to show the ways of the world, how folly is punished, cleverness rewarded, and saintliness praised. They are entertaining, no doubt, but entertaining to a particular purpose. They are to teach the listener or reader how to conduct himself with a minimum of peril and a maximum of success. A very great number of Indian stories are indeed success stories, or, to put it into Indian terms, they are designed to teach *nīti*. The word translates simply as "conduct," but this is not the *ācāra* or conduct on which the Law Books, the *dharma-*

śāstras, expatiate. The domain of these stories is not that of *dharma*, but frankly and instructively that of Profit. A better rendering of the term, then, might be "how to succeed in life."

The view of life in the stories is a bleak one, but not without hope. It is a life where everyone is out to get his neighbor, where the only protection against fate is one's presence of mind. In one story in which the hero is inveigled into a sumptuous brothel, and he suddenly finds himself in the presence of a dazzling courtesan, he brings his hands to his forehead in involuntary greeting. "A curse on my presence of mind and my voice," is his first exasperated thought when he has collected his wits; "they were surprised off guard, and blessed be my hands which went through the motion of greeting! I am nothing but my hands–my mind and tongue have perished on me! For only the vigilant live, and he who is found off guard is already dead!"[1]

Seldom must the hero allow his mind to be distracted. When he does, and danger, always lurking, assails him, it is his own distraction he blames, not the forces that beset him. A master burglar has been drinking with his wife and in his drunkenness decides in one fell swoop to clean out the city: "I burst loose," he recalls later, "like a rutting elephant from his chair, and with no other weapon than my sword I set out in a fury of violence. When I fell in with a patrol of the town guard I fought without thinking. Crying 'Thief!' they attacked me. More playful than angry I killed off two or three of them before the sword slipped from my drunken hand and I collapsed with rolling bloodshot eyes. The emergency sobered me up and my head cleared at once. In a moment I collected my senses and thought: 'Aho! I am in dire trouble, and only because of my own lunacy.' "[2]

It does not do at all to lower one's guard in this world where no quarter is ever given. A prime minister has framed a girl for the killing of a neighboring king's son; the ulterior purpose is to have the girl banished so that the prince can have her. It all works out, the girl is banished and eventually collected, but her doting parents, naturally assuming that she has perished, die from grief. The question is: who, the king or the minister, is to blame for their death? The answer is: the king who banished her, for he should have been wise enough to know of the minister's plot, especially as he had a complete espionage system at his disposal.

In this world, no quarter is given; no quarter is asked either. Generosity is so precious, so rare, that it is the prime virtue. The world is, perhaps, one big marketplace, where everyone comes for external needs –the groceries of rice, flour, and dried beans–to disappear again into his own private world that is to him his refuge and to others his ambuscade.

Within this world of his own, fallen back on his own reliable resources, he is not only a monarch but a benevolent one. Inside it, order must reign, on pain of extreme displeasure; and this harmony allows the householder to appear benignly at the door to extend his promise of security to one that begs for asylum. "To the one that comes for refuge, let there be no fear!" is the standard expression. This benevolence is more easily demonstrated if rarely provoked. Only in dire stress does the stranger throw himself as a supplicant at the doorstep of another's world. And if he does, the host is no longer the head of a family; he is the austere sage exercising his inalienable right to be without suspicion and to extend to the resourceless beggar the inviolable protection of his private hermitage.

Once one looks for it it is indeed amazing how little happens indoors. Indoors is a walled garden that is taken for granted—except when one has a marriageable daughter who may elope, or an unsatisfied wife. While the modern Western story seems almost inevitably and unnoticeably to proceed within the four walls where a more or less congenial group of people turn traitor upon each other—bedroom, bar, living room, office, elevator, penthouse, stateroom, wherever it may be, but always in an atmosphere of privacy—the Indian story thrives in the outdoors. As indeed in real Indian life, privacy is not to be had, nor is it ever expected. One always moves in a crowd. So much is this taken for granted that, whenever a conversation or an encounter takes place between two people outside the range of interested observers, a special point is made of it. Where the Western author would point out that someone overhears a conversation, the Indian story would point out that no one overhears it.

There is a heartwarming safety within one's house; it is outside that things move threateningly in the night, and even go wrong in daylight. Thus the scene of the Indian story is essentially the street scene, or public places generally, like a king's court or a courtesan's vestibule. And it seems as though the hero, once venturing outside, has donned the harness of relentless vigilence. Having left his haven, he knows that he is out on his own and acts accordingly.

It is amazing the kind of people one may meet in the street. And so various are the characters that one cannot escape the suspicion that the storytellers play on the unconfessed sense of boredom of the listener. Bull elephants fly into rut and wreak havoc. Patrols of town guards, little different from the ranks of thieves from which they are recruited, roam on the Royal Road—main street—assailing the passer-by before he has a chance to give an account of himself. Girls in love, unable to indulge their sentiments at home both because of the lack of privacy and the impropriety of forestalling parental privilege, hasten to the house of the lover, at the mercy of anyone with dishonorable intentions. Thieves are abroad, as versed in making holes in mud walls, inserting dummy heads, releasing bugs to blow out candles inside, and detecting buried treasure as they are in invoking the God of thieves and quoting the handbook on thiefcraft.

Outside, one encounters people, reluctantly at best, who belong to classes and castes whose way of life one has no way of fathoming. Worst are the homeless ones, those unpredictable mendicants who may turn out to be wizard, thief, or even saint, to all of whom it behooves the wayfarer to pay a cagey respect and eloquent homily. All of this is bearable on the familiar roads of one's own country. It takes more than usual fortitude to venture outside that country and to brave strange roads in timid caravans that may disperse at the first shout of the barbarian. But even these foreign trails are still relatively hospitable, for no one would travel far enough between October and June that he could not return safely home to his wife before the onslaught of the monsoon that makes travel impossible and puts him in mind of his pining and painstakingly superintended wife.

Most terrifying, and most romantic of all, is travel to truly distant lands, embarking on precarious ships to ply uncharted and storm-tossed seas. It is here, far from home, that the seafaring hero undergoes his most shattering catharsis: the extreme mortifications he suffers more than balance his lowly motivation of worldly profit, and he may well consider that his *dharma* outweighs in cleansing travail the safe *dharma* of the mendicants who right now are probably begging and sermonizing at his door. The perils he undergoes are illustrated in this episode. A party of merchants is crossing a ledge on what seem to be yaks:

> The travelers bathed and prayed in loud voices to Śiva and Kṛṣṇa. Thereupon the long train of yaks carrying the travelers started along, moving fast enough, yet precisely balanced like a becalmed ship on the high seas. I was the seventh from the rear, and our leader, Merchant Ācera, immediately behind me, the sixth. As we were riding along, we heard in the distance ahead of us the loud clatter of bamboos striking against one another—zing zing!—and the cries of men and beasts—meh meh! and aah aah!—as they fell into the abyss of darkness and mud, terrifying even to a brave man's heart.
>
> A moment later the line of the enemy was annihilated save for one man, and in our own line the seventh from the rear had suddenly become the first in line. Our leader prodded me from

> behind, "Come on, what are you waiting for? There is only one enemy left. Send him to heaven!"
>
> The man facing me threw his bamboo stick away, folded his hands at his forehead, and, now that his entire caravan had been destroyed and he was left unprotected, sought my protection: "My family is perishing," he cried, "and I am the only one left to continue it. Don't destroy it completely by cutting down the last branch! My parents are blind, and I, their only son, their only love, am the stick to guide them. Brother, don't kill me!"
>
> I thought, "Damn the life that is smeared with the filth of sin, thrice damned the gold that must be won by killing the living. Let the wretch kill me. He clings to his life and his life means sight to the dead eyes of his parents."
>
> Red with rage and pale with despair Ācera sneered at me between clenched teeth in a harsh and hissing voice. "Ayi! Stupid ass, have you no sense of time? This is not the time to use pity, this is the time to use a sword! Bah, you and your theories: we know all about your pity in practice! Are you going to kill sixteen for the sake of one scoundrel? Kill him and his yak, and at least fourteen lives will be spared. If you don't, he and you and the yaks and all of us will perish. A man's life is sacred and should not be sacrificed to save one criminal. "One must always protect one's self, with one's wife and one's wealth" and so forth and so on. He read me a sermon as long as the Bhagavadgītā, prompting me to an act of cruelty as Viṣṇu prompted Arjuna. Deeply ashamed, blaming myself for the cruelty of the deed, I struck my enemy's yak very gently on the legs. And as the animal sank like a ship in the ocean of darkness, the traveler who sailed it drowned with his cupidity. We came away from the perilous road like the survivors of the Mahābhārata wars: our thin ranks annihilated, seven saved their souls but lost their hearts.[3]

In short, there is in the stories a sense of adventure that nothing in the rest of Indian literature—except to some extent plays like *The Little Clay Cart*—has prepared one for. The books on *dharma* would prefer one to look upon a man as a hieratic shade blithely and mindlessly observing the ever-increasing list of duties, obligations, and injunctions that start from the moment of his conception, insure his being born male, ritually confirm his entry into the world, legislate his adolescence into pious years of Vedic studies, lay down whom he should marry, according to what ceremony, with what formulas spoken and with what gifts received, instruct him when to cohabit, what sons to engender and how to treat his wife, and admonish him at the ripeness of years to retire to the forest and if necessary to relinquish all his worldly goods. While the books on *dharma* put man into place, hoping he will stay there, the hero of the story is essentially a free man.

What qualities adorn his nonconformist character? The primary one is, as has been seen, presence of mind. He is a man of purpose, even if he does not know what his purpose is. Not at all atypical is one hero who lusts after a princess who happens to be a fallen nymph and can only be attained by one who has set eyes on the mythical City of Gold. The hero lies, saying he has seen it, is unmasked and despicably thrown out; whereupon he sets out to find the City and does so. The hero is unwaveringly consistent in his course. An unkind fate may place him in a subordinate position; but soon his virtue will be rewarded, and he is loyal to a fault. Dedication is the word for him, whether he be committed to his own interest that beckons as an ideal or to the cause of a friend.

His resoluteness makes him relentless, even ruthless in taking advantage of an adversary's lack of control. The hero is one of the perils lying in wait for one who lowers his defenses. The master burglar who fought in his drunkenness mercilessly ruins the wealthy and greedy merchant Arthapati. The moral is not so much that the merchant should have been less greedy, but that he should have been better prepared.

Like the god who can strike, but graciously fails to strike, the relentless hero may also be generous. Generosity is in fact the most prized virtue throughout the story literature, but it has its own peculiar tone. It is less a function of magnanimity, though this is often there too, than of a hero's capacity to relinquish. The word for relinquishment is often used for generosity as well. Compassion frequently, but not necessarily, also enters into it. In one of the tales of the collection called *The King and the Corpse* a little boy sacrifices himself for the king of his country in order to appease the wrath of an ogre. He does this not out of *dharma*, as Rāma sacrificed himself for his father's word. Nor does the nobility of the boy's gesture stem from other-directed compassion. It springs from the self-directed merit of the action: his motivation is primarily to add this merit to the balance that is carried forward from life to life, and the boy is quite explicit in his contempt for the motivations of those who are involved in his self-sacrifice.

Perseverance and constancy have as their function dependability. The hero has a poise and a mental equilibrium that is frequently likened to the repose of the ocean deep that, despite minor disturbances on the surface, remains largely unperturbed. Thus his poise and equilibrium become synonymous with wisdom as it is expressed in action and a man will be called "deep." His depth denotes less the penetration of his intelligence than the profundity of his imperturbability.

This then is the hero of the Indian story, effectively armed to take on the world. And the world he takes on is of the most grandoise variety: it is a vast panorama of cities, courts, underworlds, literally and figuratively, oceans, mountains, hermitages, and celestial regions. In it the supernatural mingles freely with the natural, but often, too, the hero of the story exploits the gullibility of his fellow men and uses their superstition for his own ends. It is in this world that the fantastic, the romantic, the grandiose, which have for so long determined the Western image of fabled Ind, are found. It glitters, and much of its glitter is found in the district of the courtesans. In one story, Gomukha recalls that he saw a large bazaar

> entirely paved with long stones, where mostly such wares as perfumes, jewelry, incense, and the like were being sold. Passing by the bazaar I saw a landscaped avenue of charmingly terraced villas which looked like architects' dreams come true. Then I saw a big mansion, as high as Mount Mandara and not unlike the Royal Seraglio in appearance. Guards were posted at the gates, and throngs of women and eunuchs mingled with persons of quality. Young girls ablaze with pearls and jewelry came out and surrounded our coach, challenging the fresh beauty of a lotus pond. Thereupon, like a wild elephant lured into the stockades, I was led by the courtesans through the heavy doors into the first enclosure; and there I saw a young cow elephant, point perfect at the lip of her trunk, which was being put through training exercises. Entering a second enclosure I saw a tiny lady's carriage and coach and a well-designed palanquin, which bespoke the skill of its artisans. In a third enclosure stood horses from all countries, perfectly built and excellently trained, shaking their bridles and harnesses. The fourth contained an arena of cages full of shrieking cakoras and parrots and blackbirds, and paraded by a troop of crowing cockerels. In the next enclosure I saw highly skilled metalsmiths work gold and silver and copper into various forms and shapes. In the sixth I saw expert perfumers impregnate with incense and scents the materials that in the seventh enclosure were tailored by specialists into garments of all descriptions—ribbons, veils, silken shifts, and so forth. In the eighth enclosure I saw jewelers bore, cut, and set

> pearls and precious stones which glittered brilliantly. And everywhere the masters and their apprentices barred my way to sing the praises of their own skills.

The best way to look at the popular type of the courtesan is as an Indian geisha. In a culture that had banned married women of quality to their own quarters where they were left to the company of their husbands and other women but never of other men, the courtesan played the indispensable feminine role, providing companionship, pleasure, and the delights of civilized life to the man deprived of culture. Her profession was hereditary and often also involved attendance on a god as a temple servant. Her education was strict.

> It is the task of a courtesan's mother to look after her daughter's person from the moment she is born; to teach her the science of love with all ancillary disciplines; to educate her adequately in the art of singing, dancing, and playing the lute; to educate her in acting, painting, perfuming, and garland making, as well as to teach her such accomplishments as the art of writing and perfection of diction; to impart to her a working knowledge of Sanskrit grammar, logic, and philosophy; to acquaint her in profound detail with the vocational sciences, with the repertory of sports, and with the varieties of gambling, both with live animals and lifeless pieces; to make her apply herself thoroughly under the guidance of experts, to the more refined arts of love.[4]

This courtesan is a favorite topic in the story literature. Indian listeners were obviously fascinated by these wicked goings-on involving free women, who themselves might be stars of the stage or concert hall, and urban wits who frequent their establishments as well as their performances. This fascination suggests that the type of the courtesan was a projection of a woman both desired and feared; her licentiousness, which to some extent could be excused by her dharmic obligation to her hereditary profession, is offset by her characteristic faithlessness and rapacity. To get his own back, as it were, the storyteller likes her to fall in love, by preference with a penniless man—the theme of *The Little Clay Cart* discussed in the chapter on drama.

While the more "official" literature likes to show the Indian woman in the light of *dharma*—the many saintly wives who retrieved their husbands from death, who followed them through the most outrageous perils—as striking examples of how a woman should behave, the story literature displays its women in the light of *artha,* of practical profit and wit. The result is a far more human picture. The woman of the story literature appears as a spirited, quick-witted, lusty creature who often can think rings around her men. The modesty so interminably enjoined upon her by the sacred writings is about as common as the frequency of the admonitions might lead us to suspect. If she is a wife, there is a constant suspicion that she might be unfaithful.

Ample illustration is provided of this presumption of her lack of faith. There is one collection, the *Seventy Tales of the Parrot*, which is devoted to it. The topic, not unexpectedly, proved popular, and there is a translation of this collection in the Persian *Tuti-nama*. The frame narrative is a simple one. A man must travel, and leaves his wife in the company of his parrot, which is a very intelligent bird. In the evening the lady prepares to go out; the parrot asks her where she is going, and she explains, on an errand of love. The parrot says that this reminds him of another woman who was able to extricate herself from an embarrassing situation. Curious, the woman asks what happened, and as the parrot tells the story, the night goes by. The same thing happens sixty-nine more times, until the husband returns.

This collection has a common theme. Another very popular collection has a common structure: the *Twenty-five Tales of the Vampire*. The vampire, or *Vetāla*, is a somewhat prankish spirit who at times takes possession of a body. In these stories a king, under an obligation to a wizard, is to take a certain corpse and bring it to him. The corpse happens to be haunted by a *Vetāla*. Undaunted, the king lifts the corpse to his shoulder. The *Vetāla* then tells him a story to entertain him on the way. Every story ends with a riddle that the king has to answer on peril of his life, and when he does, breaking his silence, corpse and spirit return to their starting point. Twenty-four stories are thus fitted into the frame narrative.

In their immediate appeal the stories provide a healthy corrective to the piety, mysticism, and introversion of much of the Indian literature. Overwhelmingly they illustrate that life was inspired by more than *dharma* alone. Hinduism, which likes classifying, has classed all human goals under four rubrics: Virtue, Profit, Pleasure, and Salvation. It is in pursuit of pleasure and profit that we find most of our characters living. And in doing so they give us a fascinating insight into another aspect of the workaday morality and the workaday reality of classical and medieval India. (JABvB)

6 The Persistence of Classical Esthetic Categories in Contemporary Indian Literature: *Three Bengali Novels*

Views of Bengali literature

It can be argued that certain contemporary literary and cultural modes of expression, notably the novel and Indian film, can better be understood in their esthetic impact by reference to the well-developed, indigenous, classical traditions of esthetic criticism; they can be better understood, that is, than they often are when treated primarily as derivative responses to, and in the context of, recent Western literary and cultural modes.

Conventional wisdom on the subject is exemplified by the otherwise admirable *Bengali Literature* published in 1948 by J. C. Ghosh.[1] This is a book easy enough to decry, for its author exaggerates Western impact on the modern literature precisely in order to minimize the classical inheritance, and so justify his subject to an Imperial audience. "The medieval night had already set in when Bengali was born, and it did not end until the nineteenth century. For over a thousand years the Indian intellect slumbered, and produced no new thought or knowledge . . ." (p. 22). The stereotype of the "middle ages," itself borrowed from Western sources, and so useful to Indian romantic reformers like Ghosh, is coupled with disrespect for the modes of "medieval" culture: "When . . . Sanskrit ceased to be a living language, it came under the exclusive care of the pandit. It then became . . . over-sophisticated, hide-bound, sterile, and snobbish . . . it was . . . inevitable that the modern spirit would rebel against the pedantry, rigidity and obscurantism into which that tradition had degenerated . . ." (p. 19). Ghosh finds nothing bizarre then in claiming for modern Bengali a status analogous to that of a minor European literature. "In quality, as well as quantity, this literature is comparable with the contemporary literature of minor European countries . . . its main bulk bears the mark of Western influence in some form or another" (p. 115). This is not so much a conclusion—a "validation" of Bengali's claim to literary status—as it is an expression of Ghosh's premises, and is neither more nor less remarkable than they are. His view of the nineteenth-century "renaissance" of Bengali letters is the contrapositive of his apologetic view of Bengali preceding Western contact: "Bengali was the literature of the common people, and it led a second-hand existence on themes and modes almost all derived from Sanskrit. It was deficient in taste and refinement, in the sense of form and style, and it had the limited range of ideas and experience of a folk literature. It had no prose—and prose is the backbone of literature—no critical, historical, political, or scientific writing, no works of thought and knowledge" (p. 117). It is impossible not to feel some embarrassment at this sad portrayal of Bengali recumbent—a spectacle that is more a function of Ghosh's methodology than it is of the nature of things.

It is in emphasizing the novelty of modern Indic literature vis-à-vis the classical heritage that it is possible so to stereotype the classical heritage as unproductive. Ghosh identifies this opposition at every important juncture: "In addition to the narrow range of outlook and expression there was the narrow range of subject-matter. It will be no exaggeration to say that the literature subsisted on starvation diet in the nine or ten centuries before 1800. . . . The main reason for the poverty of the literature was that it had no independent, secular life. . . . The writers were prompted by religious rather than artistic motive, and were more interested in glorifying the deities and saints of their own sects than in studying man and nature. . . . Being a literature of escape Bengali had little interest in, or contact with the actualities of life" (pp. 117–18). A number of conflicting themes are combined to orchestrate this opposition: secular-religious, descriptive-prescriptive, art-propaganda, modern-medieval, human-unnatural, naturalistic-pedantic; together they define for Ghosh not so much a historical gap as the gulf between East and West—a gulf he has not done much to untwain.

It would not seem fruitful, twenty years and several degrees of sophistication later, to propose to beat the dead horse of neocolonial romanticism. Yet this point of view, however discredited it may be in the more vigorous social sciences, lingers on in certain backwaters of literary scholarship, particularly among Indians themselves, who are also defending their own position as "modern men" in the process. The alternative is simply to show in what senses, to what important degree, continuities of theme and feeling join medieval and modern Indian literature. Bengali does constitute a test; as Ghosh says, it "was the quickest and the most whole-hearted of the Indian vernacular literatures in responding to Western influence . . . its influence still extends over all the other Indian literatures, and next to English, it is the greatest modernizing and vitalizing force in present-day India" (p. 110). There may be some doubt as to the truth of this claim now, but at least the works cited below date from the period during which, according to Ghosh, Bengali carried the banner forward.

Clearly, it would be foolish to appear to deny the seriousness of the impact of Western culture on Indian (Bengali) literature in the nineteenth century. That is not the present purpose. The question is one of literary approaches: whether in fact it is still useful so to overemphasize the gulf between old and new that certain key evidences of the *modern* literary form are misapprehended or ignored. If this possibility can be established, an added dimension of the critical task will be identified, and through such criticism, it is hoped, the work of art itself will be more correctly and sympathetically perceived.

Modern literature is modern in several evident senses, in its thematic and referential content, in the adoption of certain formal styles or standpoints (as in the novel), perhaps even (as Ghosh would have it) in demystifying itself, in establishing itself as a genre "literature" vis-à-vis traditional religion. This has happened before in India. The classical age itself can be seen as the product of an earlier desacralization of language; even during the so-called medieval period, the chief features of the developing "sciences"—logic, grammar, ritual semantics—seem to consist in their separating themselves from the soteriological context in which they had come to be, to present themselves as objective "methodologies" of knowledge, universal, and so, secular. Such a process even if pushed to the extremes that Ghosh welcomes, would not in itself argue against the maintenance of certain basic continuities, any more than the classical literature can be judged wholly different from the epic and upaniṣadic that preceded it. But the crux is: what continuities (if any) can be found within the latest literary revolution; how significant are they as critical categories in understanding the esthetic or literary force of the new forms?

Ghosh again provides the needed entree, this time by his silence: in his work of nearly two hundred pages (devoted to the entire history of Bengali literature, not just the modern period) he fails to mention even once (*sauf erreur*) the chief and dominant esthetic concept of the Indian tradition: the *rasa*. How far is he then from understanding the possibilities of criticism implied thereby! It is true that in his discussion of the medieval *bhakti* cults and their poetry, Ghosh does at least *three* times refer to the theological adaptation of *rasa* that was their peculiarity; but even here he seems unaware on the one hand that the *rasa* is in fact an esthetic category, and is on the other chiefly interested in casting doubt on the poetic quality of the poetry that derived therefrom. "For the representation of feelings and sentiments the Pad [lyric] writers closely followed the Rasa-tattwa. As already stated, the Rasa-tattwa was the exposition of the Vaishnava cult of love and devotion. It was the work of the Vaiṣṇava *rhetoricians*[2] such as Rup [*sic*] Goswami, who followed, and refined upon, the classical Sanskrit rhetoricians. The rasa-tattwa had some good things in it, such as the stages and forms of love mentioned above, but it was too vague and misty to be called philosophical. It had more ingenuity than substance, and was given to the accumulation of petty distinctions without a difference" (p. 60). On the poetry, which we now judge one of the authentic moments of Indian literature:[3] "The great defect of the Padkarttas [lyric poets] is their crudity, their lack of detachment and intellectual abstraction, and that is why they are incapable of transmuting their material into poetic values of a high order" (p. 61). Ghosh's trenchant criticisms reveal not only his insensitivity to the medieval poetic fact, but his view that whether or not there was an esthetic involved, it has no bearing whatsoever on the modern literary phenomenon.

An examination of the *rasa* theory, as expounded by its chief partisan, the Kashmiri Śaivite Abhinavagupta[4] (eleventh century), will attempt to identify those aspects of the theory that would permit a judgment of literary form; three Bengali novels of the "renaissance" will then be examined, to see in what way they might appear to be judgeable in those terms, and whether the three novels appear to be illumined in any essential or characteristic way from this point of view. If they are, it will not be so easy to ignore the possibilities implicit in an esthetic or literary continuum.

The actual agency of such a continuum is, of course, not at all difficult to specify. The medieval refraction of *rasa* in the Vaiṣṇava theologies not only constitutes the chief distinctive contribution of Bengal to Indian intellectual history, but has determined the cultural milieu down to and even throughout the imposition of European culture by the British. Bengal can be seen as a crucial case, for it is precisely here that the *rasa* has most vigorously survived and put forth cultural blossoms; it would be surprising if this cultural climate had not left some reflex in the literature, however overlaid by forms of explicit Westernization. These aspects of continuity may not in every case be taken as subjects of a literary apologetic, but may even constitute a virtue in themselves.

The novels, it is hoped, will illustrate a range of type wide enough so that some generalization will be possible and meaningful. From the nineteenth century, *Krishnakanta's Will*, one of the characteristic works of the father of the novel himself, Bankim Chandra, has been chosen; two more recent efforts, more "refined" in Ghosh's terms, which seem poles apart in theme and manner, balance the examples: the programmatical social realism of *He Who Rides a Tiger* (Bhabani Bhattacarya) and the folk romanticism of *Pather Panchali* (Bibhuti Bhushan Banerji).[5] (EG)

The rasa theory of Abhinavagupta and its application

The *rasa* is a principle of esthetic organization that imposes its character on the elements that compose it, conceived of as means to its expression or realization. The notion of *rasa*, further, defines an esthetic ideal different from those Westerners have been accustomed to regard as authoritative—those that in various ways derive from Aristotle's view of tragedy as the architectonic poetic genre. Forms and expression of *rasa*-like ideals are not unknown in Western criticism—but when they are met they are generally regarded as typical of esthetically minor or derivative genres (as, for example, in melodrama or the detective story). It is this contrast—and not the question of mere existence—that is culturally significant and must be examined in order to justify the *rasa* as important in Indian literary history. The *rasa*, indeed, for the last ten or twelve centuries, at least, has not only been the dominant mode of literary appreciation, but has been viewed as an ideal whose perfection is the perfection of art itself.

Earlier historians more culture bound tended to discount this evidence with a view that pre-modern Indians had not matured sufficiently to recognize the limitations of their esthetic principles. These writers—many of whom were or are Western-educated Indians—are thus engaged in an apologetic of the *rasa* as a partial and one-sided principle certain to be abandoned when further contact with developed Western ideals filtered down into Indian esthetic and cultural consciousness.[6]

The congruence of these views with colonial and imperialistic modes of thought is not emphasized here; nor is their refutation put simply in terms of one current and understandable reaction against such one-sidedness. The attempt will be rather to define the sense in which the *rasa* can be understood as an esthetic ideal in its own terms—one that needs no external apology to be seen as authoritative for an entire culture, an ideal that reflects characteristic positions of Indian intellectuality dominating the history of the last two milennia; and it will be argued that the ideal persists even today and informs many of the apparently anomalous qualities of such contemporary Indian literature and, to an even greater degree, Indian film art.

The *rasa* is a generalized emotion, one from which all elements of particular consciousness are expunged: the time of the artistic event, the preoccupations of the witness (audience), the specific or individuating qualities of the play or novel itself, place and character, and so on.

Portrayal of the events within the work and characterization are thus the most delicate issues before the writer; inadequate portrayal—persistence of elements of particular consciousness—amounts to an *obstacle*, just as adequate portrayal constitutes the chief *means* to generating or realizing the sentimental awareness that is *rasa*. Abhinavagupta is at pains to establish that the idealized personalities we see before us (e.g., Rāma, Sītā) are not understood as the actors portraying them, for the actors experience no grief or longing as such; no more are they understood as the "historical" Rāma and Sītā in the *actual* forest of Daṇḍaka, at some far distant remove from the play, expressing individuated grief and longing (i.e., the notion of "sympathy," union of particular awareness, is irrelevant and would be an *obstacle* in the sense defined above); no more are they seen as gods who have transcended the human condition and presumably grief and fear itself: we do not fall down and worship them. What then is the nature of our understanding of these *events* and *characters*?

Rāma and Sītā are neither the same as the actors, nor of the same nature, nor different and incommensurate. For in each of these possibilities the awareness of the audience remains distinct, concrete, a mirror of, but essentially separated from the dramatic events that are "there" and "then." The audience "understands" as Kant might say, but does not perceive. As long as the audience itself remains a discrete factor in this sense the process of generalization is incomplete—it has not canceled *that* particular awareness that is self-awareness. The mysterious transcendence even of the audience's own form of limited or natural consciousness is *rasa*. In it, Rāma and Sītā are no longer Rāma and Sītā who manifest love and terror, but love and terror themselves, not understood, but directly and intuitively perceived; they are Rāma and Sītā acting out their timeless *līlā* through the puppet gods before us—but their love and terror are *no different* from that which constitutes the very ground of the audience's emotional being. A member of the audience too becomes a puppet in this elemental drama. Generalization is in fact inversion of the "real" condition.

"Generalization"—of character, of event, of response—is thus the key to understanding the continuing Indian esthetic. Many reflexes of this doctrine in the work of art are patent, and amount to a statement of radical antirealism. Intuition is seen as direct apprehension of reality—generalized emotional being; and the only important function of the esthetic work is to enable that apprehension.

As for *characterization*, easily recognizable types help, for they involve fewer idiosyncracies; the personal peculiarities of Rāma have either been filtered out by hagiographic tradition or have themselves been made significant as symbols of his persistent character (bending the bow; leaving Sītā behind). Such types (that they are not stereotypes will be seen later) are known to a larger audience and require fewer idiosyncratic explanations as to time, place, and motive to be understood. Another "obstacle" relating to characterization is that of *confusion*: the character must himself in some sense remain constant, for the play clarifies that constancy as a means to generalizing the apprehension of the character. A character such as Hamlet, who is unsure of himself and "wind-tossed on the seas of fate," gives no scope to the development of a *rasa*, for we do not know what he *is*. The *rasa* is developed, of course, not monotonously, by iterative statement, but by essential contrasts that set the generalized character in opposition to contrary characters and events, viewed as subordinate; and that thus reaffirm and rediscover that character. In fact, no *rasa* can be developed "denotatively" by statement, but only as its inherent contrasts are continually clarified and refined. But if the character itself be confused, no dramatic progression is possible. It is in this sense that absence of change in fundamental character is a crucial feature of the art form itself.

This view of character limits and informs the structural possibilities for *plot*, of story. It will be seen that if character is, however clarified, fundamentally unalterable, plot, the structure of dramatic events, will not appear as *development*, as change in state, but rather as happening, external, having an impact, to be sure, but not provoking reformulations. The chief function of plot, in classical terms, has been seen as a *test* of character; but since it is a foregone conclusion that the character survives the test,[7] through his heroism, his wit, or his virtue, the interest can lie only in *how* it happens: the test itself will be cast in terms that *suggest* its external status: often as mixup or mistake, as in *Śakuntalā*[8]—the loss of the signet ring—or in the *Mṛcchakaṭika*[9]—the substitution of carriages. Oedipus too makes a "mistake" in killing his father and sleeping with his mother—but these "errors" are first of all to force a disjunctive change in the constants of Oedipus's ethical life, when "discovered"; and, second, they constitute in themselves changes of state that cannot be "reintegrated": Oedipus leaves, his physical and his moral body desecrated: he is blind and in exile. Plot in Aristotle's sense *means* change and development—of fortune, status, outlook, in man's essential and individual nature. In Shakespearean tragedy, the change is even more extreme: death (Othello) or madness (Lear). In the Western examples, and in the Western theory, there is no question about the reality of the change; but in the Indian theory of plot, it seems equally clear that change is illusory: the mixup or confusion is resolved; what the characters were all along (and this is usually known to the audience, and not discovered) is realized more forcefully. The denouement of a Sanskrit play or story thus appears anticlimatic: one is led to expect poor Cārudatta[10] to suffer the most horrible of deaths—but in fact an impressive series of *dei ex machina* (in the tenth act) not only save him from being impaled but restore the kingdom to its original, dharmic, rule. Though we often speak of Indian "drama," the very term is counter-expressive; it would be better to invent a term for plots that are essentially nondramatic.[11]

The plot determines the kind of action required. The *nature* of action, of event, in this context, is itself curiously unchanging; it is, paradoxically, a non-event. Since the *rasa* requires that character be inherent, predictable, and merely reaffirmed in the course of the action, it follows that the audience's interest can consist only in the discovery of that character as truth—or put in another way, in *how* the character survives his test. The action is itself extrinsic; action itself becomes the chief (but not only)[12] means of stating and affirming character. Action that is done under the compulsion of a mistake, an erroneous apprehension, thus states categorically that it does not *belong* to character. Nothing *happens* in a Sanskrit story. The character's involvement in the plot is not only *pro forma*; from the point of view of the denouement, the "truth" level, it is often, in fact, noninvolvement; it is false involvement in actions that did not really exist because they do not properly demonstrate character (e.g., Duṣyanta's mistake; Agnimitra's infatuation with a girl whom he in fact could legally marry).[13] The cobwebs blow away at last.

The theory of action is thus easily reduced to *abhinaya*, look or gesture: actions are signs, as it were, stylized gestures that do not so much express the inner, the concrete man, his commitment and passions, as they convey, through a general theory of appropriateness (*aucitya*), important aspects of the latent emotional tone. They signify and are understood, but they are not in themselves representative of the true or real.

This absence of development of character, even this dependence on the non-event, are curious features of most of the novels of R. K. Narayan —the most respected and in many ways the most traditional of modern Indian storytellers.[14] The crisis is just somehow averted, or if it comes, it turns out not to have meant much anyway. A "crisis" in Aristotle's sense is unthinkable, for it is there that the issues are clarified that provoke reassessment, modification in selfhood and character. Particularly interesting is Narayan's use of "American" themes (e.g., Vasu in the *Man Eater of Malgudi* or the young wife in *The Vendor of Sweets*), for even these do not really induce any profound reconsideration or confrontation of values; they are treated merely as irruptions of the demoniac into a settled and self-validating existence—and as always, as Vaiṣṇavite theology so convincingly iterates—if the Demon is evil enough, he cannot fail before long to reassemble the forces of stability. Denouement then is reintegration, clarification of those elemental (and therefore both insolvable and permanently fascinating) issues there in the beginning. This "Aristotelian" idea finds its Indian counterpart in the antidramatic notion of fate (*vidhi*). Śaktideva[15] was destined to become king of the Vidyādharas; his consorts were already his queens in a former life, all made to descend into this earthly life by the archetype of all ontological mixups: the curse. Fate represents in popular terms the idea that man's character cannot change, or at least cannot change very much in this life; *karma*, "act," has become "nonact"; action now is ipso facto superficial and external to man, and can play no role in determining his nature. There is hardly any sense that man's actions, within the compass of the drama, determine or cause his reward; on the contrary, his situation, as distinct from his character, is accident, and even that will ultimately be understood as reflecting, not formulating, his character; and his character is, of course, largely determined by the events of past lives. And so, for Śaktideva also, when the curse has run its course, and he has confronted and surmounted all of the trials imposed by his journeys to magical realms beyond the sea, he finds that the princesses he has married one by one on the course of these journeys are really his queens and that he is in fact their king. The elaborate veil of incident and confusion is withdrawn, and this withdrawal is the end of the curse.

The theme of the curse is most easily integrated into the popular Indian mythos as a translation from one mode of being to another. Character is constant, but in cosmic terms; this life is character seen through a glass darkly. Former or transcendent states of existence are not only true to character, but demonstrate character truly. Even Narayan has recourse to this puranic theme in *The English Teacher*.

The esthetic problem that can now be confronted is implied by this view of the work of art as reflecting, or restating, a more permanent, a truer mode of being than that which is given, and appears to constitute the framework of our individual and contingent existence. The eleventh-century philosopher Abhinavagupta's statement of and his solution to this problem have become authoritative for all subsequent literary speculation in India, and thus provide the key to understanding the persistent Indian esthetic.

In Abhinavagupta, the *rasa* itself is likened to a transcendent or inverted mode of apprehension; it is transcendent in that the character of the apprehension subordinates its own content instead of vice versa, which is the normal mode of awareness. In this generalized apprehension, which is *rasa*, neither the audience, the author, nor properly the actors, identify themselves as different in kind. Abhinavagupta considers here an ancillary problem—but one that nevertheless is important for understanding the *rasa* as a psychological reality as well as a critical or literary concept: the question of how the *rasa* becomes manifest or is realized in the audience. From Abhinavagupta's classic exposition[16] a number of key terms have already been advanced. Abhinavagupta asserts that the reality of emotional life not only can be separated from the determinate contexts in which emotion is normally realized, but is, when thus perceived *in se*, the very same thing as esthetic pleasure. This apparently paradoxical esthetic hypothesis involves an element of reciprocity with the work of art that constitutes an extraordinarily compelling and convincing demonstration of its psychological and critical validity: for, the *rasa*, successfully realized through the work of art, can in fact be realized nowhere else, and in no other way. The theory thus formulates and justifies the unique character of artistic expressionism that constitutes its necessary and sufficient test.

The theory is justified not only by its internal congruence with the work of art; this argument is, after all, circular: the *rasa* is realized by those works of art that alone are suited to realize the *rasa*; Abhinavagupta resorts to the surer dialectical method of examining in detail alternative theories and showing how the defects in each of them, when properly understood, imply stages in the psychological process of esthetic enjoyment whose end product is the apprehension called *rasa*. Again, from this point of view, the *rasa* is a capacity inherent in all men, which requires the art form in conjunction with other peculiar cultural factors to affirm it, to realize it. But not all men are equally capable at all times of engaging this propensity, and so the first question concerns the proper clientele for the art form, those who are by training and sensibility suited, as Aristotle might say, to apprehend the universal.

The classic definition of the *sahṛdaya* ("the man of heart or taste") is found in Abhinavagupta: "the connoisseur participates in the consensus of minds and is one who has perceived the natural appropriateness of what is represented. His mind has become lucidly receptive like a mirror, through effort and constant practice of poetry."[17]

But even when the poem has its proper audience, one capable of realizing the potential of the "office"—compassionate apprehension—this serves only as a limiting condition and does not explain the process of the apprehension coming to be. The arguments of Abhinavagupta insist on the one hand that the *rasa, per se*, cannot be understood as any type or mode of "normal" (given) awareness; it is *alaukika* (transcendent). On the other hand, the modes of normal awareness are in fact "obstacles" to the progress of the mind towards esthetic pleasure, and they are *ipso facto* canceled in any successful esthetic event. Abhinavagupta examines the theories of *rasa*-production of his predecessors in order to identify the nature and kind of obstacles that inhibit the utterly free delectation of *rasa*. Each theory in turn is shown unsuccessful in explaining the necessary transcendence of the human condition, which is the proper joy of art; each such theory reposes upon some notion of natural causation and thus itself portrays such an obstacle. The *rasa*, in this sense, is nothing but apprehension free from these obstacles.

The four writers whom Abhinavagupta criticizes (one his own teacher, it is thought) espouse theories that, as presented, constitute a kind of dialectical progression. Abhinavagupta, by recognizing the deficiencies in an earlier theory, forces us into accepting another, and so forth, until his view is itself the only one left in the field. It was Bhaṭṭalollaṭa (early ninth century) who first tried to explain the production of the *rasa* and his view is a caricature of the "naturalistic" position. The complex of elements that makes up the dramatic work are "causes" (*kāraṇa*) of the *rasa*, which is their effect (*kārya*). Śrīśaṅkuka (late contemporary of Lollaṭa) is assigned the task of refuting this extreme position, which in no way takes account of the audience as a crucial and independent variable. In his view, the *rasa* itself may be achieved by different combinations of causes: but the causes being present, the *rasa*, by some defect in the audience, may not be realized at all. The immense variety of shadings in the apprehension of *rasa*, as well as the fact that the cause of the increase in one *rasa*-emotion may be nothing but diminution in another—implying reciprocity and contrariety in the *rasas* themselves—suggests that a simple cause and effect theory is inadequate. Śrīśaṅkuka's great advance over his predecessor's theory (approved, within limits, by Abhinavagupta) is to consider the causal factors of the dramatic presentation not as realistic causes but as fictives, which through their *resemblance* with real causes suggest in the audience the model reality that lies behind them. The *rasa*, in this view, is indeed made specific to the work of art, for it is the apprehension of the work as an imitation; further, the audience is now a central factor in the esthetic theory, and its capacity to understand the symbology in part determines the successful realization of the esthetic effect, the *rasa*.

Śrīśaṅkuka's view turns out to be crucial, and the understanding of its inadequacies in effect amounts to a demonstration of Abhinavagupta's own doctrine. Abhinavagupta of course accepts the key element in Śrīśaṅkuka's theory, that the "causal factors" are not *real* and that this nonreality is an essential aspect of their effectiveness. But he finds the consequence that Śrīśaṅkuka draws, that *rasa* comes to be through imitation, is surreptitiously another form of naturalism, for it amounts to identifying the process of *rasa* apprehension with some form of inference. Moreover, though the causes are "artificial" they are not in the course of the play understood as such, for this would vitiate their effectiveness: "I conclude that this figure before me dressed in crown and carrying sword represents Rāma, the presence of Sītā, and the words she speaks (though not the real words of the real Sītā) cause me to represent the situation of Rāma's leavetaking, and hence to apprehend sympathetically or secondarily the sentiment of sorrow implied therein."

Much of the subsequent discussion concerns the character of the apprehension "This is Rāma" and attempts to show that inference is unable to explain the unique poetic qualities of that apprehension and, *a fortiori*, of any more complex apprehension derived therefrom.

The views of Abhinavagupta's own teacher are employed to establish the one-sidedness of Śrīśaṅkuka's viewpoint. The radical assertion of Tauta is simply that in no acceptable sense is the proposition "This is Rāma" meaningful, and that therefore, in no sense is anyone imitating anything. Neither the audience nor the author is the locus of the imitation, for their apprehensions are either derived from or manifested through the agency of the actors. But neither can the actors be said to imitate Rāma, for a variety of reasons that have to do with the incommensurability of the actor and Rāma, who is after all a God, or at least a supramundane hero. The actor cannot be said to have experienced at any time the emotions of Rāma, or indeed to have any subjective basis for identifying himself with Rāma (Stanislavsky to the contrary notwithstanding). Further, on the stage, it is dubious that in any sense the actor can be said to have the slightest emotional commonality with Rāma, in other words, that he experiences anything even resembling real love or sorrow. All that can be said, and this is in fact a presupposition that the audience takes to the theater, is that the actor, relying either on *śāstra* or his own past experiences, is able to convey by an entirely fictive nondenotative, "generalized" set of words, gestures, and the like, which presumably conform to those of the "real" Rāma, the understanding in the audience of love or sorrow. There is no imitation, in the sense that the only standard of representation and association used is this presumptive conformability, or "appropriateness" as Abhinavagupta says, of the portrayal and the original event. The original event then does not exist in any sense except as a hypothesis; it is not "real" and since it is not real it cannot be assumed to be the basis of any operation such as inference.[18] The basic elements of the portrayal, the character identification "This is Rāma," are not grounded in the particular conditions of the events presumably referred to, but are already apprehended in their essential meaning as more general than those events. They are pretext rather than context. The portrayal is only appropriate; the character Rāma, insofar as he expresses a dramatic function, has already been transcended in the audience's understanding and represents an aspect of character common to all men, to all trained men at least, insofar as all men must face common emotional issues and live lives of love and sorrow.

Bhaṭṭanāyaka, whose views were presumably accepted by Tauta expresses this view explicitly, and is obviously approved by Abhinavagupta in his insistence on the proper antinaturalism of all art, even the elements which transcend their presumed natural analogues. The notion of "generalization" referred to above is apparently due to Bhaṭṭanāyaka. Tauta's criticism of Śrīśaṅkuka specifies its implications. It remains then only for Abhinavagupta to identify the transition from nature to art as *rasa*, to explain in what sense the elements, now understood as generalized symbols or functions, combine to produce the unique esthetic effect, which like its "causes" is itself transcendent; and finally, to explore the psychological and ontological implications of that transcendence.

The entire drama has now been translated from the theater to the audience; the theater is no longer "object," but pretext for the interior play whose success is nothing but a state of mind, cleverly evoked through suggestion, realized as those latent aspects of the audience's emotional being that are the common and recurrent heritage of mankind. These aspects are implied by and present in every emotional circumstance, every concrete emotional situation, but are never, in ordinary life, grasped in themselves, apart from their specific determinants. It is the function of the play, of linguistic art, so to free the very conditions of emotional life; and it is in precisely this sense that the *rasa* is not a concrete emotion (*bhāva*), but rather the inversion of an emotion; the specific determinants of the emotion (place, time, circumstance, etc.) are so cast as to appear themselves as functions of the latent emotional state, and are generalized. A process of communication has taken place wherein the raw and largely incommunicable stuff of life has been transformed into a device for stating and exploring the very boundaries, the conditions of life itself. The *rasa* is thus inherently pleasurable, delectable, for it is nothing but a possibility—an anticipation sure of its freedom. Bhaṭṭanāyaka attempts to define the *rasa* functionally in just these terms, thinking it a special type of delectation or generalized potency, which are aroused in the special province of art. This explanation has the advantage of appearing to save something of a cause and effect relationship, but Abhinavagupta will not accept even this remaining element of "realism," however diluted, refined, and "transcendentalized." He argues that the *rasa* is nothing but its own manifestation, given the conditions of the artistic work, and the cancellation of all the obstacles that inhibit it, such as persistent memories of and reference to particular historical or personal states of existence, either in the *sahṛdaya* or representation. The *rasa* is not a function at all, but is itself the real basis of emotive life, which simply is, and requires only the peculiar "clarification" of art to be grasped as such.

It is chiefly for his discussion of the psychological implications of this theory of *rasa* that Abhinavagupta dominates the history of Indian poetics. As has been seen, much of his operational theory is borrowed from earlier writers; but the analysis of the transcendental state is developed here for the first time[19] as a unique problem. Abhinavagupta's exposition in its coherent authoritativeness is decisive; and its psychological insights add a dimension to philosophical theories that were developing and refining the basic outlook of medieval India.

Rasa, as a state, is not only the terminus of esthetic process—the reading of the poem, or the viewing of the play under ideal conditions—but is also a peculiar form of consciousness, which though intimately related to and in fact inseparable from the work of art, is, in the very terms of the esthetic theory, more real (or, differently real) than the work of art. This realization calls for comment in somewhat broader terms than those provided by poetic theory itself, even as seen by Abhinavagupta. The philosophical status of the *rasa* is at issue. The general possibility of positing such states of consciousness—real though abstract—is provided by the very philosophical systems then (and to a certain extent still) in vogue, particularly that of Advaita Vedānta. Advaita provided much of the backbone of the Kāśmīri Śaiva speculation. The homology in one sense is so patent it hardly requires extended exposition. Advaita does very little more than spell out in general and ontological terms the theory of levels of reality (based on consciousness) that has already been appealed to in the poetics of *rasa*; in this sense *rasa*, though it is not *mokṣa*, is (or can be seen as being) its anticipation, its prefiguration in analogous but dissimilar circumstances. The inversion of the "real" world that in philosophy is achieved by stern reflection and inflexible discipline is here "suggested" within the walls of the theater—equally a boundary vis-à-vis reality. The homology (it is more than a pretty simile) rests on the theory of persistent consciousness that is part of the notions of rebirth and saṃsāra, but whereas the philosophy achieves maximum generality, and stark realism, by presuming to "realize" in consciousness the basic condition of all experience whatsoever (the *ātman*); the poetic experience seeks nothing more than the realization of those persistent modes of experience or emotionality that are the agency of samsāric transmission, which in their concrete form are enumerated as the *sthāyibhāvas* of the poetic theory. The conditions of concrete experience are in a sense freed from the specific environment in which they normally come to be; but they are not realized (in the theater) as unrelated to experience, as the *ātman* itself. Abhinavagupta, in one passage, discussing the ninth *rasa śānta*, speaks of the *sthāyibhāvas* as being projected upon a "wall"—the wall being the *ātman* itself. The poetic experience stops short of the philosophical: the *ātman*, though close to "explicitude," remains in the background, the unchanging referent against which are played the first and most universal possibilities of human experience, the *rasas*. It is, of course, for this reason that poetry is not philosophy; the *rasas*, though they prefigure immortality, last only as long as the play. The latent possibilities of experience remain in poetry the chief focus of interest, and the emotional multiplicity inherent in the human condition is an essential element in theater. It was certainly not Abhinavagupta's wish by this analogy to hypostatize, to realize the *rasa* in permanency, as the *ātman* is permanent. The beauty of his view is that it both rationalizes the sense in which the *rasa* is possible (vis-à-vis the concrete reality that is its reference), and restates even more forcefully the very transiency of the *rasa*, which is its charm, its *āsvāda*.

And so, in developing the analogy between *brahmāsvāda* and *rasāsvāda* this branch of Indian poetics reaches its culminating moment. Whether Abhinavagupta's "explanation" be adopted or not, the notion of *rasa* that he canonized has remained to this day the chief concern of Indian poets and artists. The sequel will attempt to demonstrate in what sense this remains true.

But we might add, in conclusion, that Abhinavagupta's conception of the relation between poetics and philosophy was certainly not the only one explored or to achieve currency in the eight centuries since his definitive statement. Particularly in the writings of the Bengali Vaiṣṇavas of the sixteenth century, a curious variation, indeed an inversion, of the relation between art and truth was proposed. The Gosvāmins, particularly Rūpa, found in the esthetic terminology of Abhinavagupta a vocabulary that could be used to express the very concepts of the Kṛṣṇa devotionalism then reaching its apogee. *Mokṣa* has not only become an ideal open to all men, recast as the perfection of the most human of relations, love, but this new "emotional" transcendence—*bhakti*—has become the essence of *rasa*. Poetics and theology are fused, or rather theology has become a kind of poetics in response to the universalization or popularization of the formerly withdrawn and ascetic ideal of *Mokṣa*. The real *śānti* that for Abhinavagupta was only dimly reflected in the drama has become for Rūpa Gosvāmin the central issue of the drama that all men act out. Abhinavagupta's own view in a way reflects the growing importance of the *bhakti* devotionalism in suggesting a parallel between ascetic ideals and those of literature.[20] But in Abhinavagupta's view the ultimate reality—*brahmāsvāda*—is still essentially different from emotionality, and not reachable through it. The analogy is suggested by the growing parallelism between religion and literature, but "religion" is conceived through the intellectualized remoteness of the Vedānta, and is not the immediate and compelling vision of divine love of *The Gīta-govinda*.[21]

Rūpa Gosvāmin's deification of esthetics may help to account for the currency of *rasa*-related expressions in the art forms of Bengal, but it does not help to explain the esthetic quality of those works—for aid in which task we must return to the writings of Abhinavagupta himself, and the canonical interpretation of the *rasa* theory. (EG)

Three Bengali novels in the light of the rasa theory

The first of the three novels fits into the *rasa* framework almost too well. *He Who Rides a Tiger* with its presumably Marxist, egalitarian message would appear about as modern or nontraditional as a novel could be—at least in terms of the stereotypes of the Indian tradition involving necessarily the social institution of caste. But the classical esthetic categories are not limited to the exposition of certain kinds of ideas; they have much more to do with the manner in which characters and ideas are represented and the message understood. It would be proof only of their flexibility were they successfully harnessed to an uncompromisingly "modern" message. Further, an important distinction recognized by all the classical writers and emphasized by Abhinavagupta is precisely that content per se is not "esthetic"; it is a "factor" in a complex that presumably occasions an esthetic pleasure, but even this must be understood in a certain way to be functional. The proper understanding of content, along with characterization and the rest of the factors, involves as has been seen a process of what Abhinavagupta calls "generalization," by which is not meant stereotype so much as the realization of another, metaphysical, relation of the soul to content than is involved in ordinary experience. Generalization involves both content and characterization, and expresses a new relationship between them—a relationship that constitutes the real poetic vision and is a necessary prerequisite of the arousing of the peculiar pleasure called poetic.

In *Tiger* we see adequately expressed this notion of generalization.

Bhattacharya's treatment of character and theme appears to involve precisely the metaphysical standpoint demanded by the *rasa* theory. In Kalo and Chandralekha we meet the perfect blacksmith and the perfect daughter; the idyll of chapter one sufficiently establishes both Bhattacharya's view of primeval time, wherein the karmic idealism of the *Gītā* is permanently realized, and the qualifications of both main characters to participate in that golden age (even if it is only Bengal in 1941). The model certifies their happiness; in what follows, neither Kalo nor Chandralekha deviates from the character pattern thus established; they do not suffer within themselves any fundamental change. The author is at pains to show on the occasion of each trial that degradation and evil are forced upon the hero and heroine by the "times," which thus appear in myriad ways tests of their constancy and unbending authenticity, rather than as elements requiring growth and development and revision in point of view. The Hariścandra motif is evident. Famine and hunger force the blacksmith to abandon his smithy for the metropolis; hunger forces him to fall morally for the first time, to steal, but even here the author is at pains to emphasize Kalo's "madness": "His eyes were trapped by the fruit, it gave him an unbearable ache. He could not look away. His hunger seemed to grow a hundredfold. He could no longer stand on the footboard . . . All at once Kalo lost his head" (p. 30). Kalo is not responsible for his fall, which is therefore not a sin but simply a lapse of convention. He is thrust in prison and given a maximum sentence for telling the truth to the judge (pp. 30–32). He is subjected to the fires of torment, hunger, prison; even his first "job" is hellish—hauling away corpses—but he does it all thinking only of Chandralekha. As if this were not enough, he descends even further into the abyss and becomes a pimp—all for Chandralekha—but even more because the times will it: a second "hunger" rages in Bengal, the "hunger of the all-owning few for pleasure and more pleasure, a raging fever of the times" (p. 53). "Kalo lay down in the dust, repeating the questions he could not answer. And the questions spread like some corroding acid over the faith, the values by which he had lived" (p. 52). But like Kalo, inevitably, the innocent daughter is tricked into a fall, tricked by a procuress who pretends to bring a message from Kalo. She even sells her silver medal. A crisis impends, both for the *rasa* theory and for Chandralekha: her proper defilement is impossible from both standpoints for it would involve a real change in her innocence. Of course it must be avoided. Bhattacharya withdraws from the ultimate degradation, preferring a few pages of Victorian melodramatics during which Kalo thinks his daughter has fallen. Kalo, in fact, is the agent of her rescue, proving his real worth as well. She emerges, her chastity salvaged, Kalo reflecting again on his own ultimate innocence. "Society, red-eyed with rage, had branded him as evil when he had done nothing truly wrong. . . . No, he could see no meaning in this state of things. He was baffled. Since they would not let him live honestly, did they actually want him to be a criminal?" (p. 71).

By Abhinavagupta's doctrine of characterization in generalization, a character is not uninvolved in events, but he is undetermined by them. If such a character is saved from stereotype it is precisely because of this distinction. A stereotyped character in effect determines his own events: the plot evolves from the character. Here the emphasis is on the character as unaffected by events, which thus have the aspect of arbitrary, lawless chance, and which function episodically as environmental tests. In classical stories this view of the relationship between man and event is often formulated as error in its various guises: mistake, duplicity, metaphysical delusion.[22]

Without trying as Hiriyanna[23] does to develop this poetic viewpoint in terms of Advaita vedānta, it is still not far-fetched to note the parallels: "generalization" is best understood in terms of what it is not; any portrayal that suggests that the author, the players, even the audience is aware of their particular individual situation is proof that an obstacle is operating. The poetic vision begins where the view of ourselves as concrete personalities ends. Abhinavagupta is at pains to establish that any doctrine of naturalism is incompatible with this artistic form: the poet is not imitating or portraying his condition, his emotions; the characters are not portraying the historical Rāma; the audience does not reflectively appreciate as individuals the particular events portrayed. Generalization involves on the other hand the liberation of character from such precise eventual determination. The characters on the stage are simply a means to understanding a sense in which the audience is not bound by the conditions of its bodily existence, even in its emotional life. This emotional or sentimental realization is the *rasa*, expressed in one sense as the ground of our emotional being; freed precisely in that it is per se and not determined in the myriad complexities of limited concrete existence. "Character" then, to suit the *rasa* must eternally demonstrate the possibility of such freedom; it must be, in other words, changeable only as appearance. Development, "perfectability," historically based, is anathema.

The view of characterization implies a view of plot. Since events cannot be structured, in Aristotelian terms, as development, as reorientation of character, they run the risk of being portrayed in their unvarnished natural state, an arbitrary chaos of pure externality. Order is required, of course; fiction imposes its own laws, but they again appear in a different valuation. The only way of making sense of the world in these terms is as appearance. A theory of levels of reality is implied by the esthetic, in terms of which the character not only tests his authenticity, but proceeds to reestablish it by piercing the veil of appearance. The "plot" insofar as it holds our ongoing interest is caught in the tension of real/unreal, rather than in the typical "modern" dialectic of the achievable.

This view of plot would on the face of it present certain difficulties for the socially programmatic novelist. Yet the general notion of plot implied by the *rasa* theory's notion of characterization explains the structure of *Tiger* almost too well. Though Kalo's moment of truth (p. 77) seems to commit him to a social program—"They hit us where it hurts badly. We've got to hit back. *We've got to hit back*"—in fact that program turns out to be a parody of the plot structure outlined above: Kalo "hits back" by turning himself into a fraud, a fake Brahmin. Instead of being victim of the fraud (as Gomukha),[24] he perpetrates it, but for the plot the effect is the same: the destiny of the characters is worked out in terms of a complexly unreal tissue of lies. Kalo emerges whole from his own deception (p. 243) in what would appear in Western terms the weakest aspect of the plot; but the Indian *rasa* admits of no other possibility, for the fraud is one version of the veil that masks our true character. That the hero is the author of the deception might appear a novel element, for in classical terms the deception is strongly tied to a view of *karma*, of fate, that holds the outcome to be prefigured and independent of the narrow personal interests of the actor. But Kalo, in effecting his fraud, and in getting away with it for so long, is not really exempt from the law of *karma*. Bhattacharya states this in two ways, quite cleverly: on the one hand Kalo begins to take himself seriously as a Brahmin, on the other, his reaffirmation in truth is finally shown to require—oh paradox!—the public recantation of his Brahminhood! In other words, Kalo's Brahminhood, though voluntarily assumed, becomes the very *jāla*[25] or web that he must himself realize the falsity of in order to reintegrate the primeval unity prefigured in chapter one, and which has been destroyed by the dislocation of man and society. Kalo himself becomes an example of the ultimate unreal for Bhattacharya; and here the author has given an extraordinarily clever twist to the literary structure we have been discussing (and shown how forceful a "modern" adaptation of it can be) by reifying the fraud that Kalo has perpetrated personally. The very institution of Brahminhood, for the author, is a deception: the real society, in other words, ultimately becomes the delusion through which the characters must pass to truth. It is this recognition, of course, that forces Kalo to give up his personal fraud, just at the crucial point when it begins to consume his own children, at the point when he must contemplate perpetuating the fraud by giving his daughter to a Brahmin. His personal deception, to continue, must become "real." But rather than travel that path of willful connivance, he grasps instead the truth that his fraud—with its realizing implications—is all the "real" there is; the network of convention he thinks he has been mocking was in fact mocking him, and almost stole his soul away. Fidelity to Chandralekha, as before, and throughout the book, constitutes the bedrock of Kalo's character, which saves him in the end, as it gave him his very being in the beginning.

Though it might appear a clever twist on an old theme, that society itself is the deception that must be penetrated, it is clear as soon as the proposition is put that a more traditional view of the nature of society could hardly be framed. The main force of Indian philosophical speculation for the past millenium, as well as the leading traditions of esthetics, has insisted that such a point of view is in fact a necessary precondition to achieving whatever insight or pleasure is deemed real or essential. For both traditions truth and beauty are characterized by a transcendent vision in which narrowly personalized or "socialized" attitudes of existence are seen for what they are: partial and limiting, in a word, falsifying factors. Even the philosophical position of Bhattacharya is impeccable. Perhaps it could be inferred that Marxism, with its de-emphasis of personal initiative in favor of corporate action, might find more suitable ground in Indian speculative categories, which also express in one way or another not only the qualified existence of the individual but that the qualified individual is properly an obstacle to his own betterment. But this is a proposition that makes no sense in a value system that sees no category more ultimate than the "worth" of each particular man per se.[26]

If *Tiger* is considered an almost embarrassingly dramatic illustration of Hiriyanna's first or lower type of *rasa*-inspired art work,[27] one in which the categories of the *rasa* define the structure but in which the *rasa* itself is subordinated to the expression of an "objective factor," a content or message, *Pather Panchali* is an example of Hiriyanna's second or higher type of *rasa* poetry, in which no theme apart from the fundamental emotional tone of the work serves as unifying factor.[28] And this indeed seems to explain much of the evident difference between the two works, perhaps more coherently than the usual discussions of style and thematic realism. For in *Tiger*, whatever correspondences with the expectations of the classical esthetics are elicited, it would be difficult to say in which sense this work justifies the *rasa* theory. The plain fact is that it does not; yet the theory makes provision for and adequately explains the force of such works. Though *Tiger* strives not for the expression of a *rasa*, it is nevertheless understood how the requirements of the *rasa*, generalization, levels of reality, fate, and the like, are employed for another purpose, which is in the broadest sense to tell a story, and here specifically, to demonstrate the falseness of Brahminhood. That idea, as specific content, dominates the work, and it is in this sense that Abhinavagupta allowed this kind of "poem" a subordinate place in the poetic universe. The categories of *rasa*, the *rasa* itself in effect, are used to convey a specific idea, of intellectual substance, intelligible apart from the work of art. If it be asked what *rasa* is so subordinated, the reply might be *bībhatsā*, loathing, disgust.

To observe the *rasa* in a more congenial milieu, wherein it is worked out in its own terms and for itself, one must turn to what for the classical esthetician was pure art, as opposed to applied art. Pure art has no other purpose than to arouse in the beholder that peculiar form of pleasurable excitement that is in one sense the very ground or possibility of all emotional experience, but is in another demonstrable in no other way than by the work of art itself; the experience thus constitutes its characteristic function. It is the glory of *Pather Panchali*, in the fine translation by T. W. Clark and Tarapada Mukherji, to have expressed as few other modern works the excellences implicit in the classical esthetic form. As in *Tiger*, the "modern" world is not left in sterile opposition to the "traditional" but is used in deft and knowing fashion to show that the opposition itself need not be final: a "modern" theme, intensely vivid because the expressive capacities of an ancient, timeless form are released from the bondage of dated conventions.

The novel, Banerji's only really successful effort,[29] owes its distinctive charm not, as would be supposed, from Satyajit Ray's film version, to its authentic and unvarnished portrayal of village life, but rather to its unique point of view, which is that of a small boy, Opu, growing into consciousness. The recurring theme is the boy's awakening awareness of the world around him, on the one hand expressed extensively, as his field of experience becomes increasingly differentiated, but also intensively, as each new "limit" serves to focus more sharply the boy's overriding sense of the wonder in life.

The banyan or the bamboo outside the porch is associated with the ancient epic legends the mother tells her infant child: ". . . Opu's young heart was stricken with grief, and there was no holding back the tears . . . but as he wept there was born in his mind a sympathetic insight he had not experienced, and with it a feeling of happiness, happiness that comes of weeping for another's sorrow. There is a road through life which leads to compassion . . . and the signposts which pointed the way for Opu were the midday sun, the musty smell which spread through the air from the torn pages of that old book, and the gentle music of his mother's voice. . . . Opu went out and stood on the verandah, staring at the distant banyan tree. . . . More than anything else, it was the sight of the tree stained with the red colors of evening that filled his mind with grief; and in the far distance, beyond the banyan, where the sky leant down to the earth, he could see Karna, his hands laboring to drag the chariot wheels out of the mud. . . . Karna, the mighty hero, the object of a pity which could never end" (pp. 75–76). The village itself defines the familiar world, in one sense, and all beyond is marvelous: "All he knew was a little plot of land with trees all round it, . . . but outside this tiny circle was the ocean of the unknown, endless and unfathomable, where there was no bottom the feet of a child could stand on" (p. 117). Mount Prasravan, site of Sītā's exile, for a moment becomes the center of that beyond, and such marvelous objects as the distant railway line symbolize the familiar limit and the boundary: " 'The railway line?' he echoed. 'But it's a very long ways off, isn't it, Didi? How can we possibly go as far as that?' . . . 'I can't see anything,' said Opu. 'How shall we get back home if we get too far?' But his eyes were peering thirstily into the distance" (p. 133). The two children run and run and run; they pass the limits of the known: "For the first time in his life he was really free, free of all 'don'ts,' free of the restrictions of the small circle which had hitherto imprisoned him; and his young blood thrilled to the joy of release" (p. 134).[30]

The beauty of the rural Bengali countryside, just like the pathos of the old epic, becomes for Opu a moment of awakening, an aspect of the boundary of the marvelous. But it is not the developing self of the child that interests the author; this is not Proust savoring subjectively each morsel of outwardness—it is rather the non-self, the other, that is evoked artfully by the focus on the familiar, much as the pebble is chiefly seen in the ever-widening circle of ripples that divides it from the still water.

Opu's wonder becomes more concrete as he grows older, but the ancient myth and the ever-present landscape never lose their spell (p. 283); Opu tests again his thirst in the realms of literature ("The Lotus and the Princess, the Bandit's Daughter, Poisoned Nectar, The Mystery of Gopeshvar" (p. 265)) and history. Opu finds in Jeanne d'Arc a reflection partly of his own innocence, partly a souvenir of the eternally foredoomed valor of Karna (p. 270).

To speak of awareness itself as the theme of a novel may appear paradoxical; yet it is fundamentally consonant with the *rasa* theory of art. It was a stroke of genius for Banerji to select a child as his protagonist, for in the child's mind all things happen in a timeless continuum of nearly pure significance.[31] From one point of view, the adult *sahṛdaya*, or the adult philosopher, seeks nothing so much as the reintegration of the honesty and selfless immediacy of the child. Banerji has captured the sense in which the adult world, the world we take for granted, is for the child, as well as for the eternally innocent, an inexplicable happening, a limitation, but at the same time a powerful stimulus to mythologize and make significant. In this novel, what appears as the veil of falsehood counterbalancing the verity of character is nothing so concrete as a particular social system (Brahmanism); it is the eternal fraud of being an adult: being on the other side of the boundary.

The nature of the veil is expressed by Banerji in terms that are not strictly those of a child; yet his view of the adult world is not inconsistent with his protagonist's point of view. The reader is only too aware of the acute sufferings and disappointments, of the all-too-human inadequacies, of the parents' lives, and Banerji is alert to contrast the brief moments of happiness with the inevitable succession of pain and terror: "A wave of gladness broke over her [Durga's] heart, the wedding was so near now. There would be the night watch in Ranu's sister's room, and there would be songs which she hoped they would let her stay to hear. She was so happy she felt like running right across the open fields. . . . If only she could fly!" (p. 183). But immediately the contrast: "Ahead of her, not far away, a bullock cart creaked its way along a rough track which led across the plain in the direction of Shonadanga. . . . Inside a little girl was crying with a thin high-pitched wail. It was probably some peasant's daughter being taken from home to live in her father-in-law's house. . . . If she got married it would be like that with her. She would have to leave her mother and father, and Opu" (p. 184). The adult world, heralded by marriage perhaps, its initiatory ritual, is an inextricable skein of pleasures and pains, without any certain rationale. It is this latter qualification that marks Banerji's work as traditional, and it is in this sense that his view of the adult world, though more sophisticated than Bhattacharya's, was not inconsistent with the child's outlook. For the child, as well as the philosopher, a thing is not judged in terms of its consequences; a man does not act with a view to his responsibilities; sequential action chains represent bondage, but the moments in them exist; and it is Banerji's thesis perhaps that they exist more truly as random and necessary moments in an inexplicable whole called life. As one of the minor characters says, ". . . there's nothing we can do about it. . . . To tell her the truth would only lead to a quarrel" (p. 290).

The rages of their mother, Shorbojoya, as well as the transports of the two children appear equally unmotivated, or rather equally unprovoked, for the motivation seems grounded in the constants of character-based relationships, not in the circumstances of the emotional manifestation. Her unreasoning, cruel anger at the old woman who comes "home" to die (p. 56) is to be understood not so much as blameworthy—implying a circumstantial personal relationship as locus—as an instance in extremis of the elemental irruption of passion that is founded in character itself. But the father, Horihor, also has "character" in this sense, though its leading themes are his ineffectuality and his intellectuality: he is certain to muff his opportunities—if indeed they exist outside his imagination. The "decision" with which the book closes, one of the few that actually proposes to change something, is intended more for its ominous than for its hopeful overtones. Still he is not pictured as a bumbler—that would too obviously attribute his faults to his circumstantial actions—he is, to cite the old saw, a person enjoying the fruits of his former existences.

It is to emphasize this view of adult life structured by its inherent sorrows and joys that Banerji begins his story of childhood with an account of old age and hopeless death; for out of Indir's ashes arises the joy of Opu. Opu sees, but does not yet reflect, the world of opposites, and is thus (as is every child) a harbinger of liberation itself, as the *Gītā* says. The book, structurally, is not quite finished; one continues to wonder whether Horihor will, as we expect, find his hopes dashed in Benares, thus reintegrating the "original condition" of the old aunt—one generation later. But the translators as well as Satyajit Ray have chosen to truncate the book in terms of a dramatic esthetic that does not have much to do with the book itself: the last "path" must be kept open ended, says the translator, for the book is about a series of paths—"a road broken into a series of stretches divided from one another by bends which conceal what lies ahead" (pp. 13–14). It is only too clear what lies ahead; Banerji's traditional view of character makes the action a demonstration of character at first implicit, then manifest, but never "final"—except in the sense that life itself has an end. The important thing, for the plot, is that nothing done really leads to anything else, in sequential historicistic time. The great "event" of the book in these terms is the death of Durga, which Banerji takes great care to convey with all the ominous mood forebodings at the command of the Indian poet: Horihor is inexplicably absent, his family left without means of sustenance; a great autumn storm terrifying in its elemental fury, devastating to the defenseless inhabitants of the old house, brings the end near in a crescendo of horror. The total view of this "event" is thus more a view of its cosmic implications than its medical sequence; and this death is even more "inexplicable" morally, for the girl is a free spirit, embodying with her forest escapades and her love of natural things as antisocial an attitude as would be demonstrable in a Bengali village. Even her propensity to steal—about which others' doubts were resolved by the discovery of the golden box after her death—is judged in this light, for she steals "possessions" just as she collects leaves of the forest, for their intrinsic loveliness. The visit of death to such a one in her first bloom is again proof that the happenings of the story are not significant in the plot structure; perhaps Durga's death means, if it is more than mere randomness, that such a free spirit cannot possibly "grow up," cannot accept or come to terms with her concrete social character, which is the prison of adulthood.

The view of adult character as pleasure and pain determining their occasions thus explains the structure of the work itself, and again identifies it as consistent with the traditional esthetic. Again, a modern "twist" is most convincingly appended, for the "veil" of seeming consequent action is not in terms of some simple-minded mythology baldly projected on a more ultimate plane of reality, such as that of the *vidyādharas* in "The City of Gold."[32] It is not transcended in a final termination of the curse of partial vision—here, the curse is growing up itself—and we are left to wonder whether the veil of adult life, that we suffer for our pleasures, will ever again be rent apart and the child's immediate and percipient penetration of the very sense of things will ever again be realized. Possibly it will be, at the end of life, but not by such as the old aunt or Horihor or Shorbojoya, for they have become victims of their suffering.

Nor is the episodic plot a weakness. In the higher forms of *rasa*, where an emotional communion of a certain sort is the coherent unity, the ground, and the goal of the work, the notion of action objective, rationalized, suited to and exhausted by cause and effect, vanishes. Actions are not so much caused as motivated by other actions. Or better, they become outward signs of a reality that provokes and sustains all, yet cannot become more explicit except through action. The *Gītā* says blessed is he who gives not a damn, yet does his duty. Opu and Durga exemplify such activity before it succumbs to the onslaughts of adult rationalization. Children make their own toys. Plots make their own episodes.

This work is hardly that of a "naïve genius" (p. 16) in the sense that the translator attributes to the term, at least; for his view is that Banerji has achieved success without really understanding why—and so goes on storytelling after his story is over, keeping up the skein of episodes after their "dramatic" force has been exhausted—"His naïve genius could not have realized the dramatic quality of his creation." In the portion of the book presented in this translation, there is no modern example of a literary work more totally and responsibly coherent to its esthetic ideal. The art form not only continues, it prospers, and grows stronger with new challenges.

In *Pather Panchali*, then, Hiriyanna's and Abhinavagupta's notions of high *rasa* art are observed to perfection. Again, characterization is carefully expressed as undetermined by events, which thus have ontologically a status of chaotic outwardness of which esthetic sense can be made only in terms of a theory of appearance, as test and touchstone of character. We have spoken of events, of plot, as a veil, through which the characters do not so much progress as achieve rediscovery, a discovery of what they were, in fact, all along. The plot itself is thus reduced to appearance, and the possibility of "dramatic" development is absent. But what of the esthetic result itself? In *Pather Panchali*, the generalized standpoint is that of a child; the effect, the *rasa*, can be nothing else than the sympathetic translation of the everyman in us back to that state that preceded involvement, wherein all things were understood for what they were and not for what they could profit us. Banerji's *défi* has been first to amalgamate the esthetic standpoint of pure *rasa* with the social proposition that such a standpoint is naturally manifest in a child's outlook. In precisely the same terms as the *bhakti* cults wed beauty and truth, poetry and love, art is wedded to nonart: "There is a vow which leads man to serve at the shrine of beauty for ever; and slowly, without knowing what he was doing, open-hearted Nature had led Opu to take that vow" (p. 283). "Day by day, as the years of his childhood passed, Opu had walked with Nature. . . . Ever since he was born Nature's vast and lovely canvas had been spread before his eyes" (p. 283). Second, the classical form is somewhat distorted, for the generalized emotion is realized more perfectly in the audience than in the character of Opu for the simple reason that they can see him in themselves, but he cannot see them in him. Still, this is implicit in the attempt to recapture the wonder of childhood in art. The deficiency, if it is one, may also have prompted Banerji to attempt the sequels, wherein Opu loses, then regains, his view of the world[33]; the trilogy is thus more complete, esthetically, than this first part. But all its elements are present in each.

No message constitutes the aim of this work; the emotional medium itself, purged of individual consciousness in the ways indicated, alone serves as esthetic effect. Doubtless the sense of wonder and joy at being alive is very close to this effect, and of the classical *rasas*, *adbhuta* (wonder at the marvelous) is most clearly expressed. Still, the *rasa*, generalized emotional consciousness, awareness of the grounds of emotion itself, is in a way modernized, as it was in *Tiger*, by being interwoven with themes of descriptive reality such as a contemporary Indian would admit as such. Opu is not about to pass beyond the veil of circumstances, as did Śaktideva, but he is about to learn that he must discipline them to his inner vision and remain, in some sense, forever a child.

Krishnakanta's Will can be discussed briefly, for it is not a very good work of art and does not lead us far in these speculations. But its defects are not so much a function of its thoughtless retention of traditional Indian stereotypes as they are due to Bankim Chandra's eclectic and imperceptive adoption of Western stylistic techniques that sit ill within the basic Indian esthetic framework, present here too in its entirety. The characters of the novel turn out to be inexplicable in either a dramatic or a timeless esthetic, for having introduced them as paragons of fidelity and honor, the author makes Govindalal run away from his wife and take up with a concubine, only to shoot her in the head (with a pistol!), and further to escape justice (de jure) by becoming an ascetic; Rohini is prompted by remorse at her original sin, caught and punished more severely for her virtue than for her sin, and is finally shot by her lover. Throughout these inexplicable alterations of character, for which the reader is never prepared, and which violate the sensibilities of the *sahṛdaya* (for there is not a single character of irreproachable constancy) the oldest tricks are employed. No change ever takes place *en pleine conaissance de cause*: it is provoked by rumor, backbiting, deception. The tissue of lies, rather than testing character, disaggregates it, and this is consistent with the demands of neither East nor West; the former understands not the changes, the latter condemns the antinaturalism and superficiality of the plot. There is here a far greater reliance (however superficial in appearance) on Sir Walter Scott than on medieval Vaishnavism; still, Bankim Chandra could not bring himself to part with the usual pyrotechnics of the Indian plot, which were doubtless pronounced in the folk dramas of the period. But in attempting to deal with character in Western terms—he appears to understand only that change for its own sake is the rock upon which the romantic West stands—his works fall between two stools; the trials *are* fictitious, yet character disintegrates. (EG)

7 The Modern Hindi Short Story and Modern Hindi Criticism

Most of what the reader has seen to this point suggests that there is a strong continuity between classical literature and criticism and contemporary writing. But, when writing about India, one cannot afford to oversimplify. We will have failed if we have not made it clear to the reader that at no point is there anything that can be identified as *the* Indian tradition. There are always many traditions, sometimes seeming to work in conflict with one another, but always somehow resulting in a viable synthesis.

So it is with modern Indian literature. As this chapter shows, contemporary critics of Hindi fiction do not see themselves in quite the same way as the writers of this book, most of them non-Indian, might be inclined to see them. Throughout the book, the attempt has been to allow the literature to speak for itself. This final chapter lets the writers of literature and its critics speak for themselves, and what they say does not sound like what the reader of this book might have been led to expect. It is true that one attempt of the contemporary Hindi writer is "the depiction of moods," a concept that will sound familiar to the reader, and that this in fact sounds like a reversion to older forms, a moving away from plot-centered stories that might be taken to represent more modern tendencies. But at the same time, the stress on originality and "realism" might come as a surprise to the reader who has accepted the argument of the book thus far. Nothing is simple in India, and the editors feel that the assessment of Hindi fiction offered in this chapter might help to redress the balance of an argument consciously weighted on the side of traditional and classical values. As for a precise formulation of where contemporary Indian literature stands in relation to the tradition-modernity conflict, the reader is left to make that formulation for himself, if he cares to do so.

Although the subject of the chapter is a particular genre in one of many languages, here as elsewhere in the book, the particular is considered a paradigm for much larger statements. What is true for Hindi fiction might not be true in detail for Bengali or Tamil, and what is true for the short story might not be exactly the case in poetry or drama; but despite its diversity and the unique traditions of each of the regional languages, India is on another level still a cultural unity. The same forces, the same stresses, have worked on all parts of the subcontinent, and the solutions of these have been more often than not similar. "Indian writing," a recent sage has said, "is what is written by Indians." That is one of the points of this book.

—The editors

An introduction to a literary genre in a modern Indian language and to its recent criticism may help to temper expectations of extensive continuity between early and modern Indian literature. Undoubtedly early Indian literature can at times be seen reflected, clearly or dimly, in nineteenth- and twentieth-century Indian writing. And at times an understanding of the early literature can certainly help to illuminate one's understanding of modern literature, through both similarities and contrasts. Traditional imagery, a love of word-sounds, an interest in arousing esthetic sentiments, an awakening of familiar responses can all be found in certain modern literary and also in much of the early Indian literature. Similar connections could also be made with the use of nature to reflect human states of mind, the presentation of such characters as the hypocritical ascetic, the narration of romantic adventures, and the vivid description of sexual exploits.

The role of cultural continuity perhaps needs to be recognized as helping to sustain certain types of literary continuity. The modern writer who breaks with "purely literary" conventions seems less likely to arouse hostility than one who also breaks with basic cultural patterns. When a poet is seen by society and by himself as a torchbearer, his work is likely to reflect those cultural and literary expectations. A modern poet who sees himself as a pallbearer would inevitably move away from traditional literary and cultural expectations. A modern fiction-writer who skillfully describes feelings but does little with analyzing motivations could be seen as reflecting the persistence of a total cultural milieu that incidentally has led also to a persistence of certain traditional literary elements. In a culture that is more philosophically than psychologically oriented, a modern writer who delves into psychological analysis runs some risk of being charged with writing imitative Freudian case histories; and a modern writer who deals with alienation is likely to be accused at times of pandering to a derivative taste for fashionable, Western, or salable themes.

Whereas literary or cultural continuities may be striking to many Western readers, the discontinuities may appear more striking to many Indian readers of modern literature. A relatively recent Hindi novel, for example, translated as *To Each His Stranger*, has been described by many Westerners as "so Indian I can't really understand it" and by many Indians as "so Western I can't really understand it." The modern Indian writer may find himself in a peculiar no-man's-land, being not quite traditional enough for his local audience and not quite universal enough for a world audience. The Indian audience would probably exert the most immediate pressure, leading a writer such as Shrikant Varma to declare that

> The sense of non-belonging has made the modern Indian poet a stranger in his own land. He speaks a language which is absurd to the people. His conception of the world is irrational. His vision is limited and his understanding is only immediate. The only thing that makes him significant is his assessment of his own destiny, his acceptance of death, and his power to reject.[1]

One young Hindi writer and critic suggested in 1965 that in the previous decade stories had been discussed as much or more than they had been written. The need for such extensive discussion can perhaps be traced not only to new interest in the story genre but also to an attempt to justify the direction in which that genre had been moving, a direction not generally acceptable to writers or readers whose cultural and literary patterns were more in line with traditional expectations.

In the Hindi literary world since Independence, the short-story genre has become a primary focus of attention. Heightened critical interest in the story since Independence is partly attributable to the fact that "new poetry" fought for and largely won critical acceptance, and that the novel and drama have been less consistently distinguished, thereby not commanding equal attention with the short story.

Discussion of the Hindi story in the fifties began largely as an attempt to distinguish the *nayī kahānī* or "new story" from the stories of the previous two decades. Consciously at least, the discussion of recent fiction has shown almost no concern with classical Indian literary norms. Justifications for literary forms and trends have been sought in a more universal framework, comparing the fiction of each new generation with that of the previous generation, with that of writers in other Indian languages, and with that of writers in other world languages.

The modern Hindi short story, despite the presence of fiction in Sanskrit and Prakrit literature, and despite the early Hindi prose fiction in the nineteenth century, is considered by most scholars to be a twentieth-century development, with the first "original Hindi story" being placed somewhere between 1900 and 1915. There seems to be general scholarly agreement that the model for the modern Hindi story was a Western one, transmitted to some extent by way of Bengali and Urdu. In the '20s, '30s, and '40s, stories were written extensively and were popular with readers; but few Hindi writers chose this genre exclusively, and few writers received critical attention for their stories equal to that given their poems or novels.

In the 1950s, however, a large group of new Hindi writers began concentrating entirely on fiction, primarily on the short story. A number of them also began writing about their work, and critical interest in the genre grew rapidly. Some scholars point to the short history of the Hindi story to explain its relative neglect by earlier critics. More significant might be the scant attention given that genre in college and university curricula, where the study of nineteenth-century English literature meant concentration primarily on the novel and on poetry, whereas the short story had received more attention in nineteenth-century Russian, French, and American literature. A familiarity with poetic theory and analysis, developed over centuries in which poetry had been the dominant genre in Indian literature and almost the sole genre in Hindi, no doubt added to the critics' neglect of fiction, especially short fiction. Exhaustion with the debate over experimental and new poetry may have helped decrease the controversy over poetry, though not necessarily its production, in Hindi literary circles by the early '50s.

Discussion of the short story was assisted in the '50s by the rise of several critics who focused their attention on this genre; but perhaps it was assisted most by short-story writers themselves who became editors of story magazines and other literary journals, thereby being in a position to influence the selection of material for publication and to write extensive comments themselves on the story literature. The sheer number and quality of story writers who had begun to publish, and the calling of literary conferences to discuss the story, also helped draw attention to that genre. Whatever the combination of reasons, the new popularity of the story was being noticed in print by the early 1950s, and in 1957 the critic Namwar Singh raised the question as to "whether, like *nayī kavitā* (new poetry), there is also such a thing as *nayī kahānī*."[2]

A brief but bitter part of the initial discussion of the new story revolved round the question of whether rural or urban themes were more appropriate; but larger literary issues soon came to the fore. *Nayī kahānī* was debated and analyzed for about a decade, by which time there was greater critical definition and greater critical acceptance of the term and the stories that it covered. Then the new writers who had emerged in the 1960s began trying to set off their stories as belonging to a *nayī pīṛhī*, a "new generation" significantly different from that of the previous decade. Other attempts have been pursued subsequently—to define the "new new story," to define a "story of consciousness (or awareness)," to classify the "nonstory." Recently an attempt has been made to identify certain writing as "noncommercial" rather than "commercial," a category into which many established writers of the '50s are consigned. Some writers have accepted the term *sāṭhottarī kahāniyān* (post-'60 stories) to establish that this decade of stories deserves to be distinguished from the writing of the previous decade, and that the earlier definitions were too difficult to defend.

Some of these distinctions have obviously involved personal or literary factions at least as much as they have involved literary criteria. It is worth looking past the labels to identify authentic literary directions, and this is what many Hindi critics have been trying to do. A point to note again, though, is the extent to which these modern Hindi writers and critics are trying to analyze recent developments in the literature by comparisons with the work of immediate predecessors or even of contemporaries. Hindi critics may at times compare current short stories with those of Premchand, produced some forty years ago; but they do not seem to use Sanskritic literary canons, or premodern Indian fiction, as a basis for comparison. Sanskrit literature can be viewed as a sort of general background for most of Indian literature and for much of Indian life. To use it as a specific basis for evaluating the Hindi story, though, would be like discussing the contemporary Western story in terms of biblical narration or of Greek and Latin epics. The principles expounded in the *Nāṭya Śāstra*, as would be the case in the West with the principles of Aristotle's *Poetics*, can initiate interesting speculations about contemporary literature or society; but writers and critics are unlikely to see either Bharata or Aristotle as a particularly relevant source by which to evaluate or to understand contemporary literary developments.

In evaluating the post-Independence story, Hindi critics and writers naturally differ widely in their criteria and their conclusions. A survey of the critical literature suggests, however, that criteria related to newness, realism, authenticity, and the reflection of a "modern consciousness" are most highly valued. Any one of those terms could be used to incorporate the other three, but a discussion of these criteria individually helps to identify areas of agreement and disagreement regarding developments in the modern Hindi short story.

A concern with newness could be expected, since the first center of critical discussion involved the identification of the stories of the '50s as *nayī kahānī*, new stories. Critics debated whether these stories were new if compared with those of such writers as Premchard, Yashpal, Jainendra Kumar, and "Agyeya," and they also argued as to whether any newness found in the story was comparable to that found in recent poetry. Whether critics argued that these stories represented something entirely new in Hindi, something partially new, or nothing new, they tended to accept an underlying assumption that some element of newness is desirable in a story, that there should be some progression or development from the forms and themes of the '20s, '30s, and '40s.

Some critics have felt that newness in the story represented a natural development whereas newness in poetry had represented a revolt. Whether comparable or not to the poets' breaking of traditional metrical rules, there has been recognition of the new forms taken by the story. Plot-dominated stories tend to be viewed as old-fashioned and inappropriate; and involuted chronology is expected instead of a clear beginning, middle, and end. The new story is portrayed as shifting from a narration of incidents to a presentation of human states of mind, taking varied forms such as the sketch, diary, letter, outline, interview, or depiction of moods. The story with a strong climax has been replaced generally by a story with looser structure and with greater ambiguity.

In the new story form, similes and metaphors are usually rejected as contrived decorative devices. Modern, original, and meaningful symbols are valued, especially when a whole story can be seen as a symbol. Originality of language is appreciated, though experimentation with language is only very recently becoming a conspicuous feature of the new story.

Using "newness" then to suggest primarily the appreciation of newness in form, one may use "realism"—or "increased realism"—to describe the appreciation of newness in the author's point of view. A kind of realism has been accepted as an important value in Hindi fiction ever since Premchand. Nevertheless, as Namwar Singh points out, what is the truth of one age becomes the falsehood of another age.[3] Critics agree that the good modern story should reject sentimentality, melodrama, and romanticism. All these elements would negate realism. But differences in cultural and literary appreciation lead to differences in the application of the terms sentimentality, melodrama, and romanticism to particular stories.

The realism of the post-Independence story is sometimes contrasted with earlier Hindi stories that were based on ideas, where authors appeared to be manufacturing characters and plots in order to illustrate or to promote particular philosophical, social, or political views. Again, though, in the evaluation of particular stories, it is difficult to ascertain whether critical objections are aimed at the presentation of ideas as such, or whether objections are aimed more at the nature of the idea presented. The major Hindi critics do still generally appreciate stories that suggest some larger significance, though they ask that the larger significance be inferred through the author's presentation of a personal and unique situation, and a realistic situation.

Nirmal Varma, one author who rose to prominance in the '50s, questions the capacity of a writer even to identify reality, much less express it. He describes reality as a bird hidden in a bush. "To extract it alive is as unlikely as to say anything definite about it while it is hidden." The most a writer can do with realism, he suggests, is to "beat around the bush":

> If you apply too much pressure, it dies or flies away. We can only wait, poking here and there. At some unexpected moment when it is unaware of us, some contact may be possible—but always from outside. This is the curse of the writer who is also the artist. For one who is truly a realist, reality is always hidden in the bush.[4]

One expectation of modern realism, then, may be that the author show an appreciation for the complexity of reality and be able to reflect that complexity in his stories.

The demand that a good story reflect a "modern consciousness" can be viewed as an attempt to pin down the specific nature of realism. The writer who openly proposes specific answers to political, social, or philosophical questions in his stories was rejected in much of the critical writing of the '50s. New stories tended to raise questions rather than to give answers. The writers of the '50s, in turn, have been criticized by some later writers for imagining that there were such things as values, for showing nostalgia for meaningfulness. The younger the writer, the more likely he appears to propose that a modern consciousness necessarily reflects total disbelief, where an earlier group reflected disillusion and still earlier groups of Hindi writers reflected hope.

Writing since Independence speaks of the increased conflict, disillusion, complexity, fragmentation, and alienation in Indian life, often implying that older writers have not fully absorbed these experiences or reflected them in their writing. "They live cut off from life," says one young critic, "being still concerned with a sense of guilt and of moral conflict."[5]

Some difference in approach can be detected in the recent decades of the Hindi story literature, though the progression is not necessarily consistent nor chronological. Stories of the '30s might be described very roughly as proposing ideals, those of the '40s as testing ideals and proposing values, the stories of the '50s as mourning the loss of values, and those of the '60s as trying to establish the absence of such a thing as values. The most recent writers tend to deal less with conflict, trying to record meaningless meetings between people, pointless events, taboo activities, without moral judgment. The critic Bacchan Singh gives this description of the environment of the newest stories:

> . . . when a person locates himself, he sees that he is nowhere, that he has no identity. He has nothing but boredom and hatred. Once committed to the environment, he becomes uncommitted, but this path is a dead-end alley. There are only two options—to stop or to go back. But neither of these alternatives is possible, so the alley will have to be torn down.[6]

As previously taboo themes appear increasingly in modern stories, a curious critical reaction has sometimes occurred. Writers who themselves once claimed that no subject was taboo, and who defended themselves in the '50s against charges of obscenity, begin accusing the more iconoclastic generation with obscenity. Not wanting to rule out particular themes as completely inappropriate to literature, which could contradict their liberal stance, the somewhat older writers and critics say that it is not the subject of a story that disturbs them but that the youngest writers are dealing with aberrations, violence, and horror with which they have had no direct experience and which is therefore derivative and inauthentic. Similar charges had been leveled at the earlier writers by their elders who claimed that the depiction of alienation in the '50s represented a phony intoxication with Camus, Kafka, and Sartre.

One difficulty in using "modern consciousness" as the test of good literature is recognized in a Hindi critic's statement that "Every story-writer expresses the modern sensibility within his own context, and this has been true ever since Premchand."[7] The changing points of view can, however, help illuminate social and literary changes even when they fail to serve as solid criteria for evaluating specific works of literature.

The attack on phony, derivative themes brings up the other major criterion used in modern Hindi criticism of the story—that of "authenticity." A primary basis of the controversy in the early '50s over urban, as against rural, stories was a conviction that contemporary writers were not equipped to give authentic portrayals of village life since they were mostly from an urban background. Writers about urban themes have dominated the later story literature, but many of them were accused of writing stories about a sort of alienation that was not a part of their own lives. The newest writers in turn are criticized for depicting vulgarity and violence "about which they know nothing." The good writer, the realistic writer, is expected to concentrate on the areas of life with which he has primary experience. Such a definition of authenticity has tended to narrow the world of the Hindi story to that modern middle-class urban North Indian life that is the immediate world of the writer himself. Most recently, however, the world of the younger writers seems to be expanding; or at least they show a determination to depict unexplored aspects of Indian society—especially at its lower levels.

Some critics question the value and purpose of the modern Hindi story. Though few now urge that the story establish ideals, many feel that it should at least reflect some search for values, whether through positive or negative means. It is frequently pointed out that values can usually be identified even in stories that appear to deny or to oppose values. When an author appears to be promoting or accepting immorality, however, many critics reject his stories as "unhealthy."

In literary circles, the definition of the purpose of the modern Hindi story or of its counterparts in other languages appears to be growing broader. Some explain that such literature helps the reader to identify some awareness about life through creative representation. One critic says that the new stories diagnose "the cancer of the age" and provide the medicine of self-awareness,[8] somewhat echoing Namwar Singh's suggestion a decade earlier that a story should put its finger on the place that hurts.[9]

Developments in the story literature, as in most other literary genres of Hindi, have tended since Independence to precede acceptance of those developments by the general literary community and especially by the general public. In the mid-'60s, a writer and critic deplored the new story for not being a truly "national story," not reflecting in breadth the sorrow, conflict, hopes, and desires of the people, not encouraging healthy and progressive tendencies in life and society through an understanding of one's cultural heritage. "This kind of literature," he declared, "is the true representative of the nation's people."[10] The president of India in 1966 suggested a similar literary ideal when he said, during the presentation of the annual Sahitya Akademi literary awards, "Only men of letters can rescue humanity from further degradation by showing men a cause to live and die for."[11]

It may be true that there is stronger negativism, greater revolution, more complete lack of faith in statements about the story literature than there is in the literature itself. Nevertheless, the last few decades have shown the story moving generally in those directions, exploring more and more the possibilities of meaninglessness.

One might be tempted to say that a single *rasa* increasingly dominates the modern Hindi story. Hindi critics would be more likely to avoid the term *rasa* and use the English word *mood* instead. The awakening of detached esthetic sentiments is far from the aim of most contemporary writers. Given the strength of cultural continuity, however, Shrikant Varma eloquently expresses the predicament of the modern Indian writer who feels that his personal and literary responses conflict with an Indian tradition that is "not only an assertion of certain values and ideals cherished by the society during the millennium, but is also a rejection of the values which do not conform to it . . . not only an homage to the past but also a fortress of the present." Shrikant Varma then asserts:

> . . . the destiny of an Indian writer can only be painful. Alienated from his own tradition, the Indian intellectual wearing a western coat finds himself in a dilemma. Has he to choose or has he to relate? And if he has to relate the complex and self-surviving Indian tradition with the materially meaningful situation today, has he the power to do so? . . . An individual, and even more so a writer, is not a product of his own imagination. He is a reality, and reality can be interpreted only within the framework of tradition. The superimposition of ideas alien to the basic requirements of a tradition, however unproductive it might be, makes the creativity of a nation anti-self and anti-being.[12]

Without such pressure from long-standing cultural and literary traditions, modern Indian writers might feel less conflict over expressing trends common to much of world literature today. It is partly the intensity of national traditions, however, that adds meaning to the expression in the modern story of tragic tension. Only with an understanding of the tradition can a reader of modern Indian literature appreciate fully the magnitude of the accomplishment of recent writers in the Indian languages. (GR)

Epilogue: *The Modern Film*

The fact that many modern novels have been subjects of transformation into another modern art form, the film, might lead to speculation on the blending of esthetics implied by this amalgam of East and West. But the study is qualified by a number of serious difficulties, and it can be offered here only as an epilogue. Chief of these difficulties is the absence of extensive documentation on the Indian film. But even many non-Indians now have seen one or more of these spectacles and treat them with the sentimental condescension they deserve; fortunately, one of the few nearly flawless films to date is Ray's version of one of the novels under discussion: *Pather Panchali.* The few remarks here will be largely based on intuitive recollections of the films seen, and to some extent on the only easily available resource book, Erik Barnouw's *Indian Film,*[1] a wholly inadequate document for present purposes. Despite the extreme novelty of the film form, it is in principle far more adaptive to and consistent with a whole range of vigorous and popular indigenous art forms, *yātrā, Rām līlā,* and so on (pp. 68–71); it may not present that many difficulties of interpretation. Certainly its instant popularity in India is prima facie evidence that the public at least sees no great problem of adaptation to the new genre. Though Barnouw is chiefly interested in the Indian film as an extension of the art form in an exotic area, surprisingly he makes little effort to relate that exotic film style to the artistic circumstances of its locale. Rather, the book is by and large a technical history of the sort of things film historians find significant (which are mostly extra-film), economics of the industry, production statistics, the star syndrome, camera and directional innovations; only rarely does he discuss the film from the aspect of content or as an art form.

The first properly Indian film seems to have been Phalke's on Raja Hariscandra (1912); and thus the mythological was born (though the inspiration seems to have been an imported film on the life of Christ; pp. 11–14). Socials were not long in coming; among the first the satire

"England Returned" (1921; pp. 25–27). The early attempts at film-making seem to have been compromised by the Victorian taboos against the arts of dance and drama that had achieved peculiar virulence in British India at the time. But the Indian film did not really become a cultural idiom in its own right until the coming of sound, until, that is, traditional Indian art forms could be integrated wholly into it: "In 1931 and 1932 at what seemed a dark moment in Indian film history, song and dance—in part derived from a tradition of folk music-drama—played an important role in winning for the sound film an instant and widening acceptance. 'With the coming of the talkies' wrote a contemporary observer, 'the Indian motion picture came into its own as a definite and distinctive piece of creation. This was achieved by music' " (p. 69).[2] Despite the little Barnouw has to say on the general question of esthetic form, a few of his asides are suggestive for the thesis here proposed. "Meanwhile in Bombay, formula was king. The formula, as dictated by exhibitor and distributor, called for one or two major stars [*scil*, character], at least half a dozen songs, and a few dances. The story was of declining importance. It was conceived and developed toward one objective; exploitation of the *idolized star* [italics ours]. The subject matter, with increasing concentration, was romance. An overwhelming number of Bombay films now began with the chance acquaintance of hero and heroine, often in unconventional manner and novel setting. In backgrounds and characters there was strong bias toward the glamorous. *Obstacles* were usually provided by *villainy* or *accident*, not by social problems [italics ours]. Dance and song provided conventionalized substitutes for love-making and emotional crisis" (p. 148). Barnouw points himself to the parallels with classical works (if not to the classical esthetic that explains them); the mythologicals hardly need justification as supreme exemplifications of survival in a superficially new genre. "In Śakuntalā too, we find the erotic balance with decorum. Śakuntalā also began with 'boy meets girl,' with the introduction arranged in novel style by a troublesome bee. . . . The obstacles, as in the formula film, were provided by villainy or accident. And the humdrum background was shunned in favor of sylvan glade or palace" (ibid.). Oddly enough, all this is explained as "Hollywood infiltration" (pp. 148–49). Other aspects of traditional influence are noted by Barnouw: "As in other centers, auguries of various sorts were highly respected in Madras. Producers consulted not only distribution reports but also astrologers. A new production was generally launched on a day and at a time set with astrological help. The industry was thus star-dominated in more ways than one. Productions were often started with appropriate observances, serving religion and personnel relations simultaneously.

Trade papers often carried such items as: 'The camera was switched on at 10:09 A.M. by the star's mother' " (pp. 168–69). The films, being popular par excellence, often stereotype what in fact is legitimate survival. Even in the "socials" the "modern world"—represented again by the demon Hollywood—takes the place of the traditional paradise, the ultimately real behind and beyond the qualified and painful existence we know as individuals: "During this decade (1950s) Professor Asit Baran Bose, sociologist at Lucknow University, did a content analysis of sixty Hindi feature films. He found the films dealt primarily with the unmarried and educated young of the upper and middle classes living in cities. In roughly half the films the hero had no occupation, in almost two-thirds of the films the heroine had no occupation. In most films the *obstacles* were provided not by a social problem but by an *evil character* [italics ours]. . . . In roughly half the films the hero lived alone; in one-third he lived in a family, the heroine generally lived with a family. Rarely did the hero or heroine live in a joint family" (as reported in *Statesman* [India] 12 December 1959).

"The young people whose love for each other was the main concern in these films moved through a diversity of settings, exuding vigor and radiant health and usually surrounded by consumer goods. . . . Always the lavish background, radiant health, laughter, seldom the joint family, the arranged marriage, work and poverty" (pp. 158–59). If anything, the films represent escapism in the Indian sense: no longer concerned with the tension between the real and the unreal—but wholly devoted to making the audience forget the real. Even here the reflection of the effect, if not the force, of the *rasa* esthetic is palpable. (EG)

Notes

Introduction

1. The term "medieval" is a rough usage and does not correspond to that time period generally meant by the term in European history. We mean here the period between the twelfth and mid-eighteenth centuries.
2. *Rabindra-racanavali* (Calcutta: Visvabharati, 1940).
3. In W. T. de Bary et al., *Sources of Indian Tradition* (New York: Columbia University Press, 1958), p. 382.
4. Edward C. Dimock, Jr., "Rabindranath Tagore—'The Greatest of the Bauls of Bengal,' " *Journal of Asian Studies* 19 (no. 1; November 1959), p. 42.
5. Ibid.
6. Kabir, *Au cabaret de l'amour*, translated by Charlotte Vaudeville (Paris: Gallimard, 1959), p. 52.
7. In Humayan Kabir, ed., *Green and Gold* (New York: New Directions, 1970).
8. A Bengali wife never speaks her husband's name, for fear it will detract from his life. To some ways of thinking, a name and the object named are somehow one; each time a man's name is spoken, a little of the fixed quantity of life is exhausted.

1. *The Indian Epic*

1. References are to the critical edition of *The Rāmāyaṇa* by the Oriental Institute of Baroda. The passages quoted, in a translation by Edwin Gerow, are R. 2.23.1–34; 24.1–19; 27.1–33.
2. R. 3.44.15–27.
3. R. 3.53.10ff.
4. R. 3.54.1ff.
5. R. 5.19.3ff.
6. *Rāmāyaṇa* 1:1–3.
7. *Rāmcaritmānas* 1:4:5–6.
8. *Rāmāyaṇa* 3:45.3–5.
9. *Rāmāyaṇa* of Kṛittivāsa, Sāhitya saṁsad edition, p. 143.
10. Kṛittivāsa, p. 143.
11. Kṛittivāsa, p. 144.
12. Kṛittivāsa, p. 144.
13. Kṛittivāsa, p. 144.
14. S. K. De, *Bengali Literature in the Nineteenth Century* (Calcutta: University of Calcutta, 1919).
15. De, p. 296.
16. De, p. 318.
17. De, p. 341.

18. D. C. Sen, *The Bengali Ramayanas* (Calcutta: University of Calcutta, 1920), pp. 109, 110.
19. Ibid, p. 110.

2. *The Classical Drama*

1. This chapter, in different form, appeared as the Introduction to J. A. B. van Buitenen, *Two Plays of Ancient India* (New York: Columbia University Press, 1968). References are to this translation, with the permission of Columbia University Press.
2. *Minister's Seal*, Act three, p. 219.
3. *Little Clay Cart*, Act five, pp. 112–14.
4. *Minister's Seal*, Act three, p. 222.
5. *Sakuntala* (ed. Pischel), 4.8.
6. *Little Clay Cart*, Act three, pp. 85–87.
7. *Little Clay Cart*, Act three, pp. 90–91.
8. *Minister's Seal*, Act two, p. 202.

3. *The Indian Poetics*

1. Kālidāsa, *The Cloud Messenger*, translated from the Sanskrit *Meghadūta* by Franklin and Eleanor Edgerton (Ann Arbor: University of Michigan Press, 1964). *Meghadūta* 19 (p. 21).
2. *Meghadūta* 18 (p. 19).
3. *Meghadūta* 41 (p. 35).
4. *Meghadūta* 32 (p. 29).
5. *Meghadūta* 80 (p. 61).
6. *Meghadūta* 108 (p. 79).
7. *Meghadūta* 100 (p. 75).
8. *Meghadūta* 11 (p. 15).
9. Daṇḍin, seventh century. *Kāvyādarśa* 2.311.
10. Kālidāsa, *Raghuvaṃśa* 18.4.
11. See Diwekar, *Fleurs de Rhétorique* (Paris, 1930), chap. 7, pp. 95ff.
12. The latter is of obvious importance to the drama, whose characters speak several languages within the same play.
13. Bharata, *Nāṭyaśāstra* 6 (pp. 31–32).
14. M. Monier-Williams's translation of *Sakoontala* from Kālidāsa is used throughout. Originally published: *Hindu Literature* (New York: P. F. Collier and Son, 1900); in John D. Yohannan, ed., *A Treasury of Asian Literature* (Mentor Book, 1958).
15. NŚ. 6 (pp. 18–21).
16. My translation of Sylvain Lévi, *Théâtre Indien* (Paris: E. Bouillon, 1890), p. 32.
17. Lévi, p. 33.
18. Ibid.
19. Ibid.
20. Lévi, pp. 33–34.
21. After Pierre Meile, *L'Inde Classique*, #901.
22. Meile, #903.
23. Dhvanyāloka, chap. 1.
24. George Keyt, translator, *Shri Jayadeva's Gita Govinda* (Bombay, 1947), cited from Johannan, canto 5, p. 282.
25. Canto 3, p. 279.
26. Canto 2, p. 279.
27. Canto 8, p. 287.
28. Canto 10, p. 288.
29. Canto 2, p. 277.
30. The *rāga* and *tāla* notations associated with the poem are ancient, but not necessarily original.
31. Adapted example from Ānandavardhana.

4. *The Lyric Poem: Various Contexts and Approaches*

1. R.V. 10.127. The translations in this section are by the author, following generally the editions of the Nirṇayasāgar Press, Bombay.
2. Therīgāthā. The original is in Pālī.
3. Śakuntalā 1.7, in *Subhāṣitaratnakoṣa* (ed., Kosambi), 1149. The anthology has been translated by Daniel H. H. Ingalls.
4. "Natural"—a generic term for the literary forms of the various vernaculars that by the time of the classical period had diverged significantly from the artificially preserved mother language, Sanskrit "perfected."
5. Bhartrihari, *Poems.* Translated by Barbara Stoler Miller (New York: Columbia University Press, 1967); she has also translated another famous erotic anthology, attributed to Bilhaṇa, the *Caurapañcāśikā,* as *Phantasies of a Love-Thief* (Columbia University Press, 1971).
6. The *Gītagovinda* has been translated in its entirety by George Keyt (Bombay, 1947).
7. *Raghuvaṃśa* 13.2; 13.14–19.
8. The stotras of *VSS.* 34, 36, 43.
9. John Frederick Nims, translator, *Poems of St. John of the Cross* (New York: Grove Press, 1959).
10. Moshe Lazar, *Amour courtois et fin'amors, dans la litterature du XIIe siècle* (Paris: Librairie C. Klincksieck, n.d.), p. 72.
11. Edward C. Dimock, Jr., and Denise Levertov, translators, *In Praise of Krishna* (New York: Doubleday, 1967), p. 16. *Kohl* is a dark ointment used around the eyes by Indian women as a cosmetic.
12. Dimock and Levertov, p. 58.
13. Dimock and Levertov, p. 23.
14. In Humayan Kabir, ed., *Green and Gold* (Asia Publishing House, 1957), p. 126.
15. Translated by Daniel H. H. Ingalls, "A Sanskrit Poetry of Village and Field: Yogeśvara and his fellow poets," in *Journal of the American Oriental Society* 74, no. 3 (1954). This and other poems by Yogeśvara and others appear in later versions in Ingalls, *An Anthology of Sanskrit Court Poetry* (Cambridge, Mass.: Harvard University Press, 1965).
16. Dimock and Levertov, p. 69.
17. Yatīndramohan Bhaṭṭācārya, *Bāṅgalār vaiṣṇava bhāvapanna musulmān kavi* (Calcutta: Book Society of India, 1950).
18. S. K. De, *Bengali Literature in the Nineteenth Century* (Calcutta: University of Calcutta, 1919), p. 295.
19. De, p. 317.
20. Bengali text quoted by S. K. De; translation by E. C. Dimock, Jr., p. 343.
21. De, p. 340.
22. De, p. 314.
23. Rabindranath Tagore, *Gītāñjali* (New York and London: Macmillan, 1912).
24. A. K. Ramanujan, *Speaking of Śiva* (Penguin Classics, 1973), p. 142.
25. For a general introduction to Vīraśaivism and the vacanas of Mahādevīyakka and other saints see A. K. Ramanujan's *Speaking of Śiva.* Pp. 111–42 contain a biography of Mahadeviyakka and translations of her vacanas.
26. Ramanujan, p. 141.
27. Ramanujan, p. 134.
28. Ramanujan, p. 122.
29. Ramanujan, p. 139.
30. Ramanujan, p. 137.
31. Ramanujan, p. 120.
32. Ramanujan, p. 131.
33. For translations from classical Tamil poetry and technical discussion of Tamil poetics see A. K. Ramanujan, *The Interior Landscape* (Bloomington: Indiana University Press, 1967, and London: Peter Owen, 1971), and "Form in Classical Tamil Poetry," in *Symposium on Dravidian Civilization,* edited by A. F. Sjoberg (Austin, 1971), pp. 73–104.

34. Ramanujan, IL, p. 37.
35. Ramanujan, IL, p. 51.
36. Marianne Moore, "Poetry," in Oscar Williams, *The Pocket Book of Modern Verse* (1954), p. 342.
37. Ramanujan, IL, p. 19.
38. Ramanujan, IL, p. 41.
39. Ramanujan, IL, p. 93.
40. Ramanujan, IL, p. 45.
41. Ramanujan, IL, p. 94.
42. Ramanujan, IL, p. 64.
43. Ramanujan, IL, p. 22.
44. Ramanujan, IL, p. 112.
45. Nicol Macnicol, *Psalms of the Maratha Saints* (Calcutta, 1919).
46. F. E. Keay, *Kabir and His Followers* (Calcutta: Association Press, 1931), p. 76.
47. Edward C. Dimock, Jr., *The Place of the Hidden Moon* (Chicago: University of Chicago Press, 1966), p. 263.
48. "Three Voices of Poetry," *Selected Essays*.
49. Rabindranath Tagore, *Songs of Kabīr* (New York: Macmillan, 1917), pp. 108–9.
50. Edward C. Dimock, Jr., *The Place of the Hidden Moon*, p. 262.
51. Ibid.
52. Ibid.
53. A song of Madana Bāul, quoted in Rabindranath Tagore, *Bāṅglā kāvya paricaya* (Calcutta B.S. 1345), p. 70.
54. Kabir's Bijak sabda 4.
55. *Caitanya-bhāgavata* of Vṛndāvana-dāsa (Calcutta: Gauriya math, 1934), *Ādi-līlā* 16, pp. 70–85. See Edward C. Dimock, Jr., "Muslim Vaiṣṇava Poets of Bengal," in *Languages and Areas: Studies Presented to George V. Bobrinskoy, 1967* (Chicago: Division of the Humanities of the University of Chicago, 1967), pp. 28–36.
56. A. Kinany, *The Development of Gazal in Arabic Literature (Pre-Islamic and Early Islamic Periods)* (Damascus, 1951), passim.
57. Muhammad Iqbal, *The Reconstruction of Religious Thought in Islam* (London: Oxford University Press, 1934), pp. 17ff.
58. L. M. J. Garnett, *Mysticism and Magic in Turkey* (London, 1912). Quoted by Margaret Smith in *The Sufi Path of Love* (London, 1954), pp. 13–14.
59. For more on this subject see C. M. Naim, "Traditional Symbolism in the Modern Urdu Ghazal," *Languages and Areas: Studies Presented to George V. Bobrinskoy, 1967* (Chicago: Division of the Humanities of the University of Chicago, 1967), pp. 105–11.

5. *The Story Literature*

1. J. A. B. van Buitenen, *Tales of Ancient India* (Chicago: University of Chicago Press, 1959), "Gomukha's Escapade."
2. *Tales*, "Two Kingdoms Won: the First Prince's Story."
3. *Tales*, "The Travels of Sānudāsa."
4. *Tales*, "Two Kingdoms Won: the First Prince's Story."

6. *The Persistence of Classical Esthetic Categories in Contemporary Indian Literature: The Case of Three Bengali Novels*

1. London, 1948; following page references are to this edition.
2. Italics mine; in 1902 Jacobi (*ZDMG* [56] p. 392, n. 1) warned against the inappropriateness of using this term to apply to Indian poetic traditions.
3. See *In Praise of Krishna*, translated by E. C. Dimock, Jr., and Denise Levertov (Garden City, 1967).
4. See *infra*, pp. 216ff. and n. 16.

5. *Krishnakanta's Will*, by Bankim-Chandra Chatterjee (tr. J. C. Gosh [*sic*]; New York: New Directions paperback, 1962); *Pather Panchali*, by Bibhutibhushan Banerji (translated by T. W. Clark and Tarapada Mukherji; London, 1968); *He Who Rides a Tiger*, by Bhabani Bhattacharya (New York, 1954). All page references given are to these editions.

6. The most recent and possibly the most persuasive representative of this point of view is S. K. De: see his *Sanskrit Poetics as a Study of Aesthetic* (SPSA), Berkeley, 1963. But De merely sums up a tradition of interpretation that finds its spiritual mentor in Macaulay.

7. "What is the point of killing off your hero?" Bhāmaha, *Kāvyālaṃkāra*, 1.22–23.

8. Of Kālidāsa, translated by Monier-Williams, Ryder et al.

9. "The Little Clay Cart," of Śūdraka, translated by R. Oliver, J. A. B. van Buitenen et al.

10. Hero of the "Little Clay Cart."

11. Dramatic: "Characteristic of or appropriate to the drama, especially in involving conflict or contrast of character; vivid; moving . . . highly effective, striking. Syn.: startling, sensational" (RHD, p. 401).

12. I.e., language itself, poetry.

13. Heroes of *Śakuntalā*, and of *Mālavikā and Agnimitra*, a harem intrigue also by Kālidāsa.

14. See my article, "The Quintessential Narayan," *Literature East and West* 10:1.

15. See "The City of Gold" of Somadeva, translated by J. A. B. van Buitenen, *Tales of Ancient India* (Chicago 1959), pp. 79ff.

16. His commentary on the *rasaniṣpattisūtra* of Bharata. Our references are to the Gaekwad text (vol. 36), edited by M. R. Kavi.

17. *Locana* to *Dhvanyāloka* (Kāvyamālā, ed.), p. 22. Cited in De, *SPSA*, p. 54.

18. The term "imitation" is properly used only where there is a real basis of similarity.

19. Nāyaka did characterize "bhoga" (enjoyment) as "like the experience of the Supreme Brahma" (*NŚ* p. 277).

20. Which fact we also see in the virtual collapse of the old classical genre distinctions *kāvya* and *nāṭya*, in the devotional lyric—by Abhinava's time the only vital literary mode.

21. Of Jayadeva, translated by George Keyt, *Shri Jayadeva's Gita Govinda* (Bombay, 1947).

22. Compare "The Quintessential Narayan," *Literature East and West* 10:1.

23. M. Hiriyanna, whose short essay "Art Experience II" (republished in the collection *Art Experience* [Mysore, 1954]) is still the best account available in English of the *rasa* theory as literary criticism. His exposition we feel supports our understanding of Abhinavagupta's position as given above (pp. 216ff.).

24. See "Gomukha's Escapade," translated by J. A. B. van Buitenen, *Tales of Ancient India* (Chicago, 1959).

25. "Jāla, indrajāla," "net, web (of Indra)," hence "sustained illusion."

26. As expressed, e.g., in the "inalienable rights" of man; compare the interesting development of similar propositions in the work of Louis Dumont, *Homo Hierarchicus, La Civilisation Indienne et Nous*, etc.

27. *Art Experience*, p. 35.

28. These are in fact the first and third types of Ānandavardhana; the second, "alaṃkārapradhāna," is not mentioned here.

29. *Pather Panchali*, Introduction, p. 12.

30. Regretfully, we pass over the metaphysical implications of this passage.

31. Compare some interestingly parallel statements in Jung, *Memories, Dreams and Reflections* (New York: Random House Vintage Books, 1963), pp. 20, 244.

32. Translated by J. A. B. van Buitenen, *Tales of Ancient India*.

33. The Bengali title of Part 3 of the trilogy is simply, *Apur samsār*.

7. *The Modern Hindi Short Story and Modern Hindi Criticism*

1. Lecture at the University of California, Berkeley, November 1970; printed in *Times of India*, 14 March 1971.
2. "Āj kī Hindī Kahānī, New Year issue, 1957; republished in Namwar Singh, *Kahānī: Nayī Kahānī* (Allahabad, 1966), p. 19.
3. Ibid., p. 218.
4. "Nayī Kahānī: Lekhak ke Vahī-Khāte se," *Dharmayug*, 19 January, 1964, p. 19.
5. Vijaymohan Singh, *'60 ke Bād kī Kahāniyān* (Agra, 1965), p. 21.
6. *Samkālīn Hindī Sāhitya: Ālocanā ko Cunautī* (Varanasi, 1968), p. 126.
7. Indranath Madan, "Ādhūnikta aur Hindī Kahānī," in Devishankar Avasthi, *Nayī Kahānī: Sandarbh aur Prākṛti* (Delhi, 1966), p. 187.
8. Nityanand Tiwari, "Hindi Kahānī kī Diśā," in Avasthi, *Nayi Kahānī*, p. 113.
9. Namwar Singh, *Kahānī: Nayī Kahānī*, p. 32.
10. Shivprasad Singh, "Āj kī Hindī Kahānī: Pragati aur Parimiti," in Avasthi, *Nayī Kahāni*, p. 139.
11. *India News*, 4 March 1966.
12. Lecture at the University of California, Berkeley, November 1970; printed in *Times of India*, 14 March 1971.

Epilogue: The Modern Film

1. New York, 1963. S. Krishnaswamy is coauthor. Citations below refer to this edition.
2. The quoted passage is from Desai, in *Indian Cinematography Yearbook* (1938), pp. 291–93.

Index